Summer 2002   Vol. XX
ISSN: 0276-0045   ISBN: 1-

THE REVIEW OF CONTEMPORARY FICTION

Publisher

JOHN O'BRIEN
Illinois State University

Editor

ROBERT L. MCLAUGHLIN
Illinois State University

Book Review Editor

TIM FEENEY

Guest Editors

TAKAYUKI TATSUMI, LARRY MCCAFFERY, SINDA GREGORY

Production & Design

NOAH LARSEN

Editorial Assistants

JENNIFER ANDERSON, SARAH MCHONE-CHASE,
LAYNE MOORE, LAINE MORREAU

Cover Illustration

TODD MICHAEL BUSHMAN

www.centerforbookculture.org
www.dalkeyarchive.com

The Review of Contemporary Fiction is published three times a year (January, June, September) by the Center for Book Culture, a nonprofit organization with offices in Chicago and at Illinois State University in Normal, Illinois. ISSN 0276-0045. Subscription prices are as follows:

   Single volume (three issues):
      Individuals: $17.00; foreign, add $3.50;
      Institutions: $26.00; foreign, add $3.50.

DISTRIBUTION. Bookstores should send orders to:

Dalkey Archive Press, ISU Campus Box 4241, Normal, IL 61790-4241. Phone 309-874-2274; fax 309-874-2284.

This issue is partially supported by grants from the Japan Foundation and the Illinois Arts Council, a state agency.

Indexed in *American Humanities Index, International Bibliography of Periodical Literature, International Bibliography of Book Reviews, MLA Bibliography,* and *Book Review Index.* Abstracted in *Abstracts of English Studies.*

The Review of Contemporary Fiction is also available in 16mm microfilm, 35mm microfilm, and 105mm microfiche from University Microfilms International, 300 North Zeeb Road, Ann Arbor, MI 48106-1346.

www.centerforbookculture.org
www.dalkeyarchive.com

THE REVIEW OF CONTEMPORARY FICTION

BACK ISSUES AVAILABLE

Back issues are still available for the following numbers of the *Review of Contemporary Fiction* ($8 each unless otherwise noted):

Individuals receive a 10% discount on orders of one issue and a 20% discount on orders of two or more issues. To place an order, use the form on the last page of this issue.

Call for Casebook Editors and Contributors

www.dalkeyarchive.com

Dalkey Archive Press/The Review of Contemporary Fiction is seeking editors and contributors for its new web-based casebook series: Studies in Modern and Contemporary Fiction. Each casebook will focus on one novel. It will include an overview essay on the book (its place in the author's oeuvre; its critical reception; the scholarly conversations about it) and four other essays looking at specific dimensions of the book. (Recommended length of essays: 20-25 double-spaced pages.) Also included will be a selected bibliography of critical works on the book. The anticipated audience includes professors teaching the book and graduate and undergraduate students studying it.

All casebooks will be refereed. Successful casebooks will be published on the Dalkey Archive Press website.

The duties of the casebook editor will be to write the overview essay and develop the critical bibliography, to coordinate the other essays, especially avoiding overlapping among them, and to coordinate with the series editor.

The following are the books for which we are seeking casebook editors and contributors:

Felipe Alfau
  Locos
  Chromos
Andrei Bitov
  Pushkin House
Louis-Ferdinand Céline
  Trilogy (*North, Castle to Castle, Rigadoon*)
Peter Dimock
  A Short Rhetoric for Leaving the Family
Coleman Dowell
  Island People
Rikki Ducornet
  The Jade Cabinet
William Eastlake
  Lyric of the Circle Heart
William H. Gass
  Willie Masters' Lonesome Wife
Aldous Huxley
  Point Counter Point
Tadeusz Konwicki
  A Minor Apocalypse
José Lezama Lima
  Paradiso
Osman Lins
  The Queen of the Prisons of Greece

D. Keith Mano
  Take Five
Wallace Markfield
  Teitlebaum's Window
Harry Mathews
  Cigarettes
Nicholas Mosley
  Impossible Object
  Accident
Flann O'Brien
  The Poor Mouth
Fernando del Paso
  Palinuro of Mexico
Raymond Queneau
  Pierrot Mon Ami
Jacques Roubaud
  The Great Fire of London
Gilbert Sorrentino
  Mulligan Stew
Piotr Szewc
  Annihilation
Curtis White
  Memories of My Father Watching TV

Applicants should send a CV and a brief writing sample.

Send applications to:

Robert L. McLaughlin
Dalkey Archive Press, Illinois State University, Campus Box 4241, Normal, IL 61790-4241

Inquiries: rmclaugh@ilstu.edu

RCF Call for Contributors

www.centerforbookculture.org/review

The Review of Contemporary Fiction is seeking contributors to write overview essays on the following writers:

Michel Butor, Julieta Campos, Jerome Charyn, Emily Coleman, Stanley Crawford, Carol De Chellis Hill, Jennifer Johnston, Gert Jonke, Violette Le Duc, Wallace Markfield, Olive Moore, Julián Ríos, Joanna Scott, Esther Tusquets.

The essays must:

- be 50 double-spaced pages;
- cover the subject's biography;
- summarize the critical reception of the subject's works;
- discuss the course of the subject's career, including each major work;
- provide interpretive strategies for new readers to apply to the subject's work;
- provide a bibliographic checklist of each of the subject's works (initial and latest printings) and the most;
- be written for a general, intelligent reader, who does not know the subject's work;
- avoid jargon, theoretical digressions, and excessive endnotes;
- be intelligent, interesting, and readable;
- be documented in MLA style.

Authors will be paid $250.00 when the essay is published. All essays will be subject to editorial review, and the editors reserve the right to request revisions and to reject unacceptable essays.

Applicants should send a CV and a brief writing sample. In your cover letter, be sure to address your qualifications

Send applications to:

Robert L. McLaughlin
Dalkey Archive Press, Illinois State University, Campus Box 4241, Normal, IL 61790-4241

Inquiries: rmclaugh@ilstu.edu

Contents

BRIDGE

NUMBER FOUR APRIL 2002
INTERVIEWS: ALEX SHAKAR JEANNE
DUNNING FICTION: JOE MENO
ELIZABETH CRANE RYAN KENEALY
CURTIS WHITE CAITLIN O'CONNOR
CREEVY CULTURE AND CRITIQUE: KEVIN
BLASKO JAN ESTEP MICHELLE GRABNER
ART: WILLIAM CORDOVA GEAN MORENO
SHANA LUTKER POETRY: D. A. POWELL
PETER RICHARDS JOYELLE MCSWEENEY

WWW.BRIDGEMAGAZINE.ORG

SPECIAL REVIEW OF CONTEMPORARY
FICTION / GILBERT SORRENTINO 20TH
ANNIVERSARY PORTFOLIO ISSUE!

FEATURING ESSAYS BY NICOLAS MOSLEY,
TOBY OLSEN AND OTHERS...

Editors' Acknowledgments

In fact, the whole of Japan is a pure invention.
—Oscar Wilde, "The Decay of Dying"

This special issue of the *Review of Contemporary Fiction* could not have been assembled without the assistance of many different people, Americans and Japanese, translators, transcribers, advisors, and so forth. A big *domo arigato* first of all to all the authors included here for their willingness to meet with us and talk about their lives and writing seriously. Also indispensable to this project were our Japanese colleagues and pomo enthusiasts, Yoshiaki Koshikawa, Yoshiaki Sato, and Toshifumi Miyawaki who—with the assistance of their wives, Kazuko, Jinko, and Hisami—helped us arrange to meet with several of these authors and who also accompanied us during the interviews themselves, serving as both intermediaries and translators during the q & a sessions, and in some instances, as transcribers and translators of the interviews. Takayuki Tatsumi's wife and co-spirator, Mari Kotani, not only attended and contributed to most of the interviews included here, but was always the perfect hostess during several later visits by McCaffery and Gregory to Japan; her warmth, good humor, and keen knowledge of recent developments in Japanese literature were absolutely essential to the completion of this project.

We'd also like to acknowledge the ongoing encouragement and insights provided by numerous Japanese and American academic specialists in contemporary literature, including Jerry Griswold, Dan McLeod, William T. Vollmann, and Tateo Imamura. Assisting with the translations and transcriptions were Takafumi Akimoto, Reiko Tochigi, Pam Hasman, and Hisayo Ogushi; Hisayo Ogushi also wrote several of the individual author introductions. A special word of thanks also goes out to Takashi Yamaguchi, chauffeur extraordinaire and good buddy, who also took us to several of Tokyo's hippest nightspots, pipe bars, and Mexican restaurants. National Endowments for the Humanities funding in the form of a summer fellowship allowed Sinda Gregory and Larry McCaffery to spend several months in Tokyo in 1992, during which this project began. The San Diego State University Foundation and the College of Arts and Letters also provided minigrants which funded the transcription of several of these interviews, while the College of Arts and Letters granted Gregory a sabbatical leave and McCaffery a leave of absence which permitted them to spend the fall of 1998 in

Tokyo, where they completed work on this project. We would also like to thank the Japan Foundation for its generous support of this issue.

Our thanks, too, to all the authors and translators included here for granting us permission—without any payment at all—for use of the English translations of the following works:

"Soft Clocks," by Yoshio Aramaki was originally published in Japanese as "Yawarakai Tokei," and first appeared in the Japanese SF fanzine *Uchujin* (The Cosmic Dust, April 1968), reappeared in a revised form in the Japanese monthly, *Hayakawa's SF Magazine* (February 1972), and was later reprinted in his collection called *Shirakabe no Moji wa Yuhi ni Haeru* (The Writing on the White Wall Shines in the Setting Sun, Tokyo: Hayakawa, 1972); the stylized English version by Lewis Shiner (translated by Kazuko Behrens) originally was published in the British bimonthly SF magazine *Interzone* 27 (January/February 1989).

"Oedipus City," by Kiyoshi Kasai, translated by Kazuko Behrens and stylized by Larry McCaffery and Sinda Gregory, was originally published in Japanese as "Edipusu no Machi" in *Hayakawa's SF Magazine* (August 1984) and then reprinted in his collection by the same name, *Edipusu no Machi* (Tokyo: Kodansha, 1987).

"The Human Factor," by Goro Masaki and translated by K. Odani and Steven Ayres, is an excerpt from his novella *Evil Eyes,* which was originally published in Japanese in *Hayakawa's SF Magazine* (January 1988) and then later included in his collection by the same name, *Evil Eyes* (Tokyo: Hayakawa, 1988).

"Murder in Balloon Town," by Yumi Matsuo was originally published in Japanese as "Baruun Taun no Satsujin" in *Hayakawa's SF Magazine* (March 1992) and later reprinted in her collection by the same name, *Baruun Taun no Satsujin* (Tokyo: Hayakawa, 1994). Translated by Amanda Seaman, © 1998.

"Mental Female," by Mariko O'Hara, translated by Kazuko Behrens and Gene van Troyer and stylized by Michael Keezing, originally was published in Japanese as "Mentaru Fiimeeru" in *Hayakawa's SF Magazine* (December 1985) and later reprinted in her collection by the same name, *Mentaru Fiimeeru* (Tokyo: Hayakawa, 1988).

"Stalled at a Kiss," by Masahiko Shimada and translated by Kenneth Richard, is an excerpt from his novel, *Master and Discipline,* which was originally published in Japanese as *Higan Sensei* (Tokyo: Fukutake, 1992).

"Time Warp Complex," by Yoriko Shono, was originally published in Japanese as "Taimu Surippu Kombinaato" in Bungei-Shunju's literary monthly *Bungaku-kai* (June 1994) and later included in her collection by the same name, *Taimu Surippu Kombinaato* (Tokyo: Bungei-Shunju, 1994); the English translation by Adam Fuller, with assistance from Takahashi Yuriko and Ito Nobuji, first appeared in the Japan PEN Club's *Japanese Literature Today* (1995).

"The Rumors about Me," by Yasutaka Tsutsui, was originally published in Japanese as "Ore ni Kansuru Uwasa" in *Shosetsu Shincho* (August 1972) and later reprinted in his collection by the same name *Ore ni Kansuru Uwasa* (Tokyo: Shinchosha, 1974); the English translation by David Lewis originally appeared in *The African Time Bomb and Other Stories* (Tokyo: Kodansha, 1986).

Dedication

For Ken Akiyama, Masao Shimura, and Shigeru Koike—for their many personal and professional contributions to Japanese-American understanding and friendship

The Japanoid Manifesto: Toward a New Poetics of Invisible Culture

Takayuki Tatsumi

One day I couldn't help but fall in love with Invisible Culture. Ten years ago, in New York City. I'm not sure if you are alive and well, but I need you more than I love you.

No, I'm not talking about either an abstract notion or a specific person, but just recollecting the day the video artist David Blair took me to a fantastic live show of the multiethnic (black, white, and yellow) rock 'n' roll band Invisible Culture at the club Knitting Factory in the East Village. What drove me crazy was the music of Invisible Culture, which was not only ethnoracially hybrid but also dangerously erotic. In a sense, their music is a sort of dangerous, intoxicating drug; once you take one pill, you keep needing more and more. I don't know if they have released an album yet, but I am sure they continue to seduce more addicts.

Now, I'm not only speaking about the fatal attraction of the multiethnic band Invisible Culture, but also about paraliterature as an invisible culture. Such a redefinition is probably inevitable, since one of the theoretical champions of paraliterature is Samuel Delany, a great gay male New Wave science-fiction writer belonging to the race Ralph Ellison called invisible. Disguising himself as K. Leslie Steiner, Delany once remarked: "In spite of some heavy arguing by people both positively and negatively disposed toward his book, Delany has insisted that no matter how high-falutin' it all sounds, his work is not literature but paraliterature, and should be analyzed, however seriously, as such" (*SF Eye* #5, 9). What matters here is not that the discourse of paraliterature has been promoted by a writer of invisible ethnoracial and sexual identities, but that the trope of invisibility is applicable to the canonical problematics of literature. While deeply influenced by the Anglo-American literary tradition, Delany was so skeptical about the discourse of literature invented and constructed by visible intellectuals, that he felt compelled to call his science fiction paraliterary.

With this point in mind, I would like to witness what happens to paraliterature from a comparative literary perspective. Of course, orthodox approaches to literature have undertaken tremendous research on the multiple relationships between and beyond the text with the author, history, intertextuality, intercultural negotiations, international influences, and so on. And yet, what is at stake now might be the act of making these multiple relationships visible. If you take up a methodology of comparative paraliterature, just start by forgetting—or rather radically questioning—the notion of causal relationship. Delany's concept of paraliterature, which had many things in common with the concept of good, old-fashioned metafiction, was further assimilated into cyberpunk writings in the eighties, the literary status of which has been recontextualized by theoreticians like Bruce Sterling (who declared the rise of "slip-stream" literature in 1989) and Larry McCaffery (who provided us with the Avant-Pop perspective in 1991). Despite the contrast between the former's theorization of literary genre and the latter's literary marketing strategy, Sterling and McCaffery were both concerned with the idea of a literary category being deconstructed or deconstructing itself. They taught us new ways to enjoy literature, with a special emphasis, not on the relationship, but the synchronicity between what's going on in mainstream literature and what's going on in paraliterature.

Such a perspective invites us to undertake comparative literary rereading. Insofar as literature is concerned, Japan is a country of an excess of imports, not an excess of exports. This kingdom of translation is very good at translating and making visible foreign cultures, whereas this very same kingdom is largely invisible to other nations, not translating and exporting many of its own national literary fruits. Japanese literature itself, thus, is one of the radically invisible and highly paraliterary cultures. But if you take a glance at what's going on in Japanese postmodern literature, you will be amazed that the kingdom of translation is another name for the kingdom of synchronicity. The more texts you translate, the more capitalistic your nation gets and the more synchronic any two nations or any two national literatures become.

Certainly, in the 1950s and 1960s it became almost inevitable for Japanese writers to freely adopt from the latest translated Anglo-American fiction and to follow American examples produced in the Pax Americana climate. Thus the Japanese tried to import a huge number of Anglo-American cultural products and unwittingly misread their own Occidentalism as genuine internationalism. And yet, since the 1970s Japan's own excessive Occidentalism has sometimes gone so far as to simulate the most canonical discourse of Western Orientalism. However, in Japanese postmodern literature the logic of imitation has been replaced by one of synchronicity—synchronicity between American and Japanese works. It is the logic of hypercapitalism that requires us to throw away our bullshit ideas about causal relationship and to be confronted with the multinational synchronicity between literature and paraliterature.

This paradigm shift from the logic of imitation to the logic of synchronicity is especially evident in the artistic development of all the writers we include here. Let me illustrate the point with quite a few synchronic coincidences.

For example, the Japanese guru of metafiction, Yasutaka Tsutsui, started his career in the 1960s by closely examining the style of Ernest Hemingway and absorbing the pseudoevent/ hyperspectacle theory of Daniel Boorstein. His earlier short-story masterpieces, "The African Bomb" (1968) and "The Rumors about Me" (1972—excerpted in this issue), for instance, unwittingly shared much with Thomas Pynchon's representation of the V2 rocket in *Gravity's Rainbow* (1973) and Andy Warhol's Pop-Art philosophy in the age of hyperdemocratic celebrity.

Haruki Murakami, one of the most famous postmodern Japanese writers in English-speaking countries, started writing in the late seventies by re-creating the literary styles of H. P. Lovecraft, Scott Fitzgerald, and Kurt Vonnegut. His homage to Vonnegut could well be comparable to another slipstreamer, Gen'ichiro Takahashi. However, more recently, Murakami's deeper sense of the past that is characteristic of his 1990s trilogy *Wind-Up Bird Chronicle* was perfectly contemporaneous with the historical consciousness evident in the young American video artist David Blair, who stormed our late-postmodern reality studio with his avant-pop masterpiece *WAX, or the Discovery of Television among the Bees* in 1991 and who is now completing a hyperhistorical romance called *Jews in Space (Israel in Manchuria)*. These examples suggest that the more cultural transactions and translations occur between any two cultures, the more synchronic these cultures and their national narratives become.

A comparison between the American writer Paul Auster's *Moon Palace* (1989) and the Japanese writer Masahiko Shimada's *Higan-Sensei* (Master and Discipline, 1992—an excerpt of which appears in this issue), two typical avant-pop novels skillfully displacing the boundary between literature and paraliterature, will naturally lead one to note an interesting detail: their common use of a Chinese restaurant in New York City, Moon Palace, as a setting, as well as a similar plot structure weaving together exemplary orphan narratives with many metafictional devices. Without having read Auster, Shimada wrote *Higan-Sensei*, narrating a story of an orphan-seeking father, who contrasts strikingly with a father-seeking orphan in *Moon Palace*. It is also possible to discover the analogy between Auster's antidetective fiction *The Locked Room* (1986) and the post-Marxist writer-critic Kiyoshi Kasai's metadetective fiction, *The*

Philosopher's Locked Room (1992).

What is more, if you read Greek-American woman writer Eurydice's *f/32* (1990) with Japanese woman writer Rieko Matsuura's *Apprenticeship of Thumb-Penis* (1993), two typical cyborg-feminist novels radically mocking the boundary between patriarchal literature and feminist paraliterature, you will quickly find their common characterization of genitals as independent protagonists, either male or female. While Eurudice describes a woman's cunt running away from her body in the Gogolian way, Matsuura tells us about a woman's thumb metamorphosed into a penis in the Kafkaesque fashion. The same thing could be found in the comparison between the Anglo-Asian gynoid fictionist Richard Calder's *Dead Girls Trilogy* (1993-96) and Matsuura's close friend and major magic realist Yoriko Shono's representation of cyborgian identity in most of her novels, including her prize-winning novella, *Time Warp Complex* (1994), which is excerpted here. Moreover, we cannot read Yumi Matsuo's science-fiction mystery *Murder in Balloon Town* (1994—an excerpt of which appears in this issue), whose heroine is a biologically pregnant and culturally invisible detective, without recalling the contemporary heritage of invisible culture inaugurated by the African American writer Ralph Ellison's *Invisible Man* (1952) and further explored by the African American queer science-fiction novelist Samuel Delany's *Dhalgren* (1975) and other works.

In addition to such an intercultural synchronicity, the 1980s witnessed another revolutionary paradigm shift. For the first time, Anglo-American writers imitated and reappropriated "Japanesque" images; i.e., images that at once draw on and distort Japanese culture. At the same time, their Japanese counterparts came to realize that writing subversive fiction in the wake of cyberpunk meant gaining an insight into the radically science-fictional Japan. Of course, while American representations of Japan become attractive precisely because of their distortions of Japanese culture, they have often given rise to heated controversy on the part of Japanese audiences. I remember one of friends from Chiba City reacting angrily when he read the first chapter of William Gibson's *Neuromancer,* "Chiba City Blues," which seemed to him to represent the Chiba people very pejoratively. Nevertheless, another cyborg-feminist like Mariko Ohara so deeply speculated upon the rise of hyper-Orientalism that she succeeded in creating a post-Occidentalist cyberpunk narrative "Mental Female" (1985—included in this issue), unwittingly echoing the dramatic advent of Gibsonian cyberspace in the mid-eighties. Let me also note that the rise of the cyberpunk movement also helped revive interest in J. G. Ballardian speculative fiction in the 1960s and 1970s, ending up with the translation of the now famous simulation novelist Yoshio Aramaki's early surrealist masterpiece "Soft Clocks" (1971), loosely based upon not only Salvador Dali's paintings but on Puccini's proto-Orientalist opera *Madama Butterfly* as well.

What is at stake now is the canonical distinctions between Western identity and Japanese identity, Orientalism and Occidentalism, and Anglo-American narcissism and Japanese masochism. While Japanese people have persistently made every effort to imitate and import the tradition of Anglo-American culture, now quite a few Anglo-Americans attempt to incorporate the effects of postmodern Japanese culture into the origin of their everyday life. So how can we designate the chimerical identity born of Virtual Japan, which could just as well cover the new species like the "Otaku" (nerd, or obsessive collector), "Okoge" (a straight woman fan and friend of gay men), "yaoist" (women underground manga artists who reappropriate de-eroticized homosocial images of beautiful boys and queer them), "Hako-otoko & Hako-onna" (new kinds of hobos living in cardboard boxes), all of whom at first glance seem particular to Japanese culture but turn out to be global? Developing Donna Haraway's cyborg theory further, in 1993 with the help of David Blair, I came up with the conceptual framework of "Japanoid"—the post-eighties hyper-Creole subjectivity transgressing the boundary between the Japanese and the non-Japanese, and in so doing, naturalizing the very act of transgression (See Takayuki Tatsumi, *A Manifesto for Japanoids* (Hayakawa Publishers, 1993)). While the heroine of Toni Morrison's *The Bluest Eye* (1970) was dying to become white, now we, along with Michael Jackson, are all enabled by high-technology to put on, take off, and hyperconsume any skin color just like any other brand-new mode. Ethnically Japanese or not, we are all Japanoids. As a proviso, I do not want to boast about the effects of bubble economy in the heyday of Pax Japonica. Instead, let me locate Japanoid as the invisible identity specific to the post-hegemonic globalist age. Japanoid literature does not stick to Japanese literature and Japanesque literature, floating between Japanophobic Japanese and Japanophilic Westerners. We are all living and enjoying the chaotic negotiations between the Orientalist stereotypes of Fujiyama-Geisha-Sushi-Harakiri and the Occidentalist stereotypes of Kennedy-Monroe-*Gone-with-the-Wind*.

From this perspective, let me reconsider the status of an American avant-pop writer, Mark Jacobson, as a typical Japanoid. Jacobson became so fascinated by a famous Japanese gangster that in his first novel *Gojiro* in 1991 (Atlantic Monthly Press), Jacobson "re-Orientalized" Japan by making the friendship between Godzilla himself and a Japanese boy Komodo as its central topic. Indeed, in the history of Japanese cinematography, by the 1980s Godzilla had undergone a transformation in Japan. The image of Godzilla (the oversized public enemy of the fifties) was displaced with that of Godzilla as the all-Japanese superhero in the economic high-growth period. While Godzilla, the radioactive green monster of the 1950s, revived the fear of Moby Dick the white whale, he now encourages not only Japanese screenwriters but also American novelists to re-create postnuclear romances between Japan and the United States. The more synchronic the two cultures get, the more accepting the Japanese become even to the rise of postmodern Orientalism.

Thus we are also intrigued by the concept of postmodern diaspora further developed by recent virtual-reality narratives, such as Goro Masaki's *Evil Eyes* (1986—excerpted here) and *Venus City* (1992) and Alexander Besher's *RIM* (1994), both of which must have been influenced by Sakyo Kamatsu's *Japan Sinks* (1973), in which the erasure of Japan or Tokyo is scheduled to take place not in geospace but in cyberspace. The post-bubble economy in the mid-nineties has apparently made it easier for Japanese to accept other creative masochistic concepts like "Creative Defeat" (Shigeto Tsuru), the "Mental History of Failure and Defeat" (Masao Yamaguchi), and "the strategy of being radically fragile" (Seigo Matsuoka). Japanese intellectuals thus have gradually systematized a self-reflexive form of Occidentalism, which I would like to call the hyper-Occidentalist philosophy of creative masochism. In the age of post-Godzilla, this Occidentalism does not simply imitate Anglo-American precursors but radically transforms the potentially humiliating experience of an imagined Japanese diaspora into the techno-utopian vision of an affirmative construction.

Such a cultural reconfiguration will illuminate the essence of William Gibson's *Virtual Light* (1993), which was deeply affected by the Japanese neo-dadaist artist-writer Genpei Akasegawa's brilliant essay "Thomason" (1985). Gibson reappropriated Akasegawa's junk-art poetics as a postmodern aesthetic principle in his description of the disused San Francisco Bay Bridge in the near future. However, we cannot forget that Akasegawa himself had been largely indebted to a Franco-American dadaist Marcel Duchamp's ready-made theory. Thus at a certain point it becomes more difficult to distinguish between Gibson Japanized by Akasegawa and Akasegawa Americanized by Duchamp. What is evident is that both Gibson and Akasegawa clearly show us the potentiality of junk: the former jeopardized the generic difference between serious fiction (literature) and junk fiction (paraliterature); in the latter the categorical distinctions between the original and the simulacra, the natural and the cultural, the literary and the nonliterary, and the national and the nonnational were fractalized and thrown into crisis. Their allegories of junk will undoubtedly carry us to the invisible birthplace of Japanoid in the globalist age. For now anyway, my romance with invisible cultures does not seem to be cooling off.

Introduction

Larry McCaffery and Sinda Gregory

Some Opening Remarks

Art is something that exists in the slender margin between the
real and the unreal.
—Chikamatsu Monzaemon (1653-1725)

I have a theory of my own about what this art of the novel is, and
how it came into being. To begin with, it does not simply consist of
the author's telling a story about the adventures of some other person. On the contrary, it happens because the storyteller's own experiences of men and things, whether for good or ill—not only that he
has passed through himself, but events which he has only witnessed or been told of—has moved him to an emotion so passionate
that he can no longer keep it shut up in his heart. . . . Viewed in this
light, the novel is seen to be not as it is usually supposed, a mixture
of useful truth with idle invention, but something which at every
stage has a definite and serious purpose.
—Lady Shikibu Murasaki, author of *The Tale of Genji*

We are up to our necks in Western culture. But we have planted a
little seed. And just as a seed takes root and grows, we are beginning to re-create ourselves.
—Japanese Nobel Laureate Kenzaburo Oe in conversation with
Patrick Smith, 1993.

The most urgent task of contemporary art is to synthesize the
global and the particular; to understand the particular in a global
perspective; and to achieve a global perspective that is based on the
particular.
—painter and critic, Taro Okamoto, "What Is Tradition."

I want to believe that "tradition" is the driving force that can tear
down the old framework, open the field for new ideas, and allow new
possibilities for human life to emerge.
—Jun'ichiro Tanizaki, "What Is Tradition."

Man's insecurity stems from the advance of science. Never once

has science, which never ceases to move forward, allowed us to pause. From walking sticks to ricksha, from ricksha to carriage, from carriage to train, from train to automobile, from there on to the dirigible, further on to the airplane, and further on and on, no matter how far we may go, it won't let us take a breath. How far it will sweep us along, nobody knows for sure. It really is frightening.
— Soseki Natsume, *The Wayfarer*.

. . . to confuse Japan's non-modernity with the West's "postmodernism" is perhaps a serious error.
— Masao Miyoshi, Introduction to *Postmodernism in Japan*.

Fiction in the Age of Japan's Post-Millennial Twenty-First-Century Culture

Early in Yoriko Shono's haunting, dreamlike novella, *Time Warp Complex* — an excerpt of which appears in this issue — the story's female narrator, Mrs. Sawano, is talking with (or dreams she is talking with) a mysterious caller (who may be a tuna she has fallen in love with) who remarks, "You must get out there for me. . . . It is the twenty-first century, you know." Although the full implications of these remarks require a more complete context to be fully understood, what should be stressed here is a point that is made in one way or another in nearly all the interviews and fiction selections included in this issue — namely, that the frantic pace of social, political, economic, aesthetic, cultural, and technologically driven change that swept over Japan after World War II like a series of tsunamis thrust Japan into the twenty-first century prematurely; or to put it another way, the millennium arrived in Japan early, thus rendering pronouncements about the imminence of the apocalypse not only passé but anachronistic.

But if contemporary Japan already represents (to quote Michael Stipe) "the end of the world as we know it," what *sort* of brave new world has been emerging in Japan during the past twenty-five years? Certainly readers will immediately notice that the fiction included here bears few similarities to either the modernist works of Soseki, Kawabata, Tanizaki, and other major pre-WWII authors or to the innovative, psychologically complex, existentialist-oriented works of Kobo Abe, Kenzaburo Oe, Yukio Mishima, and other leading Japanese authors who emerged in the years after Japan's devastating defeat in WWII determined to develop new approaches capable of expressing a sense of postwar Japan. Likewise, the textures and allusions found in our fiction selections are almost devoid of references to those traditional features of Japanese life with which most Western readers would be familiar. Thus instead of tatami mats, rice paddies, tea ceremonies, geishas, miso soup, and samuri, readers will find a very different set of references here—to Elvis and Oedipus, Kim Carnes and Salvador Dali, Butch Cassidy and the Sundance Kid; to computers, hackers, and cyborgs; to Western brand names, rap, *Blade Runner,* and Disneyland.

But beyond the exoticism and strangeness (and banality) of these new textures and references, what sorts of narrative forms, character types, imagery, symbolic patterns, and themes have recent Japanese authors been employing to render this postapocalyptic world? In particular, to what extent have Japanese authors been able to develop literary strategies capable of representing the increasingly rapid pace of global exchange generally and the impact of Western pop culture in particular? Or the plurality of virtual worlds introduced into the daily lives of ordinary Japanese citizens by computers, the Net, VCRs, compact discs, and digital cameras, or the various other profusions of data and imagery-aspects of hyperconsumerist contemporary Japan that are today every bit as much a part of its "landscape" as its magnificent shrines and temples, rivers and mountains? In an age in which serious literature has become as increasingly marginalized in Japan as in the U.S., how are Japanese authors finding a means to write books that can successfully compete with the rise of a mass media whose proliferations increasingly seem to be offering audiences an illusion of choice that ultimately only tightens its grip on people's lives and imaginations?

Just as important, what sorts of conclusions are contemporary Japanese authors making about what has been occurring in Japan during the past twenty years? Are these developments seen primarily as utopian variations on the familiar myth of contemporary Japanese history—i.e., that of constant progress, economic miracle, and social harmony—or as something darker and dystopian? If dystopian (as nearly all of the fiction included here seems to be), what methods have Japanese authors been employing to develop a literature of resistance and opposition—this in an era when any form of cultural rebellion, no matter how extreme, can be almost instantly co-opted by the system of cultural production, replicated, and then sold back to Japanese consumers who are able to satisfy their sense of being "hip" by purchasing the latest "countercultural" product?

Finally, beyond certain obvious, often superficial similarities in form and content, what do any of these developments, both within the Japanese culture at large and within the literature that seeks to represent contemporary Japanese life, have to do with postmodernism—a concept which originally evolved in the West as a means of distinguishing the new kind of art and culture that began emerging there during the sixties and early seventies, which seemed to break decisively with the great modernist program?

Although the co-editors of this issue make no claims for being able to supply any definitive answers to these vexing, enormously complex questions, we believe that the interviews and fiction selections included here should provide American readers with a useful departure point from which they can continue their own investigations and readings. With this in mind, we have provided individual introductions for each of the authors included in this issue, as well as other, more general bibliographical information.

The writers we have selected for inclusion in this issue are highly eclectic in terms of their personal and literary backgrounds, their formal tendencies and thematic interests. What unifies their work is most definitely *not* any allegiance to postmodernism or any other movement (indeed, as will be discussed in more detail below, we feel that any attempt to associate their work with the Western-derived concept of postmodernism is highly problematic), but a more general shared acceptance of the need to break with the dominant literary conventions—including those of the confessional "I novel," realism, and naturalism found in the works of Soseki and other prewar Japanese masters and of the dense, exquisitely crafted, psychologically complex narrative modes of Kawabata, Oe, and other figures who flourished from 1945 until 1970. The authors in this issue range in age from Yasutaka Tsutsui (b. 1934)—a literary maverick and one of the first Japanese authors to begin publishing fiction whose formal and thematic concerns are comparable to the work of the first wave of American postmodernists back in the 1960s—to Yumi Matsuo (b. 1960), whose avant-pop novels only began appearing during the nineties. We've included interviews with and fiction selections by several authors such as Haruki Murakami, Yoriko Shono, Masahiko Shimada, Gen'ichiro Takahashi, and Kiyoshi Kasai who are widely read in Japan and published by such leading mainstream Japanese publishers as Kodansha and Shinchosha, while other authors, such as Mariko Ohara, Goro Masaki, Yumi Matsuo, have established their careers (and readerships) within the relatively insular world of Japanese SF and other commercial genre publishing. But with the exception of Murakami, whose books have already achieved considerable attention in the U.S. and Europe, and to a lesser extent, Masahiko Shimada (whose *Dream Messenger* appeared in the U.S. from Kodansha in 1992), most of these authors remain largely unknown in America beyond the few stories that have appeared in recent anthologies.

It goes without saying that there are numerous other deserving authors whom we would have liked to include in this issue but who do not appear here due to circumstances, space limitations, and personal taste. These include Ryu Murakami (arguably the most significant omission of all), Banana Yoshimoto, Amy Yamada, and—the author we most regret not being able to meet—the mysterious and reclusive novelist Shozo Numa, whose savagely satiric, underground masterpiece, *Yapoo, the Human Cattle,* is one of the great achievements of postwar Japanese fiction. Our aim, then, has not been to create a definitive anthology (impossible given the limitations of time, space, and resources) but to compile an issue that will provide a representative sampling of the wide range of vital, innovative fiction that has been appearing in Japan recently.

Bad News/Good News

Japanologists and other readers already familiar with recent literary developments in Japan will soon discover that this issue offers a very different, considerably more optimistic picture of contemporary Japanese fiction than the often harshly critical portrayals of postmodern Japanese culture and literature that have regularly appeared in Japan and the U.S. since the mid-1980s. Typical of such negative assessments are the viewpoints expressed by most of the contributors included in perhaps the most influential study of the topic to have yet appeared in the U.S.—Masao Miyoshi and H. D. Harootunian's *Postmodernism in Japan* (1989). These essays explore a wide range of topics including the evolution of Japanese culture since WWII, the impact of mass culture (particularly advertising) and Western pop forms on this evolution, and the various ways that the hyperconsumerist boom Japan experienced during the 1980s has influenced both the form and content of contemporary Japanese literature and culture. Most of these critics agree that by the time its bubble economy began to expand during the eighties, Japan could indeed be seen to have evolved a postmodern culture that was analogous in many ways to the ones that had evolved in the West—so much so that in many ways it represents a kind of apotheosis of the sort of postmodernism described by Fredric Jameson in his influential account *Postmodernism, or the Cultural Logic of Late Capitalism.* To support such claims, many of the essays in *Postmodernism and Japan* cite a number of key, overlapping formal features and thematic concerns evident in both contemporary Japanese fiction and the postmodernist work of a great many American and European writers from the same period. These shared features—which are also evident in many of the selections we've included here—include: the impulse toward collage, appropriation, and collaboration at the expense of notions of aesthetic order and originality (the latter being of particular significance in a society which has always worked best with found forms); the replacement of linearity, causality, and stable meanings by slippage, pastiche, parody, recycling, and randomness; the impact of poststructuralist theory (by Barthes, Lyotard, Derrida, Baudrillard) on writing practices; and the stylistic tendency toward fabulism, magic realism, and surrealism of effect. Also cited are certain ongoing thematic issues that recur in many of our own fiction selections: the role of info-overload and media-oversaturation (and the resulting transformation of nearly all aspects of art and life into digitalized data and consumable images); the incredible speed and volume at which anything "new" and "different" is now sought out, fetishized, and transformed into products; and the sense of confusion, exhilaration, fear, and euphoria that results when cultural norms, idioms, and sign systems are wrenched out of their original contexts and recast to produce new marketable constructs.

While these critics agreed that there was now ample evidence to indicate that Japan had indeed evolved its own brand of postmodern culture, the arrival of this new culture was also greeted almost unanimously with alarm, skepticism, and concern. This response was certainly understandable, particularly since Japan's mid-eighties brand of postmodernism seemed to exhibit many of the same debilitating features of pomo culture that were being described (and decried) at about the same time by Fredric Jameson, Jean Baudrillard, and many of the other leading Western postmodern theorists. Like Jameson, for example, most of the critics in *Postmodernism and Japan* expressed concern about the loss of idealism; the replacement of history by historicity; the devaluation of reading and writing (and the concurrent emphasis of data-acquisitions at the expense of knowledge); the replacement of the real by the hyperrealities generated by a media or cultural industry increasingly dominated by youth culture; and the difficulties posed for citizens in being able to locate themselves, physically and imaginatively, within such realms. Above all, these critics agreed that the success of the Japanese economy had produced a postmodern society awash in data and creature comforts but nearly devoid of any political awareness or intellectual sophistication. While it was acknowledged that Japanese citizens were still far more likely to read books and magazines than their American counterparts, the process of reading was seen as increasingly related to aspects of commodity production generally: books and ideas were now consumed just like the latest Nike tennis shoes, new burgers from McDonald's, or any other disposable items. Meanwhile, the possibility for any sort of oppositional, politically motivated art having any significant or lasting impact on society had all but disappeared. The following comments by Masao Miyoshi concerning the status of literature in Japan during the late eighties bring together many of most serious criticisms of postmodern Japanese culture into a single dismal pronouncement:

The privatized experience that once was legitimate among intellectuals is now being emptied of self-contemplation. Thus critical oppositions are now virtually nonexistent. . . .

The mark of an individual is his purchases and possessions; likewise, time passes as he labors and daydreams about advertised goods. Books, too, are consumed; that is, they are bought, enjoyed, discarded, and forgotten. No longer authors, manufacturers of books dash off two or even three *shōsetsu* a year, in addition to such lucrative media fragments as *kanso* ("impressions"), *rondan* ("op-ed articles"), assembly-line nonproducts, *taidan* ("dialogue"), and *zandankai* ("round-table conversations"). The journals of opinion, once the arena of intellectual and ideological combats, are now congenial to those in the seat of power and authority. Many journals have simply disappeared, while few have emerged. Literary magazines are notoriously in decline. Books are prompted by large publishers by means of widely publicized awards and prizes that presumably certify quality and confer prestige, but work to increase sales. While more and more people are getting bored with printed words, literature has been redefined as a serious industry and a form of entertainment in which the writers' membership in the collective enterprise is taken for granted. All three leading national newspapers have huge circulations and compete in safe reporting and conformist analyses. Paralleling the holy alliance of capital, labor, and bureaucracy is a powerful consortium of writers (*sakka*), scholars (*gakusha*), reviewers/commentators in the media (*hyoronka*), and publishers (*honya*), all supporting one another in a unified effort to advance their economic interests and power bases. Such a quadrilateral cooperative, often made closer by a shared college or publishing background, grows into an unchallenged monopoly. When several such alliances form a still larger cartel of literature, the nation's culture is ill served indeed. . . .

Under the circumstances, the literature of critical opposition is nearly invisible. (156-57)

While we recognize that there is a great deal of truth to Miyoshi's assessments, we also feel that such an exceedingly glum perspective presents only part of what has been recently occurring in the Japanese literary scene. It should be emphasized, for example, that Miyoshi and the other contributors to *Postmodernism and Japan* were responding to a somewhat earlier set of circumstances—i.e., those in the mid-eighties, when the Japanese bubble economy was still rapidly inflating—than we encountered during the nineties, while we were assembling this issue. As several of our interviews indicate, a number of things occurred during the 1990s to encourage a reassessment on the part of serious Japanese writers about their relationship to history (including Japanese literary history) and mass culture. These events—which included the rapid deflation of the Japanese bubble in the early nineties, the Tiananmen Square massacre, the crumbling of the Soviet Union (and the resulting disappearance of any system to oppose capitalism), the Persian Gulf War, the death of Emperor Hirohito and the fiftieth anniversary of the end of WWII—all contributed to a revival of Japanese fiction, particularly the sort of formally innovative, oppositional work that is showcased in this issue.

Postmodernism without Modernism?
Toward a Post-Postmodernist Literary Aesthetic

Although this issue was originally conceived as a means of showcasing postmodern Japanese writers and fiction—and although, as we've already indicated, Japanese fiction undeniably shares a number of important formal features and thematic concerns with its postmodern American counterparts—we would also like to note here that we've grown increasingly doubtful that terms like *modernism* and *postmodernism* accurately describe what has been occurring within the Japanese literary and cultural scene recently; and at least to a certain extent, this hesitancy on our part turns out to be shared by most of the writers we interviewed. This is hardly surprising, since the Japanese version of postmodernism has emerged from a very different series of historical and cultural circumstances, from equally different philosophical and aesthetic assumptions, and from signifying practices and notions of representation that are also widely divergent from those that gave rise either to Western modernism or postmodernism.

Thus, for example, the authors included in this issue agree that for all the widespread social and political upheavals that were occurring in both Japan and the U.S. during the late sixties, there was no equivalent in Japan to the postmodern literary scene that emerged in the U.S. during this same period. Indeed, how could there be, since the initial conditions responsible for the appearance of postmodernism in the U.S.—which included the rise of pop art and absurd theater, the appearance of translations of Kafka and Borges, the impact of Beckett, Nabokov, Burroughs, Barth, Pynchon, Coover, and other new American authors, the war in Vietnam, the rise of rock music, changing attitudes toward drugs and sex, the first stirrings of feminism and gay pride, the assassination of JFK—had no equivalents in Japan during this period. This isn't to say that Japanese fiction during the 1960s was lacking in literary quality or formal inventiveness—quite the contrary, by the end of the sixties, the postwar generation of authors such as Kenzaburo Oe, Kobo Abe, and Yukio Mishima, had produced a body of fiction unrivaled in Japanese literary history in terms of its formal diversity and intellectual sophistication, the depth of its psychological probings, and boldness of its sociopolitical critiques. This fiction was created by a generation who had witnessed the devastations of WWII and who shared the desire to invent new forms capable of registering not merely what had led Japan into the war and the personal and national disasters resulting from this involvement but also the impact that this national calamity had on the Japanese people following the war. As Japan struggled to rebuild itself during the fifties and sixties, the revulsion about what had led Japan to such a staggering national calamity resulted in a keen interest on the part of many leading Japanese intellectuals and artists (not to mention economists, politicians, educators, and sociologists) in Western philosophy and aesthetic norms as providing possible alternatives to traditional Japanese ways of thinking and culture. Determined to liberate the Japanese from the curse of the emperor system and to offer new models for understanding the vast transformations occurring in Japan, postwar Japanese literature became, in Kenzaburo Oe's words, "A means of giving vent to cultural energies that had been suppressed since the prewar days" (199). On the other hand, for its undeniable accomplishments and radicalism of spirit, this rich and varied body of postwar work bears little similarity with the kind of wildly exuberant, darkly comic, irreverent, and metafictional works that were appearing in the United States during the first wave of experimentalism of the sixties and early seventies.

But by the late sixties, a different generation of Japanese authors was beginning to come of age—one whose aesthetic inclinations, sociopolitical concerns, and interest in mass culture would eventually begin producing fiction that had more in common with Western postmodernism than with the postwar fiction of their parents. These authors emerged into a Japanese world that bore little resemblance to the one that had so decisively shaped the worldview and imaginations of their parents. Born after the war and maturing during the years in which student radicalism was challenging the ideals and practices of the reigning political and cultural norms that had been in place while Japan was successfully rebuilding, authors such as Murakami, Takahashi, Kasai, and Shimada were also the first generation of Japanese writers to have grown up listening to the Beatles and Bob Dylan, watching reruns of American sit coms, and reading the works of early American postmodernists like Brautigan, Vonnegut, Barthelme, Burroughs, and Coover. It is at this point—which is in fact the starting point for this issue—that one can identify enough commonalties in theme and formal approach among Japanese and Western writers to justify using the term *postmodernism* to describe them. But while using this term in this manner is undoubtedly appealing to both Japanese and American audiences, we hope that our own readers recognize that the only real way to understand and appreciate contemporary Japanese fiction is not by making any easy comparisons but by reading the fiction on its own terms. We're also convinced that what has been occurring both in Japan and in recent Japanese fiction should be of great interest to Western audiences not merely because it offers us a window into the evolution of a country whose fortunes, for better or worse, are at this point utterly intertwined with those of the U.S. but because it offers an equally valuable model for judging and assessing related developments in our own culture.

WORKS CITED

Miyoshi, Masao, and H. D. Harootunian, eds. *Postmodernism and Japan*. Durham: Duke UP, 1989.

Thinking the Opposite:
An Interview with Yoshio Aramaki

Mitsutaka Oide

Yoshio Aramaki was born in Otaru, Japan, in 1933. An architect by training, he runs an art gallery as well as a construction company in Sapporo. Aramaki made a debut with his highly speculative fiction "Oinaru Shogo" (The Great Noon) and his heavily theoretical science-fiction manifesto "Jutsu no Shosetsu-ron" (Theory on the Fiction of Kunst), both published in *Hayakawa's Science Fiction Magazine* in 1970. One of his earlier novellas, *Shirakabe no Moji wa Yuhi ni Haeru* (The Writing on the White Wall Shines in the Setting Sun) won the 1972 Seiun Award, the Japanese equivalent of the Hugo, voted on and decided every summer at Japan's National Science Fiction Convention. Two of his earlier short stories, "Soft Clocks" and "Blue Sun" were translated into English (the former printed in *Interzone* #27 in 1989, the latter in *Strange Plasma* #4 in 1991). Another story, "War in the Ponrappe Islands," appeared in English in Lewis Shiner's edited original antiwar anthology, *When the Music's Over* (1991).

Despite the unconventional and metaphysical quality of his earlier works, Aramaki in 1990 launched a hardcore entertainment series of what he designates "Virtual Reality War Novels," with the Admiral Isoroku Yamamoto, the real-life naval commander during World War II, as a central character reincarnated in alternate history. The first volume of this series, *Konpeki no Kantai* (*Deep Blue Fleet*), published in December 1990, did not seem very promising, but the opening of the Gulf War in January 1991 soon helped the series to attract a much wider audience, leading Aramaki to start a different series called *Asahi no Kantai* (*The Fleet of the Rising Sun*); the two series, totaling some twenty-five volumes, wound up selling 5 million copies. The great popularity of this emerging subgenre came to the attention of the *New York Times,* which featured on 4 March 1995 Andrew Pollack's article "Japanese Refight War in Pulp Fiction," based on interviews with Aramaki and other writers of this new literary camp. The following interview was conducted in the heyday of the Virtual Reality War Novels, by Mitsutaka Oide, a military journalist and big fan of Aramaki's fiction, and printed first in *The Deep Blue Fleet Casebook* published in 1992 from Tokuma Publishers. (TT)

Mitsutaka Oide: Could you talk a bit about your background from the time you made a debut as a writer until now?

Yoshio Aramaki: When I was young, I was involved in the SF fanzine called *Core* in Hokkaido. But since I was far from Tokyo, I made a late debut as an SF writer: when I sold my first story to *Hayakawa's Science Fiction Magazine* in 1970, I was already thirty-seven years old. Some said I came out just in the beginning of the second phase of Japanese SF writers, but I thought I belonged to the very end of the first generation. Some even said that I was the father of the restoration/revival [laughs].

As a latecomer, I also struggled a bit. The early SF works were classified into science fiction "themes" such as time travel or cultural anthropology. Each story had some kind of theme. Most of the good themes were already taken when I began writing, and just like Japan after World War II, there weren't any good ones left [laugh].

Being a latecomer, I had to have something new. In those days, no one was interested in your writing if you were simply imitating the work of others. I studied psychology at Waseda University. But when I returned to Hokkaido in 1957, I entered Hokkai Gakuen University's Construction/Engineering Department, which was necessary in order to inherit my family business. I entered the school as the top student, but I hardly went to classes. I was working at a job site during the day, you know? I had managed to attend about one-third of the classes, and I got a special permission to graduate from the school. For this reason, I have licenses in construction and architecture. Using the knowledge of this field and psychology as well as philosophy, I wrote "The Great Noon." It was first published in the fanzine *Uchujin* (*The Cosmic Dust*).[1] Then Mr. Yu Mori (pen name: Hiroshi Minamiyama), chief editor of *Hayakawa's SF Magazine* at the time, also published the story in *SF Magazine,* and I was featured as a debut writer. It was 1970. I guess I was lucky.

Most of my early short stories were collected in *Soft Clocks* and *Space 25th Hour* (1978, Tokuma Publishers). You could say that those are my early SF works and those are the ones that are now being recognized overseas.

MO: In 1989 "Soft Clocks" was translated into English and published in *Interzone,* and in 1991, "Blue Sun" was published in *Strange Plasma.* Since those stories were well received, your work was included in an SF anthology by an American SF writer. Could you talk a bit about the background of how these translations came about?

YA: Let me explain the process. Mr. Takayuki Tatsumi was serving as a liaison in this process while he was studying abroad at

Cornell University. He met Ms. Kazuko Behrens there. She was married to an American but happened to be from Sapporo and expressed an interest in translating my story. That was the beginning. But a literal translation of a Japanese SF will not work for general audiences in the English-speaking countries. So Mr. Lewis Shiner, an SF writer from Texas who was associated with the mid-eighties cyberpunk movement, rewrote or "stylized" some of my stories. "Soft Clocks" was published in the British SF magazine *Interzone*. Later, "Blue Sun" was also published in the American magazine, *Strange Plasma*. As was noted in a book review, the concept of a meta-SF, currently popular in America owing to P. K. Dick, Thomas Disch, Samuel Delany, and Barry Malzberg, had been adopted by a Japanese writer twenty years ago.

Then, when I was attending the SF World Convention in New Orleans in 1988, I met Mr. Shiner. He mentioned to me that he was planning to publish an anthology of tales against war and violence and asked me if I would write one for it. I agreed, and I wrote "War in the Ponrapp Islands" which was published in the summer of 1991. It has not been published in Japan yet.

MO: I will ask you about "War in the Ponrapp Islands" in detail later, but can you first explain your transition from your early meta-SF works to your recent compilation of your works, *Deep Blue Fleet*?

YA: For *SF Magazine,* "Tales of White Devils" series was the last of the series. A job as a writer can be quite scary, you know? When the chief editor, Mr. Yu Mori, resigned the position, there was no more work for me, so I went through a dry period.

When Shodensha Publishers in Tokyo decided to publish works other than novels, I was asked to write for them because Ryo Hanmura was writing Historical Gothic. I suppose they had been reading my "Tales of White Devils" series. So I turned around 180 degrees in "Blank" series. I probably disappointed some loyal fans, but I didn't have a choice because it was the publisher's request. This is the world of supply and demand after all, you know? Tokuma saw this change and called me. I then started the "Kinmeria" series in 1976 from Tokuma. They sold quite well. I also began writing the "Big Wars" series for Tokuma around the same time, that is, in 1978.

Meanwhile, in the mid-eighties, we entered a stagnant period in SF literature. It was around that time that I resigned from the Science Fiction and Fantasy Writers of Japan. I didn't have a choice and I was writing pseudo-Gothic mysteries for Kodansha. But with the emergence of Mr. Hideyuki Kikuchi and Mr. Baku Yumemakura, even the trend of Historical Gothic seemed to have been altered.

Later, an editor from Chuo Koron Publishers, who claimed to be a loyal fan of my work since the beginning, contacted me. He was planning a new sort of publication and wanted to feature something unique. After brainstorming, I began writing *Niseko Fortress 1986*, the first one in the "Fortress" series. This was based on "Big Wars," and in order to produce a new work, you have to follow several steps. First you get books and materials from which you gain knowledge and gather data. From this you establish a knowledge base that can be added to or modified.

Until very recently in the early nineties, I was writing the "Sarutobi Sasuke" series for Kadokawa. For this series, I explored the Sengoku period (the Age of the Civil Wars) for the first time. If I may describe my field in graphical terms wherein the vertical line stands for time and the horizontal line for space, I covered the ancient period with "Blank" series. "Sarutobi Sasuke" was the Sengoku period (the Age of the Civil Wars). Then, "Shinshu Byakuma-den" (Tales of the White Devils) treated the Hiraga clan from the Tanuma era of the Edo period. I have not yet tried the Meiji period or prewar period, but I'm planning to do so. So once I get to World War II, my work will then be all connected, covering almost every historical period in Japan. From a spatial point of view, "Big Wars" is already expanding into the space. I believe such "largeness" of the scale is quite useful. Because when you master the Sengoku period (the Age of the Civil Wars), as I explained in *The War Strategy of Deep Blue Fleet* (Tokuma, 1992), you begin to understand that the military strategy approximates that of World War II. It was based on the theory of generations. Even now, the theory of generations strategy exists as a principle of a military strategy. So now that I understand the basic principles, I can then apply them across time.

Also, for background in general, SF requires the construction of an entire world. As a result, you must gain a shallow but broad knowledge of all areas. This explains why I have books of all kinds, from pornography to philosophy, on my bookshelves. It is impossible to build an SF-like world unless you have this breadth of knowledge. So you could say my broad knowledge base is a result of being an SF writer for twenty-five years. *Deep Blue Fleet* was thus based on all of this accumulated knowledge.

MO: In 1978 you already mentioned in your interview with Mr. Tetsu Yano that you felt you should definitely write about World War II.

YA: It is true that I was feeling that way then. But I could not write without the adequate preparation. As I've just explained, a writer doing these sorts of works must first gather materials, read

books, and build a strong base of knowledge. What I was lacking
was the knowledge of weapons and tools. I gradually began gaining
this knowledge when I studied airplanes in "Fortress" series or "Big
Wars."

The reason World War II is so important is that I intend to write
about the Japanese race. When you think of the Japanese race historically, it was not until World War II that the Japanese played a
major role in world history. In other words, during this construction
of world history and international movements, Japan, for the first
time, was itself a major player. Until then, Japan was kind of a
country bumpkin located on the edge of the Asian continent. We
don't know, maybe it was marginalized in this way, but either good
or bad, Japan did participate in world history beginning in the
1930s and shook the world. From this point of view, I think that
World War II obviously was indeed a significant event for Japan.

I was in the second grade when the war broke out. It was over
when I was in the sixth grade. You could say that I spent pretty
much my entire elementary school life in wartime. We all read lots
of SF stories during the war. My parents would get mad at me, so I
used to read them under the covers with a flashlight. That kind of
feeling seems to have had an impact on readers of my generation
that remains even today. Even a professor of international politics
said that he enjoys reading my stories.

Stories that were popular when I was a child, such as "Sunrise of
Asia" or "Floating Flying Island," are so unscientific and ridiculous
if you read them now.[2] But I certainly remember how exciting they
were as a child attending a national school at that time. I want to
re-create these feelings of excitement in my stories. I try to introduce some unusual or unexpected weapons. It is the era of new
ideas so I try to come up with some of my own. Even during World
War II, the Japanese military were doing some very strange things.
I was reading some weekly magazine where I learned that they
made navy soldiers dress in women's costumes and pretend to be
bathing in the sun. Then they approached the enemies and attacked
them. They won some fights that way. They did many such silly
things that are probably at least as improbable and fantastic as
anything I have ever invented.

MO: As examples of similar kinds of impossible events that
you've invented, in your own *Deep Blue Fleet,* you have the Japanese military landing by parachute in the middle of Washington
D.C. and directly approaching the American mothership and advis-
ing them to surrender.

YA: Well, even impossible things can become possible in stories?
That's why fiction is interesting. As with Swift's story of Gulliver,

once you start thinking unconventionally you begin to discover new things. Even when you look at a world map upside down, you begin to see something very interesting.

MO: So, for example, in *Deep Blue Fleet* the captain Otaka obtained a map from England, because he thought that the strategy would become too rigid if he used a Japanese version of a map with Japan in the center . . .

YA: When you look at a map made in England, England is the center of the world. Japan is a little country on the edge of the world. But now we all recognize the world as a globe. Like geopolitics, unless you understand the world globally, your war strategy will be fatally wrong.

MO: Illusionary meta-SF, Gothic SF, military simulation: you have covered a truly wide range of world construction. Despite the variety of your experiments, does "Jutsu no Shosetsu-ron" (Theory on the Fiction of Kunst) still constitute the base for all these?

YA: Yes, it does. "Theory on the Fiction of Kunst" basically reexamines Heinlein's work. Heinlein was also involved in the construction industry like me. What's important is to create things by hand and to think as if you were at a job site in real time. At a job site in real time, there is actually an incredible amount of mental activity.

Classic literature often does not deal with the concept of jobs in real time. When they talk about the problems of the family, of man and woman, these problems are discussed as social problems, or as literary "theme." In fact, in our lives, especially for men, we spend a much longer time at work. There we use different things to write, to print, and to make things. I always wonder why most writers don't write about this. Maybe this is a weakness in classic literature. At any rate, I believe that to create things in itself provides a psychological peace or a conscious purpose for being a human, something important for living. That, at least, is the kind of SF I write.

Also, what was discussed in "Theory on the Fiction of Kunst" was a different way of handling problems. Classic literature deals with a problem in life or in society by simply presenting it. Depression may lead to a suicide or nihilism. Modern literature is especially like that. It is the victim literature of the victim. But in SF literature, especially Heinlein's stories, people aren't usually mere victims: instead, they solve these problems.

Even in the *Deep Blue Fleet* series, Japan encounters many serious problems. Many of these relate to Japan today. In other words, my series explores how Japan can remain in peace. The constitution of peace in writing or peace activity alone will not solve the world's peace problems. If that were all it took, it would have been solved during the Wilson era. When you encounter these problems in my writings, I try to simulate how we can realistically solve them. This is my major theme. Simulation is itself a rather postmodern concept. "This could be a mistake but why not try it?" This is how Prime Minster Otaka in *Deep Blue Fleet* comes up with various ideas. By reflecting on past mistakes, they do not repeat them. They don't protect an island; they do not attack the mainland. Losing is winning. All sorts of things can be created by thinking the opposite. I believe that's why people have found my work interesting. In any event, problems must be solved. Everyone—including Asahi newspapers, other newspapers, scholars, and governments—says we have to do something. But no one comes up with a detailed plan. This is a problem. Of course, I am only an amateur, so I can be wrong. I may not be accurate but I give it a try. Failure itself can be a basis for the next success! I am not a man unless I take detailed action. A job must be detailed. It doesn't help to simply criticize faults like professional critics. Anyway, under the circumstances that exist now, I've been thinking that I have to do something—and as a writer, this sort of speculative problem-solving seems worthwhile.

NOTES

[1]This fanzine was launched in 1957. Many SF writers, including Shinichi Hoshi and Masaki Yamada, made their debut in this publication. The origin of "The Great Noon" was "Time Harbor" which was published in *The Cosmic Dust* No. 140. (January 1970).

[2]"Sunrise of Asia" was written by Minetaro Yamanaka and "Floating Flying Island" was written by Juzo Unno.

The complete interview with Yoshio Aramaki can be accessed at www.centerforbookculture.org.

Soft Clocks

Yoshio Aramaki

> When I look at the stars in the sky, they appear so small. Either I am growing larger or the universe is shrinking—or both.
>
> —Salvador Dali

It was noon on Mars. The party was already in full swing under blinding equatorial sunshine. The theme was "Blackout in Daylight." Our host was DALI, surrealist, paranoiac-critic, millionaire, technophobe. His estate covered an area of the Lunae Planum about the size of Texas.

Gilbert, the producer of the affair, had left orders that all guests were to wear costumes taken from the paintings of the original Salvador Dali. Even I could not get out of it. Nearly naked receptionists, their faces made up into masks, took away the business suit I'd worn from Earth and dressed me in a plastic costume with golden wings, taken from the "View of Port Lligat with Guardian Angels and Fishermen."

I wandered out into the grounds, dazzled by the landscape. A pond of mercury and mirrors flowed at unsettling angles. A dimensionless black mountain reflected the Spanish seaside village, Port Lligat, where Dali had spent so many years. Erotically shaped pavilions stretched to impossible horizons.

"This is indeed surreal, is it not?" said a man's voice behind me. I turned around. The man's hair stood straight up, the Dalist trademark. His mustache was waxed and curled at the ends. He held a glass of Martian blue mescal, clearly not his first. "Oh, excuse me. What are you supposed to be? A donkey?"

"I'm sorry?" I said.

The man's upper body weaved from side to side, though his feet were planted solidly in the red sand. "No, wait, I see it now, you're a tiger . . ."

Not just the mescal, I thought. The hallucinations were typical of Martian Disease, a form of low-grade encephalitis. According to the literature, the victim's interpretations of an object shifted without the perception itself changing. The disease was responsible for an abnormally high level of neuronal activity and some even claimed it gave the victims telekinetic powers. The last was of course not verified.

I couldn't imagine what I must have looked like to him. He seemed to find it amusing enough.

"I'm from Tokyo," I said. "I am—or was—Vivi's analyst. You sent me a letter—"

"Ah, yes, doctor. Welcome. I'm the famous DALI OF MARS. How are you enjoying the party? Vivi should be with us soon."

"Good, that's good," I said. I'd known that coming here would mean seeing Vivi again. Now I found myself afraid of the idea.

"Gilbert should be here somewhere. He produced all this. You'll want to meet him."

"I don't remember him being on the list," I said. "Is he one of the . . . uh, candidates?"

"Ah, the list. So you're wanting to start work already, eh?" DALI was distracted by a young woman in a death's head mask and a tight suit cut away to reveal her breasts and buttocks. His eyes bulged with a look of insatiable greed.

"Yes," I said. "I'd like to get started as soon as possible. It would be much easier if I could get back my normal clothes . . ."

"Yes, of course," DALI said. "The 'candidates,' as you put it, should be in the bar." He pointed toward a building shaped like a snail's shell lying on its side.

"Thank you," I said, but DALI was already walking toward the woman with the death's head.

Dressed like a normal person again, I made my way to the bar. Chairs were set up along the wide spiraling aisle, and leather bags full of mescal hung from the curved ceiling. Several of the guests were already drunk. As DALI would have put it, they looked like "snail meat marinated in good champagne."

I found a seat in a bulge of the wall, close enough to hear the conversation. As an outsider, it sounded to me like a herd of geese being stampeded by a pig. Highly symbolic words and phrases shot out of their mouths, one after another. There was a certain harmony to it, but it didn't last. The loudest of the voices belonged to Pinkerton, the pig among the geese.

His name and that of Professor Isherwood, the rheologist, were the first two on DALI's list.

"No, no, no," he shouted. He was dressed as the artist's self-portrait, in smock and beret. "You're all wrong. The hatred of machines goes all the way back to my ancestor, Salvador Dali. His is the true paranoiac-critical view of technology. It's my perfect understanding of this that Vivi so admires. That's why the odds all show that I'm going to be picked for her husband. The odds are 92.4 percent, in fact, calculated objectively."

"Fool," said Isherwood. He sat across the table from Pinkerton, wearing a corduroy jacket over a sweater. "Loudmouthed fool."

"What?" Pinkerton came out of his chair, leaning across the table with both hands spread wide. "You're nothing but a monkey, a simpering toady to technology. You haven't got a prayer. Our engagement will be announced any day. Vivi's husband will be Pinkerton, genius painter of Mars, new incarnation of the first, the original, Salvador Dali!"

Pinkerton settled back in his chair, checking his hair in a hand mirror. Isherwood stared at him, his hands shaking. There was a glass of mescal in one of them and it shattered with a transparent sound. Blood streamed onto the tablecloth.

"Ah," Pinkerton said. "This is true beauty. I think I'll show this tablecloth in my next exhibition."

The other two at the table, Boccaccio the barber and Martin the movie actor, laughed without much conviction. Pinkerton seemed serious. "I think I'll call it, 'Jealous Donkey, with His Tail Caught in His Horseshoe, Insults an Angel.' "

"This is ludicrous," Isherwood said. He got up, knocking his chair over, and started out.

"Sir?" I said. I offered him my handkerchief.

"Thank you," he said. He wrapped the handkerchief over his cut and glanced back at Pinkerton. "The man is insane."

"Martian sickness," I said. "Maybe he's not in control of himself. Will you sit down?"

Isherwood nodded and sat across from me. "I've never seen you before," he said. "Are you from Earth?" When I nodded, he said, "You talk like a psychiatrist."

"A marriage counselor, right now," I said. "I was trained in psychiatry. But there aren't many openings these days. Not on Earth, anyway."

"My name is Isherwood."

"I know," I said. "I've read your articles on the rheoprotein."

Isherwood raised one eyebrow, but didn't take the bait. "You're here as a tourist?"

"I'm studying Martian Disease," I said. It was the cover story DALI had instructed me to use. "I want to see if there's any truth to this mind-over-matter business."

"Odd work for a marriage counselor," Isherwood said. "I think maybe you're here to test the various suitors for Vivi's hand. What do you say to that?"

I looked down. My training was in psychiatry, not espionage. I didn't know how to go about deceiving him.

"Good," Isherwood said. "So I'm to be the first. Tell me, what are my chances?"

"I couldn't tell you yet. There have to be tests and interviews, I have to compare your test data with Vivi's . . ."

"You already have Vivi's data then?"

One thing was already clear. Isherwood was in love with Vivi. I only had to speak her name to arouse his jealousy.

"I treated Vivi personally while she was studying on Earth," I said.

"Personally?"

"Needless to say, we were just doctor and patient, nothing more." His stare cut into me. I found myself rushing to explain. "She suffered from acute technophobia. It's different on Earth than it is here. There are machines everywhere. You can't get away from them. Computers and televisions and video cameras in every room. It's bad enough for an ordinary person coming from Mars, but with Vivi's special—"

Isherwood cut me off. "That's true. She has a very delicate nervous system. It was a mistake to send her to Earth in the first place."

"But your work is technological. Don't you think it would be a mistake for the two of you to marry?"

"Well, I don't think so, of course. I'll be with her no matter what happens."

"But you have powerful enemies. And are you sure she cares for you? You're old enough to be her father."

"I don't know," Isherwood said sadly. "My Beatrice's mind is more mysterious to me than the construction of Phobos."

"So she hasn't refused you completely, then?"

He looked theatrically at the curved ceiling. "No, she only smiles like the Mona Lisa." I wondered if he meant da Vinci's or Dali's.

We moved to his office so we could have privacy for the formal tests. I gave him TAT, Improved Rorschach, Super Association Test, Differential Color Test, Abnormal Sentence Completion, and everything went well. There's often a problem with defensiveness in this sort of testing, but Isherwood was open and friendly, often showing a childlike innocence.

I'd almost told him about Vivi in the bar, but he'd interrupted me. Now, the longer I put it off, the harder it was to bring the subject up again.

I'd found out about it during her analysis in Tokyo three years before. It was early summer when she first came to my office. I could see crystalline sunlight through the green leaves outside my window. By the end of June the heat and monoxide would turn everything to gray and brown.

Vivi was a student at the art college near my office. She was a referral from the local hospital, where she'd been taken after she tried to disembowel herself with an ancient short sword.

When I saw her medical records things became clearer. The plane bringing her to Tokyo had crashed, and only the replacement of her heart, lungs, and stomach with artificial constructs had kept her alive. Knowing her technophobic background, the surgeons had kept the information from her. But her subconscious had evidently at least suspected the truth.

She was only eighteen, beautiful as a butterfly. I was twenty-seven, just out of medical school, without even a nurse or a secretary, trying to make a living from referrals. I suppose I loved her immediately. Of course, I realized my position. It would have been improper for me to take advantage of our relationship as doctor and patient. More than that, though, I simply didn't have any confidence that I could make Vivi happy. A conservative attitude, but then I was young and hadn't established myself, and my future was far from certain.

I saw her for over a year, and helped her, I think. Maybe I should have told her the truth, that the technology she hated was the only thing keeping her alive. But I couldn't bring myself to do it. Her feelings were too delicate, like fine glasswork.

There were other problems I was able to help her with. The worst of them was her relationship with her grandfather. Her father had died when she was three years old. She suspected, perhaps with reason, that DALI had then had an incestuous relationship with her mother. DALI became both substitute father and rival for her mother's love. I had persuaded her to confront some of these Oedipal conflicts and begin to resolve them.

When she left to go back to Mars I thought I would never see her again. And then the letter arrived from DALI. Vivi was twenty-one now, old enough for marriage, but she rejected every man who even broached the subject. DALI had decided that she was to marry, and I was to choose from his list of candidates. The thought of selecting her husband was distasteful to me, but it would mean seeing Vivi again. I accepted.

And so far, the first candidate was doing well. There was only one serious problem. Vivi was still technophobic, and Isherwood's occupation as rheologist naturally involved machines. I tried to delicately express my concerns, but Isherwood ignored me, instead indulging in still more poetry.

"I'm the one who really loves her. Pinkerton is only thinking of DALI's fortune. A square inch of any of his paintings is worth more than a hundred square feet in Manhattan. I'm different. Vivi has taught me the meaning of life. She is a heliotrope, blooming in the red desert of Mars."

"But you must see that Pinkerton is the more obvious choice. He is younger and, forgive me, better looking. As an artist, his career would not be so threatening to her. And he seems very confident of his appeal . . ."

"So you think so, too? But there are things I can offer her. Wonderful toys. Delights for the imagination. Just look."

He reached into a desk drawer and took out a soft clock. It was the size of a dessert plate, and it hung limply over his hand. He set it on the edge of the desk, and the rim of the clock bent and drooped toward the floor.

"That's amazing," I said. I touched it with one finger and it gave slightly. The second hand moved continuously around the dial, following the deformations of the clock. "Just like in Dali's 'Persistence of Memory.' "

"Made entirely of rheoprotein," Isherwood said. "Accurate to within a few milliseconds, and calibrated for the slightly shorter Martian hour. It must be kept reasonably cool, or it will melt, just like chocolate."

"This seems impossible," I said.

"It would be, with an inorganic mechanism. The problem is that the gears, for example, must resist other gears and yet be flexible under pressure from gravity or an external touch. The protein resembles a universal joint, only on a molecular level. Plus there is an information carrying component, like RNA, that allows it to recognize other rheoproteins and respond appropriately to them."

"A very complicated toy," I said.

"It's not just a toy," Isherwood said, "It could bring an industrial revolution on Earth. Maybe you've seen some reference to it—they're calling it Flabby Engineering. Some journalist's idea of a joke, I imagine. Anyway—an internal combustion engine could be produced in virtually any shape—long and thin, like a broomstick, or twisted, like a spiral. Not to mention cybernetics. Energy or movement can be passed on—or reacted to—with the kind of smoothness you see in living tissue."

"I even find it interesting, from a psychiatric standpoint. The contrast between the hardness of machines and the softness of human beings . . ."

Isherwood didn't seem to be listening. "In factories this kind of material could contain, or even harness, the force of accidental explosions. Cars and planes would be infinitely safer." The mention of airplanes made me think of Vivi. "Submarines could be built to mimic the swimming of dolphins. With flexible machine parts all these six-decimal-point tolerances would become meaningless."

He held up his hands. "The possibilities are . . . well, beyond anything we could imagine."

For the rest of that day and all of the next I interviewed the remaining candidates. Boccaccio had little intelligence and no imagination. Martin, the actor, was driven by vanity and greed. Conrad, a well-known athlete, revealed a basic hostility toward women.

I interviewed Pinkerton late on the second day. As with all the others, I approached him in conversation and only later resorted to formal testing. He seemed eager to make a good impression once he found out what I was really up to. But under the relentless light of the personality tests he showed himself to be nothing but a dreamer and a braggart, completely self-obsessed. By the end of our session he was screaming and cursing me.

Of all of them only Isherwood was stable and sincere enough to be worthy of Vivi. His paternal nature would go well with her delicate personality and sensibilities. The only problem was Vivi's technophobia. If she married Isherwood, it might very well send her over the edge.

The party lasted two days. The last guests were gone by the time I finished with Pinkerton. The butler showed him to the door and I was alone in DALI's huge cathedral of a house.

I had no sooner showered and changed than the butler came to my room with an invitation. "My master wishes you to join him for dinner, if that would be convenient."

"Of course," I said.

I followed him down to the lobby. Through a bronze door I could see a hallway that seemed to curve upward and over itself in defiance of gravity. When I looked closer I saw it was only an illusion.

The mansion was full of them. There were so many false rooms and staircases and corridors that the false parts seemed to put pressure on the real things, distorting them into nightmare shapes.

The dining room was so large it seemed a deliberate insult to rationality. Black-and-white checkered tiles receded to infinity in all directions.

"Welcome," DALI said, "please sit down." He was at the head of the long, narrow table. His favorite crutch leaned against the side of his red-velvet armchair. But I hardly noticed him. At the far end of the table sat his granddaughter, Vivi.

She was ethereally beautiful. Her golden hair was cut within an inch of her head. Her cheeks were sunken, her eyes hollow, and the muscles of her neck stood out like marble ornaments. It was obvious to anyone that she was critically anorexic. I smiled at her, and she smiled back with what seemed to be great pleasure.

The first chair I touched collapsed and then sprang back into shape. It was clearly not meant to support my weight.

DALI smiled. "One of Mr. Gilbert's designs. They are part of his 'Revenge against the Machine Age' series. You see, if the function of a tool is removed, you have Art. Very witty, don't you think?"

I found a chair that would support my weight, and the dinner began.

DALI explained that shellfish had long been the object of his family's gluttony. "The bones, you see, are the objectivity of the animal. The flesh is madness. We carry our objectivity inside us and wear our madness for all the world to see. But the shellfish, the shellfish is an enigma. Objective outside, mad within."

He then proceeded to eat an astounding quantity of oysters, mussels, lobsters, crab, and conch. Unlike the classic bulimic he did not pause to purge himself, but kept on eating with undiminished appetite.

Vivi, meanwhile, did not even taste the small portion she had been served. "Grandpa won't listen to me," she said, her voice glistening like olive oil. "Please, doctor, won't you speak in your own behalf?"

I smiled uneasily, unsure what she was asking.

"This child wants everything," DALI said, breaking through the shell of a monstrous shrimp and attacking the soft, buttery meat inside. "I have always given her whatever she wanted." He looked at me meaningfully.

"I'm sorry," I said, "but—"

"No!" Vivi said. "Doctor, tell him that I only want to be with you! I want you to take me back to Tokyo with you!"

I was completely at a loss. It was natural for a girl like Vivi to become infatuated with her doctor during treatment. It is a common hazard of psychoanalysis. But such feelings are shallow and temporary. Vivi needed a strong father figure, someone to love her faithfully and protect her. Someone like Professor Isherwood.

"Vivi, I—"

DALI grabbed his crutch and stood up. "Vivi! You will go to your room! Immediately, do you hear me?" He turned to me. "Please try to make her understand, doctor."

"No," Vivi said, "no, no, no!" She lunged for a table knife and brought it up to stab herself in the chest. I saw that I could not reach her in time and snatched away DALI's crutch. With the crutch I knocked the knife from Vivi's hands. She sank back into her chair, weeping.

I looked back at DALI. It was as if I had taken his sanity when I took the crutch away from him. "Give me that!" he shouted and tore it from my hands.

I already knew the crutch was both physical and psychological. It appeared in many of Salvador Dali's paintings. It was the symbolic tool he needed to support his soft world. DALI and Vivi stared at each other across the table. The anger and jealousy sparked in the air between them. Vivi recovered first and ran from the room, covering her face with both hands.

We all have our crutches, I thought. Sometimes they are powerful weapons and sometimes they become dangerous dependencies. The dinner was over.

I found the butler and asked him where Vivi had gone. He said she had just taken her car into town. "Probably to the Narcissus. It's a pub where the artists all go." He gave me directions and the key to one of DALI's cars.

The pub smelled of tobacco, marijuana, mescal, amyl nitrate, beta-carboline. The Chiriconians meditated silently in the center of the room. A naked couple, tattooed with birds and snakes, wandered around until they finally found two seats by themselves. Two contending groups of monochromists formed living sculptures, the blues horizontal in a dark corner, the reds vertical under a bright light. The futurists walked rapidly around the edges of the room, talking in a truncated language which I could not understand. A pop-artist, wrapped in dirty bandages like a mummy, smelled of rotten sausage.

A fauvist woman, dressed as Matisse's "Lady in Blue," approached me. "Buy a girl a drink?" she said. I nodded and signaled to the waitress. "So what group are you?" she asked.

"I am as you see me."

"That's what I was afraid of. Non-artist. What a drag. Too practical, no dreams." She drained her absinthe in a single swallow. "Oh," she said. "Here comes my friend." I was a little relieved when she left me for the old man, who moved with robotic stiffness. A cubist, apparently. I had heard the rumor that fauvists were obsessed with wolves. Just as the thought came into my head, the woman in the blue dress turned back to me and smiled, showing cosmetically implanted fangs.

I looked away. Martian Disease, everyone was affected to some degree. If I stayed too long, it would begin happening to me. The pub reminded me of the mental hospital in Tokyo where I'd been an intern.

"Are you alone?" a woman said. "May I sit here?"

She had a firm, beautiful body, covered by a Tahitian dress out of a painting by Gauguin. There were red tropical flowers in her hair.

"Do I know you?" I asked.

"My name is Carmen. We met the day before yesterday at DALI's mansion."

"Ah, yes, you were one of the receptionists. I was here looking for Vivi, actually. Have you seen her?"

"She went for a ride with some of DALI's disciples."

"Where do you think they went? I really need to find her."

"Give it up. The desert is too big. She'll be all right."

I let her convince me. After all, I thought, if she was with friends, they would take care of her.

I bought Carmen a glass of champagne and ordered a beer for myself. The beer tasted like mouse piss. Martian water and hops were not up to the job. But it had a lot of alcohol in it, and I quickly became drunk.

Martian women were notoriously loose, and Carmen was no exception. I felt the pressure of her hips against mine. I was a long way from home, and her interest was warming me faster than the beer.

The champagne was clearly affecting her. "I have to make a confession," she said. "I have a terrible habit and I can't seem to stop it. I'm a kleptomaniac. I steal things."

It wasn't the confession I'd wanted to hear, but I nodded sympathetically.

"The guilt is really terrible," she said. "I'm suffering so much pain from it. Please, spank me, doctor." She started to cry.

No one seemed to care except a man at the next table, who said, "Why don't you just go ahead and hit her? That's what she wants." He was wearing a bowler and waistcoat and a short beard. He tipped the hat to Carmen. "Hey, Carmen, did you steal anything worth money this time?"

"You cheap old bastard!" Carmen shouted.

"Bitch!"

The man yanked her away from me, and then both of them fell onto the floor. The man straddled her waist, backwards, lifted her dress, and began to spank her shapely buttocks. I got up to pull him away and felt a hand on my arm. It was the Lady in Blue. "That's Carmen's pimp," she said. "You'd do better to stay out of it."

The pimp opened her purse and felt inside it. "This bitch, she steals the most worthless shit. What the hell is this?" The thing he pulled out hung down through his fingers like chewing gum.

It was one of Isherwood's soft clocks.

"You thief!" Carmen shouted. Without warning she threw the clock into her mouth, chewed it and swallowed it.

I was not, it seemed, going to be spending the night with Carmen. But she had given me an idea. I ran to the phone and called Professor Isherwood.

The next morning I woke up with a pounding head and queasy stomach. I hadn't realized the aftereffects of Martian beer would be so devastating. I took a hot shower and lurched downstairs just in time for breakfast. DALI was in an extremely good mood. He had already begun eating.

"Why don't you try one?" he said.

When I saw what was on the plate he offered, I panicked. I had meant Isherwood to give the soft clocks to Vivi to eat. DALI must have taken them from her.

I had no choice. I picked out a small pocket watch and ate it. It was cool and crisp, like an English wheat biscuit.

"I like to eat a full meal in the morning," DALI said. The cook brought in a sizzling alarm clock on a tray. The clock was deformed and spread out to the edge of plate, but was still keeping time.

DALI stabbed it with a fork as if to murder it and cut it into bite-sized pieces. His face was radiant with joy. Brown sauce dripped from his mouth and stained his napkin. "Doctor, this is wonderful."

"Perhaps," I suggested, "Vivi would like to try one."

"I don't want any," Vivi said.

"Please, Vivi," I begged her. "It's a gift from Professor Isherwood. He asked especially that you try it."

"No," she said. "I have no appetite. I don't want any, I tell you!"

My idea had been to warm her to the idea of technology with the soft clocks. They were so friendly and harmless looking. I had hoped she might use them to begin to overcome her technophobia. But I hadn't counted on the intensity of her anorexia.

At lunch and dinner she again refused to eat. Her loathing for the soft clocks was so intense that I was afraid she might attempt suicide with her fork. Her personal physician was forced to give her an intravenous injection of protein simply to keep her alive.

The next day I returned to Earth. I had one last plan. Isherwood had given me copies of all his notes and a range of samples of the rheoprotein, and I took them to Sony's research and development laboratory. If Vivi's mechanical organs could be replaced with organs made of the rheoprotein, so close to living tissue, her subconscious self-hatred might be brought under control. Her gratitude to Isherwood would seal their marriage.

I had to hurry. If Vivi's anorexia continued to get worse she would even refuse the injections, and then she would surely die.

The Sony scientists were ecstatic at what I'd brought them. Within a week they'd developed prototype organs and made arrangements for them to be implanted as soon as possible. Isherwood's patent applications were filed, and I was assured that he would soon be a millionaire several times over.

I sat alone in my office with a flask of warm sake. It was bitter and sweet at the same time. I had probably saved Vivi's life and made it possible for her to be married to the man I had chosen for her. I had fulfilled my mission.

Why was I miserable? Was it possible that I still loved her? Was it more than some childish infatuation?

But if I truly loved her I would wish only for her happiness. I would see her in her bridal gown. She would leave for her honeymoon with Isherwood. I would see them off. I would have the gratitude of the happy couple.

Gratitude! I smashed the sake cup against the floor. I staggered off to bed and lay there, sleepless, until long after the sun had come up.

My job, I soon learned, was not over. A telegram arrived from Vivi. "GRANDFATHER GOES MAD. MARS IS MELTING."

Isherwood was there to meet me at the abandoned shuttleport. I got into his jeep and we drove into the Martian desert, toward DALI's mansion.

"What's happening? Where is everyone?" I asked him.

"He should never have eaten the soft clock," Isherwood said. "The results have been beyond anything anyone could imagine. It's a disaster, a catastrophe."

The desert was melting, reshaping itself. It formed two human-like figures, which sank waist-deep in the sand and began to melt into each other. A twisted tree grew up to support the woman's head as it became soft and began to topple over. No, not a tree, I realized. A crutch. I recognized the scene from Salvador Dali's painting "Autumn Cannibalism."

"The rheoprotein mixed with DALI's digestive fluid, with his entire body chemistry. By the time it passed through his system the protein had absorbed his genetic message. Now everything that comes in contact with the protein becomes part of DALI and part of his madness."

"The Martian sickness," I said. "He can telekinetically control the entire desert."

"Not control, exactly," Isherwood said. "The desert has become a vast theater of his unconscious."

The sand under the jeep began to undulate. The jeep itself

seemed to soften. I sank deeper into the seat. Isherwood shouted "No!" and drove even faster. As our speed picked up the tires were less and less in contact with the ground, and the effects diminished.

"The entire space-time structure is being affected," Isherwood said. "DALI is insane, bulimic. And as this insanity spreads, his insane world becomes edible. The more he eats, the worse it becomes. His gluttony is devouring time itself."

Vivi stood outside the palace, waiting for us. Around her was an island of solidity. As I got out of the jeep she ran toward me, but stopped short of putting her arms around me. "You came," she whispered. "I'm so glad you're safe."

"Of course I came," I said. She was even thinner than when I had left. She was a skeleton, barely covered with skin. And yet she had a radiant, spiritual beauty that I could not deny.

I looked back into the desert. A herd of giant elephants, led by a white horse, was charging toward us. Their legs were impossibly long and distorted, like the legs of spiders. I recognized them from Salvador Dali's "Temptation of Saint Anthony."

"We'd better get inside," I said. "Where is your grandfather?"

"Eating," Vivi said. Isherwood ran for the house. I took Vivi's hand and pulled her in after us.

"Eating what?" I asked.

"Anything he finds. Desks, chairs, beds, he's even cooking telephones. He's started on the wall of the dining room. Soon he will have eaten the entire house."

I suddenly noticed the house. DALI had once predicted that the buildings of the future would be soft and hairy. Here at least it was coming true. As I watched, the walls swelled and softened and moved gently in and out, as if they were breathing. Fine black hairs began to grow from the walls and ceilings. I shuddered away from them.

"First the house," Isherwood said, "and then the entire planet. Perhaps the entire universe."

I didn't believe him until I saw DALI.

He was ten feet tall. Sitting with his legs crossed, his head nearly touched the ceiling. He was eating the mantelpiece when we walked in.

"So you're back," DALI said. "Will you join me?" He offered me a leftover chair leg.

"No, thank you," I said.

He continued to eat. He ate with more than mere hunger. He was not eating just to sustain himself, but with endless, thoughtless greed. It was the ultimate materialism, the ultimate desire to possess, to control, to own. To make the entire external universe a part of DALI.

"Mars has become the fantasy he inherited from his ancestor," I said to Vivi. "When he was a child Salvador Dali wanted to be a cook. As he grew older his hero became Napoleon. Now DALI OF MARS has become both. The imperialist glutton. Worlds not only to conquer, but devour."

I pictured DALI floating in space, large as a planet, Mars in one hand like an apple that had been eaten to the core.

Vivi shook her head. "It's horrible," she said. "How can he stand it? To eat so much. To become *so huge.*"

And then I saw it. Vivi's anorexia was the antidote to DALI's madness.

It made perfect sense. Classical anorexia nervosa is very much tied to the patient's concept of space. A previous anorexic patient of mine used to feel ashamed whenever anyone entered the area around her, which she defined as her personal space. On occasion she would have to spend time at her father's restaurant. If any of the customers touched her, it would send her into ecstasies of self-loathing. In time her bashfulness extended from being touched to being seen, and finally she could not bear to be seen even by inanimate objects, such as dishes.

Vivi's fear of things crossing her personal boundaries was the exact opposite of her grandfather's gluttony.

There were also her personal feelings for DALI. In fact I was beginning to see that her anorexic self-hatred was just a displacement of her Oedipal hatred for her grandfather. As Vivi grew up, the closed world of her inner space began to reach toward the outer world. The dining room played an important role in this. Receiving nutrition from one's family is like receiving trust. But the atmosphere at DALI's table, between his gluttony and Vivi's fear of him, was hardly suited to normal development.

This all came to a head with the artificial organ transplant. The anorexia was just another form of technophobia, a rejection of the outer world. Because her subconscious realized the presence of a piece of the outer world—her artificial organs—inside her, the contradiction began to tear her apart. She rejected not only food, but the bridegroom candidates, anyone, or anything that tried to cross her personal boundaries.

"Professor Isherwood," I said. "Do you still have any of those soft clocks?"

"Well," he said unhappily, "there is just one. I was keeping it as a souvenir."

"You must let me have it. It's our only hope."

DALI had eaten through the back of the house. He was now

consuming the lawn furniture, and growing steadily larger. Within minutes he would be heading into the desert.

Isherwood handed me the clock. It was a small wall model with red enamel, not much larger than my hand. Vivi, as if suspecting what was about to happen, shrank from me.

"Vivi—" I said.

"No," she said. I put the soft clock in her hand. "I can't even look at it," she said. "It's shameful, embarrassing."

"Vivi, you must be strong. You must eat it."

"No, I can't. It's shameful. I'd rather die."

"It's not just your life. It's the lives of everyone on Mars." I hesitated, and then I said, quietly, "It's my life too."

"All right," she said. She was crying. "I'll do it. But Professor Isherwood must turn his back."

"Professor?"

"Yes, all right."

Isherwood turned away. Vivi slowly brought the clock to her lips. She flushed with shame. Her eyes filled with tears. I looked away. The clock crunched slowly as she bit into it, like a cookie. From the corner of my eye I could see her chewing, slowly, keeping it in the front of her mouth.

She swallowed. "All of it?" she asked.

"As much as you can. At least a few more bites."

When I looked back she had eaten half of it. The second hand swept around to the missing half and then disappeared. Thirty seconds later it reappeared at the other edge. Vivi shook her head. "No more," she said.

"Very well. There's something I have to tell you. You should hear this too, Professor. Vivi, when you came to Earth you were in a terrible accident. You were in surgery for many days."

"What does that have to do with—"

"Please. This is difficult for me." I was sweating. "In order to save your life, your heart and lungs—"

"No!" Vivi screamed.

"—and stomach had to be replaced—"

"No!" She tried to run, but I held her arms.

"—replaced with artificial implants. Mechanical substitutes—" I couldn't go on. Vivi was screaming too loudly. I let her go. Immediately her eyes wrinkled shut and her throat began working. I saw her mechanical stomach heaving. I got out of her way.

She ran for the bathroom and flung the door closed behind her. It shut with a fleshy sound. I looked at Professor Isherwood as we heard Vivi being violently sick.

"You did that on purpose," Isherwood said.

"The rheoprotein has mixed with her digestive juices. Vivi has infected the house with her anorexia, just as it was earlier infected with DALI's bulimia." I smiled tentatively at Isherwood. "Now the battle commences."

We ran outside. I could see DALI in the distance, running into the melting desert, thirty feet tall, devouring boulders and handfuls of red sand.

"Doctor!" Isherwood shouted. I ran to where he stood, at the edge of a pond. A naked woman floated face down in the water. Her body had turned soft and her fingers and toes had begun to melt into long, thin tendrils. I helped Isherwood pull her body onto the shore and turn her over.

It was Carmen, from the pub.

"She must have come back to steal something more valuable," I said. I couldn't look away. Her softness was ripe, erotic, intoxicating. Her full, glistening breasts wobbled provocatively. The soft flesh of her thighs rubbed against the damp blackness of her pubic hair.

Isherwood was captivated too. He bent over her and gently touched one arm. "The bones are still there."

"She still has her 'objectivity,' as DALI would say. There may be time to save her."

"Her, perhaps," Isherwood said, "but what about Pinkerton?"

He pointed into the desert. A gigantic hand had risen from the dunes. Its fingers held a cracked egg with a flower growing out of it. The form of the hand was reflected in the form of a huge man, crouching in the sand. The scene was from Salvador Dali's painting "Metamorphosis of Narcissus." The face of the crouching man belonged to Pinkerton.

As I watched, Pinkerton's mouth seemed to form the words "Help me." But it was too late.

Vivi walked out onto the porch of the now firm, lifeless house. A wave of solidity flowed from her and rippled out into the desert. Carmen stirred and sat up. "Where am I?"

"Safe," I said. "Safe, for now."

They finally found DALI, deep in the desert of the Lunae Planum. He had been transformed into a hundred-foot-tall replica of one of Salvador Dali's earliest paintings, "Self-Portrait with Easel," and frozen there.

Vivi returned to Earth with me for the operation that replaced her mechanical organs with living organs of rheoprotein. Almost immediately she began to gain weight. It was a symbolic cure, but effective; my previous anorexic had been cured by a tonsillectomy.

She was willing to honor her grandfather's last wishes and marry Professor Isherwood, though she knew she didn't love him. Isherwood, however, had changed his mind. Maybe it was the fact that Vivi had asked him to turn away from her, there at the end of the madness on DALI's estate. Maybe it was something else. In any case, he had fallen in love with Carmen, and the last we heard, he was more like a bullfighter than a poet.

As for Vivi and myself, I learned to stop fighting my feelings. I completed my contract and selected myself as Vivi's bridegroom. The decision seemed to please everyone.

Someday, perhaps, we will have children, and one day we may take them to Mars to see the statue of their great-grandfather. But for the moment we are in no hurry.

Translated by Kazuko Behrens and stylized by Lewis Shiner

A Meaning in Art That's No Longer Possible: An Interview With Kiyoshi Kasai

Larry McCaffery, Sinda Gregory, and Takayuki Tatsumi

Kiyoshi Kasai was born in Tokyo in 1948. Pursuing an early interest in politics, he attended Wako University, a center of student activism. Kasai joined a new-left political organization in 1968 and under the pseudonym Ryuji Kuroki was a prominent radical activist until giving up all political involvement and expatriating to Paris in the mid-seventies. Eventually returning to Japan, he published a novel, *Bai Bai Enjeru* (Bye Bye, Angel), which won the Kadokawa Award in 1979. *Bai Bai Enjeru* launched the career of Kasai's detective protagonist Kakeru Yabuki, who employs phenomenological speculation to solve his murder cases.

His most ambitious Kakeru narrative so far is the 2,000-page novel *The Philosopher's Locked Room,* which concerns the philosophy of Martin Heidegger and the recent revelations of Heidegger's involvement in Nazism. When the interviewers visited his house in the summer of 1992, he had published the first 1,000 pages of this in serial form for *EQ,* the Japanese version of *Ellery Queen's Magazine.* But after finishing the serial, he found there was more to go and he wrote another 1,000 pages. (TT)

Sinda Gregory: Is Kakeru Yabuki a private detective acting on his own or a member of the police who somehow is part of a larger legal system?

Kiyoshi Kasai: He's a nonprofessional detective somewhat like Poe's Dupin. The theme of my new book is death—the difference between the nineteenth-century experience of death and the twentieth-century experience of death.

Larry McCaffery: Don DeLillo has also addressed this issue in his novels, like *White Noise* and *Mao II,* which both imply that technology mediates our experience of death in all sorts of ways.

KK: I agree with that idea. World War I was the first technologized war in which death was completely different from that depicted by Homer or even by Stendhal. In technologized war, people were treated just like garbage; they died without dignity; it was a mass production of death. That war was the actual beginning of the twentieth century. Until then, people were living in an extension of the nineteenth century.

LM: How does Heidegger fit into this—his connections with fascism?

KK: Heidegger was one of my favorite philosophers when I was a student, along with Gyorgy Lukács. In *Sein und Zeit* Heidegger states that the human being becomes the true self only when he is confronted with death. This philosophy was derived from the experience of World War I. Before then, people were able to die their own death, whereas after undergoing World War I, that became impossible. This wound up leaving the theme of death to the philosophers to speculate about. Anyway, I became interested in the fact that the World War I experience in Europe gave rise to Heidegger's philosophy of death and also the classical type of detective fiction simultaneously.

As you know, most of the major movements associated with modernism—for example, formalism, surrealism, dadaism, and expressionism—originated in countries like Russia, Germany, and France, where battles had actually taken place in front of their very eyes. Whereas, you don't find these sorts of drastic artistic movements occurring in countries like America and England, which didn't experience the war firsthand. Then what did happen in America and England? The fad of serious mystery novels! Let's take a serial story in a magazine or newspaper. Before the war, at least one person per day or per week or per month was killed in those stories. The way death is presented in those works reflected the way people thought about death before the war—it was routine, very easy: people simply died, very quickly, with almost no fuss at all. But in a serious postwar mystery novel, death doesn't happen so easily: the murderer scrupulously plans the killing in detail and carries out the crime with every due respect to the victim. Even after the murder, the detective works very hard to find out who had done it. This is almost like a double-authorization of the victim. The death of the individual is made very meaningful—perhaps in order to give it meaning in art that's no longer possible in real life.

SG: Are classical detective novels—the kind you associate with Conan Doyle and Agatha Christie—popular in Japan?

KK: Yes, the fad of the classical British-type detective novel is still pretty popular, even now. The reason for this popularity is that Japan is one cycle removed from the experience of war compared to America or England. That is, since Japan had not really experienced World War I, we had to wait until World War II to truly understand the meaning of the serious classical mystery novel, which emphasizes the significance of death and the horror of mass-slaughter.

SG: What about writers like Arthur Conan Doyle and Edgar Allan Poe who wrote much earlier than World War I?

KK: The backbone of the detectives of the nineteenth century is positivism. They thought that the truth exists and that they could get to that truth by experience, observation, and presumption. Holmes is a good example. However, the detectives of the twentieth century begin by doubting the truth. If there were any truth at all, it would be something that they themselves must create, rather than discover. In a sense, nihilism was pervasive. From this point it is interesting to see that Van Dine was a student of Nietzsche. While Holmes was a typical nineteenth-century Victorian detective, Poe doesn't fit into this categorization. I am not so interested in Holmes as I am in Poe. Poe was a rhetorical writer, a postmodern writer. My new book is going to be the fourth case of Dupin.

LM: Earlier when we asked about the type of the detective you usually depict, you said a phenomenological one. That makes me think of Alain Robbe-Grillet and Michael Butor. I know that you lived in Paris for a time. Were you interested in the French detective novels or the nouveau roman, and was your new story influenced by them in any way?

KK: I like Sarraute and Butor better than Robbe-Grillet. I read the antiromans when I was a university student, and I thought they were different from what I thought was a novel. I think the narrative is very important in a work of fiction, whereas the avant-garde writers try to deprive the novel of their narrative. Detective fictions or SF novels are trying to recover narrativity—that is why my interest lies in these fields. By using the narrativity system of science fiction or detective novels, I would like to present a theme of our time. By this, I hope to avoid the blind alley in which all the antiromans seemed to have trapped themselves.

LM: In the fifties and sixties there were so many discussions about the death of the novel. But now we seem to have gone beyond that. It's almost as if writers of the eighties and nineties have said, "OK, let's go back to story, we need it, it's important." Voilà: the death of the death of the novel.

KK: As a critic, I cannot ignore the hard-core literary theory which had sort of insisted on the death of the novel and the irrelevancy of story. But as a writer, I go back to Balzac and Dumas and emphasize narrativity.

LM: There seems to be a lot of connections between SF and detective fiction. And maybe some significant differences, too. Since you've worked in both of them, what connections do you see and what differences?

KK: There are two points that are similar: they are both genre novels and formula fiction. As such, they both tend to repeat certain popular motifs once they have become popular. Let's take SF novels for example. After the H. G. Wells novel *The Time Machine* appeared, almost all the novels afterward build up their story with the time machine functioning as a main gadget. The same thing can be said with the detective story as well. Once a writer uses the locked room murder, so does everyone. I think this is an essential condition for these two types of novels. They are also both concerned with epistemology. The difference is whether the writer uses the rhetoric of science dominantly and consciously, as SF authors do, or the rhetoric of logic and empiricism, which is what detective writers rely on. In both cases it doesn't matter if the science or empiricism used in a work is faulty, or even wrong, so long as the rhetoric found there is dominant.

SG: In most detective fiction the world is set up and controlled by reason. The question is answerable. This seems to me to be one of the defining characteristics of what is not postmodernism: a solution, a finality, a denouement exists and does not shift. That's one of the reasons why I would argue that Hammett is pushing the borders of modernity because what he is suggesting in his books is that the solution is one that is constructed by the detective. The truth does not exist; it's simply a construct of the detective.

KK: I think it's very unproductive to say that the only truth is that there is no truth. When they say "there is no truth," in actuality, most people automatically believe in a truth that there is no truth. Generally, this attitude characterized highly fashionable Japanese postmodernism during the 1980s. In those days college students used to carry about the texts of Derrida and Deleuze just like accessories. They often referred to "deconstruction" or "rhizome," but it was just because the terms sounded smart and fashionable. And now, no one reads Derrida. It went out of fashion. The same thing can be said about failed metafictions. Metafiction attempts to erase the existence of its author, the authority of its fictional world, who is even analogous to God. Poor metafiction, however, transgresses the fictional order of realism so easily and arbitrarily that it provides the author with much more authority than that of realistic fiction. At this point, the fiction is no longer a metafiction that implies there is no truth, but a fake metafiction that makes propaganda for the truth that there is no truth.

LM: Is there is any chance for a writer's work being able to have any real impact, either on the world or at least on the ways people think about the world?

KK: During the Gulf War, there was a controversy among the Japanese poets and critics. On the one hand, a magazine called

Hatoyo! (O, Dove!) asked several poets to write a poem about the Gulf War. So they wrote antiwar poems using motifs of the dying sea birds and so on. On the other hand, there were those who criticized these poets and poems. Of course, this reaction was not because the criticizer was approving the war but because he or she thought that it was not a very good thing for a poet to jump onto a social issue and take stands against or for it by means of poetry.

Takayuki Tatsumi: Some of these writers who came against the war just seemed to do so because it was fashionable—it was a stance that grew out of a postmodern posture and seemed the thing to do. Opposition to war just became another new thing that could be put out there to consume. There were those of us who thought this was irresponsible coming immediately after the Gulf War began. Expressing one's antiwar feeling right after the war was declared could cause problems because it is too hasty.

SG: Most people who think about these things and who are not just knee-jerk patriots had very ambivalent feelings about the war. It was a more complex feeling than the way we felt about Vietnam. Most people felt that Hussein needed to be stopped, that he was a dangerous and brutal man. But there was also a recognition that George Bush was using this for political reasons.

KK: Until the post-Vietnam era of the 1970s, people were still able to believe in truth, justice, the existence of the center of the world. Then why did postmodern skepticism or nihilism become "fashionable"? I think the boat people of Vietnam and the great massacre of Cambodia had a lot to do with it. Those incidents exposed, the "justice," that one thing you always thought you had to stand up for, suddenly turned fake. It was not until then that people started to be skeptical, in America, in Europe, and even in Japan. So comes the approximately ten years of the "noncentered world," "no absolute world," "no justice world." But then, especially in Japan, we began to get bored with that situation. That is when the Gulf War occurred. We Japanese were not the ones who were actually involved; we were the outsiders, which made us all the more "irresponsible." So some people, mainly those who could not bear the unstableness, the uncertainty of postmodernism anymore, made an attempt again to insist on the old-fashioned justice opposing to America's imperialism. This is how I see the "Anti-War Protest" of *Hatoyo!* magazine, and I think it is wrong.

LM: I completely agree with you. I don't think postmodernism or the implications of postmodernism should be used to justify nihilism. It is important to recognize subjectivity, but you also have to understand the absolute necessity to finally take positions and to make distinctions between systems that lead to death and chaos versus those that are life-enhancing and create cooperation and community. If you just say that they are all equal, you wind up saying that something that creates death is the same as what creates life. The postmodern artists that I admire are those who are absolutely taking stands.

KK: Ever since the Gulf War and the collapse of the Soviet Union, postmodern issues have become more and more critical. I think we must try to find out what kind of justice can exist on the premise that no such absolute justice exists.

SG: Since "serious" forms of literature, at least in America, are read by a very very few people, their potential for generating political action is almost nonexistent. But it seems like pop culture, which is the dominant culture both in terms of prevalence and marketplace clout, has a potential for actually affecting large numbers of citizens. The dynamic is in place for art to change things even if it's rarely used for anything other than repackaging the same old merchandise/information. In other words, pop culture could challenge the norms just as well as reinforce them—that's what Larry is proposing with his avant-pop concept.

KK: In Japan the difference between popular fiction and literary fiction is unique, compared to that of Europe or America. When Japan started its modernization a hundred years ago in the Meiji era, the bureaucrats, university teachers, and high-ranked military men were the ones who wore Western clothes. And serious fiction was read by those who wore Western clothes. Pure literature was something Western, something imported. Now, during this same time, all the ordinary people were wearing their kimonos. For them, there was Kabuki, Kodan, and other forms of popular culture which had succeeded in establishing themselves from the Edo period. This division continued for about a century. Nowadays, of course, most of us Japanese wear Western clothes. The border between serious literature and popular literature has become vague.

In Japan the role of academicism is undertaken by journalism. You would have to produce something once a year that would sell 50,000 copies if you want to make an average living. I suppose there are fewer than ten "serious writers" who are able to do that in Japan. There are five major publishing companies that turn out serious literary magazines every month. If you are prestigious enough to be able to have your short story published in one of these major magazines, there will be requests for lectures, reviews, and essays from all over. That is how you would make a living.

LM: You've said earlier that both SF and detective fiction are formulas. But when you began writing the science fiction series *Vampire Wars,* was there anything you would say that was fundamentally different about writing SF and detective fiction?

KK: I don't think there were any big differences, no. Both of them are formula fiction, and both of them are really gadget-oriented. And both of them are dealing not with the "I" but with something more general.

LM: Was there any particular reason that you used the vampire motif?

KK: My interest in vampires wasn't very abstract. The main reason for using the vampire motif was that I wanted to write a novel in which the vampire, who is usually the bad guy, is the good guy, and the human beings, who are usually the victims, are in turn the bad guys. I was trying to make a remixture of Gothic romance and SF. As a theme, I wanted to differentiate humanism by using the vampire device.

LM: You apparently were writing *Vampire Wars* primarily as popular entertainment. Would you be interested in writing "serious" SF, or do you not much consider such distinctions?

KK: Theory and practice are two different things. I just want to do something new. Having experienced the Hawaii Tour and London Tour, even Sumo has become international. The only things unique in Japan are probably No, Kabuki, and the classic puzzle-solving-type detective fiction. Nowadays, Japan is the only country that enjoys this genre. So I think we should preserve this as one of our national traditions. There are several awards for detective fictions in Japan but none for the classical type. I guess I would have to establish one. At present, in Japan, the mainstream of the mystery genre is Frederick Forsyth or Robert Ludlum, who write long political novels.

Transcribed by Reiko Tochigi; translated by Takafumi Akimoto

The complete interview with Kiyoshi Kasai can be accessed at www.centerforbookculture.org.

Oedipus City

Kiyoshi Kasai

A breeze arose at the street corner. Dried, yellow plantain leaves blown by the wind were making dry clattering sounds on the sidewalk. Leaning against the new art-styled street light, Yu was absentmindedly watching these autumn sights. This was his twentieth autumn.

Of course, this did not necessarily mean that Yu had any real understanding of the four seasons. Facts about them were easy to learn. He was taught by the computer learning machine that the four seasons were caused by the tilt of the Earth's axis.

However, this had only been the case up to the time of the Great Destruction. In the city where Yu was now living, the four seasons were merely artificial creations controlled by the computer. The entire city was completely covered by a giant transparent dome. A change of season thus no longer had anything to do with the tilt of the Earth's axis.

The domed city called Oedipus was built on the ruins of an ancient city which had been demolished at the time of the Great Destruction. The original city, once located on the coast, had a most distinct yet delicate change of seasons. Thus those who longed for the city before the Great Destruction designed the new city to include four seasons as a part of the city environmental control program.

Yu had not been feeling well for more than a month. Each cell in his body seemed to have accumulated a sensation of dark fatigue. He had no appetite, nor had he been sleeping well. He often had nightmares. When he was awake, he was distracted most of the time, accomplishing nothing.

Alone with the computer learning machine in his room, he was not in any condition to be able to focus on studying. Yu's grades, which were statistically categorized and reported weekly, continued to decline rapidly. Last night the display screen in his study room gave a message in a blinking, orange color which said, "— tomorrow, visit the psycho consultant. To prepare for the 'Silver Ceremony' —"

The computer learning machine installed in each household was connected to and operated by the city's main computer, which controlled every function of the domed city. The city computer thus played the role as teacher for tens of thousands of students at the same instant.

Yu held his breath for a moment. The blinking, orange-colored letters meant that it was not an automated response from the study program but that the main city computer was communicating directly with him. This was the third time this had occurred. The first had occurred just before the Golden Ceremony. The second time was about three months ago and had also told him to visit the psycho consultant.

All citizens of Oedipus City, regardless of their age, were expected to obey the computer's commands. It was also considered absolutely taboo to tell anyone about the computer's direct contact with you. No one ever tried to break this taboo. It would be more accurate to say that no one could. Indeed, it could be said that Oedipus citizens were raised by the city computer. The standard patterns taught by the city computer penetrated deeply into their unconscious minds. The network of the city computer extended literally everywhere into the daily lives of all citizens. It was the only available toy infants could play with, the only teacher for students—and also their only friend.

Yu came to the business district of the city as he had been instructed by the city computer. He was really not excited about this visit. The psychological disturbance he had been experiencing the past three months had actually begun when he first met the psycho consultant. What would happen this time? Nonetheless, he knew he must meet the psycho consultant this evening. It was his obligation.

In addition to the east section of the outskirts, where Yu was living, the city contained three other sections, north, west, and south. Yu, however, never stepped into the other areas. Tall stone walls one mile in length were built between each area and no entrance was visible from outside. But what blocked the way between each area was not simply a physical barrier, for on the other side beyond the wall was believed to be a taboo territory. This belief constituted a mental block buried deep in each citizen's unconscious mind and was what enabled the myth of the other side beyond the wall to be maintained forever.

The east area as a whole was shaped like a park. Nestled among the trees, grass fields, and ponds were gigantic high-rise buildings, each capable of holding several thousand households, where the countless residents lived. But even from the roof of these high-rise apartment buildings, one could not see into the adjacent northern and southern areas. The stone wall, separating each area, was that high. Yu himself sometimes thought that the actual stone walls were much lower and that anything above was a three-dimensional visual trick that the city computer was somehow projecting.

There were underground highways between buildings in the east area, and to go to the city center, you had to take the express subway. You could arrive at the station of the city center in thirty minutes once you got on the train.

The city planner designed the city to have all motorized traffic buried underground, thus leaving the citizens no choice but to go to places on foot above ground. The moving vehicles for individuals which had once existed before the Great Destruction no longer existed. The factories and power plants to support the lives of citizens were buried even farther underground. The cultured plankton farms providing food, along with the food-processing factories, were also buried deep underground.

In the middle of the east area, surrounded by greenery, was a white high-rise apartment complex where Yu and his mother had been living since he was born.

Since children's education was done by computer learning machines existing in each household, there was no school in Yu's world. When Yu was very young, he played with other kids in the neighborhood but in the last several years he had rarely seen any other children. This isolation started when Yu, like all adolescent boys, completed the Golden Ceremony and began confining himself at home with his mother. From that moment on, life's meaning began to change completely.

It was four years ago when the orange-colored message first appeared on the display screen of the computer learning machine. The night before, Yu experienced a wet dream for the first time. The beautiful naked woman who appeared in his dream, seducing the innocent boy, was, of course, his mother.

Yu had never had a girlfriend nor even any chance to get to know a girl. It was the same for all boys in the east area. All the east-area residents were families comprised of only mother and son. There was no exception.

Yu loved only his mom, and his mom loved only Yu. Since Yu had been born, there was nothing to interfere with this deep affection, thicker than butter, between mother and son. It was natural for Yu, who was at puberty, to have a wet dream. And in the east area, where he had been raised, it was also only natural that his mother was his sex object.

On the night after his wet dream, the message Yu had seen in orange-colored letters on the display screen read: "You have grown up. The Golden Ceremony will take place tonight. By midnight, prepare for the ceremony as instructed." Yu vaguely knew that the Golden Ceremony was the first ritual ceremony to become an adult. Boys who completed the Golden Ceremony were allowed to wear a gold ring on their left hand. The ceremony that took place between mother and son would begin in flaring pleasure and ecstasy. At midnight, Yu's bedroom door had opened. There was his mom, still young and beautiful; and as in his dream of the previous night, she was totally naked. The only light in the room was the dim light from the display screen. The city computer was watching Yu and his mom. Yu understood these matters.

As he was instructed, Yu, who also was completely naked, pored honey on his palm and carefully rubbed it onto her white breasts, belly, buttocks, and thighs. Then he licked off all the honey he had just rubbed over each intimate region of her body.

Yu felt something hard rising between his thighs. That night at the very peak of the Golden Ceremony, Yu was invited into his mother's body for the first time. He inserted his rock-hard penis deeply into the same dripping wet hole he had emerged from when born and exploded white liquid inside.

After the Golden Ceremony, Yu and his mother began sleeping naked every evening. Never having previously experienced sex, Yu found himself becoming more and more deeply involved in these erotic experiences; the mother, who was longing for his young body, never tired of seeking her own unlimited pleasure. From that time onward, Yu rarely left the house.

". . . Yu."

Someone was calling his name with a clear, soft voice. Yu immediately turned around and discovered a girl with a slender, gentle body standing behind the plantain tree. Her long hair was waving in the breeze. Yu called the young lover's name.

". . . Ai."

"What happened to you, calling me so suddenly?"

The girl looked into Yu's face, worriedly. The two started to walk slowly along the promenade, and after a few seconds, Yu muttered, "I must see the consultant again."

"You should go ahead and see him."

"Yeah. But . . . for some reason, I'm worried."

"Why? He is a good man. After all, we got to know each other thanks to him."

Trying to cheer this young lover who was somehow depressed, Ai squeezed his arm. By pressing part of her body against his, she was trying to channel her fresh energy directly into his soul and body.

Ai could never understand the reason for his low spirits. For his part, Yu had no intention of blaming her for what he was feeling. "It was my fault," he muttered to himself, biting his lips gently. "Last week, even after the terrible ordeal in the bedroom at the Silver

Palace, Ai is trying to cheer me up as if nothing ever happened to her. Ai is so kind and she must really love me."

Three months earlier, after receiving his second direct communcation from the computer learning machine, Yu visited the psycho consultant in the office complex in the city center, as he had been instructed. The psycho consultant had a sad and serious look on his face. Until then, he never met an adult man face-to-face at such close range.

After a meaningless short conversation regarding Yu's mother-child relationship, Yu was taken for his first visit to the Silver Palace by the psycho consultant. Until then, Yu had no idea that there was such an institution as the Silver Palace for adolescent boys and girls.

The Silver Palace was located in a park full of greenery which was rather unusual for the city center. There were big and small restaurants, coffee shops, movie theaters, playhouses, discos, bars, pool, game centers—every kind of entertainment imaginable had been set up for young people, not only for boys of his age but girls as well. The psycho consultant took Yu into the great Silver Palace, showing him everything from the basement to the roof top. Listening to the exciting music and enjoying his first alcoholic drink, Yu became mesmerized by the festive atmosphere. Eventually he was introduced to a girl—his first meeting with Ai.

"You guys can now use this Silver Palace anytime you want," the consultant told Yu and Ai.

Yu then asked, "But, my mom . . ."

"Your mother knows you are leaving home to prepare for the Silver Ceremony. She won't be in your way."

Yu spoke to the girl, his eyes cast down as if looking at something too bright, "So, Ai, where is your home? Where were you raised? How's your mom?"

The psycho consultant answered in place of the girl. "Ai does not have a mother. Girls are all raised in the protective institute in the south area. When they reach a certain age, the door to the Silver Palace will then be opened to them. This is the place for young girls and boys to find a partner."

"Why are you so down? You're not feeling well?"

"My mom took me to a hospital yesterday, but after the automated medical examiner checked me, he said there was nothing physically wrong with me."

Yu began to explain that he had gone to the hospital, without thinking much when he suddenly felt a tension from the body who was walking next to him. Feeling a terribly sharp pain in his heart, he immediately regretted what he had been saying.

"I'm sorry, Ai. I just said that without thinking. As I promised, I'll never talk about my mom. I won't."

Yu looked at the girl's face; seeing that her eyes were filled with tears, he hurriedly looked away. The girl shook her head violently like a child. Tears began to roll down her face.

Yu didn't know what to do. He felt terrible about saying something he shouldn't have. Touching Ai's shoulders with both his hands, words started to pour out of his mouth, even though he didn't know what he wanted to say.

"Ai, please listen. I like you more than my mom. It hurts when we are apart. It's true. I hate the night time. I hate to sleep with my mom naked. I want to sleep with you. And tonight, Ai, I'm sure I can. Please wait for me at the Silver Palace. I will meet you there after my meeting with the consultant.

After saying this, he felt like some enormous weight had been lifted from his shoulders. He realized the reason he was not feeling well was that he was blaming himself for feeling more attracted to Ai than to his mom. "I want to be your partner, Ai," he said solemnly. "Really, I'm quite serious."

The girl raised her face and nodded. The boy drew his lips to her eyes, tasting the salty taste of her tears.

The sun was setting; above the transparent dome, a silver arrow flew across the sky and disappeared. It was a giant spaceship which had lifted off from the spaceport located outside the dome. As the young couple began walking down the deserted street toward the Silver Palace, the girl said weakly, "I'm sorry I cried, Yu."

"You don't have to apologize. It's my fault."

"I learned for the first time the meaning of *jealousy* after I met you. I don't want to think about your mom. Such thoughts hurt me. They hurt so much that I start to hate your mom. Because she is keeping you all to herself. There is no place for me, no space between you and her."

The girl's confession eased the confusion Yu had been feeling. He thought, "Ai is jealous of mom for me." Suddenly feeling much happier, he decided to tease Ai a little. "You know, I feel jealous too. That consultant says really nice things about you."

The girl blushed and cried out softly, "That's a lie!" She then continued to talk quickly. "I was just very curious. Because obviously it was the first time that I had talked with or even seen an adult man that close."

"Me, too."

Yu drew his eyebrows closer, thinking deeply. As far as he knew, all of the residents who lived in the east area's high-rise complexes were but mothers and young sons. In other words, there was absolutely no chance to see an adult man in the east area. Around the time when a son was becoming an adult, the mother and the son apparently moved somewhere else in the city. Their vacant home was soon occupied by a new mother and a newborn baby.

When Yu was about four years old, his mother took him to a shopping mall in the city center where he saw an adult man for the first time. The mall was filled with mostly mothers and their sons, along with some boys or girls walking by themselves or in small groups. In the crowd Yu saw a strange man who was tall and muscular, wearing dark clothes and a serious look. He was so scared that he clung to his mother. The mothers with children who saw the man looked down in a hurry and cleared the way to avoid him as if it were bad luck to see him. The man's face left a sad and indelible impression on the young Yu.

Yu knew that there must be an equal number of male and female children born, and in fact, there were many boys in the area in which he lived.

"Why are there so few adult men?" Yu muttered.

"Yu, have you ever heard a rumor that all the adult men are sent to outer space? It is said that since Earth became an almost uninhabitable star after the Great Destruction—and humans can only manage to live in domes like these which protect them from exposure to radiation, poisonous gases, or viruses—mankind has no choice but to prepare for a migration that has not yet been completed. So once men have produced offspring here on Earth, they are sent to space to construct the space migration city."

"I heard the rumor too. But neither my mom nor the computer learning machine teaches us the truth clearly. I'm going to talk about my mom, but don't get mad, OK? This has something to do with our future and is very important."

The girl nodded in silence, and Yu continued to talk in a low voice. "One day, my mom told me where I was born. She said there was an ocean."

"It must have been in the west area, because that's the only area with an ocean. I once saw a map of this city before it became Oedipus City, when it wasn't yet covered by a dome. My friend and I tricked the computer learning machine into displaying it on its screen."

"Then, the west area is the place for us to go. There must be somewhere for a couple to live together. The east area is the place for mothers and sons. The south area is for girls only. Only the west area and the north areas are left."

"Yu, girls grow up in the south area; after finding partners at the

Silver Palace, they have children in the west area. If it's a girl, she and her mother will be sent to the institution in the south area; if it's a boy, they move to the east area. Boys who are raised by their mothers will meet girls from the south and fall in love and move to the west area to have a new home. When a child is born, the man who has fathered the child will depart for space . . . But, Yu, what happens to mothers who are left behind after their sons move to the west area with their wives? There's no home where only mothers live in the east area, right?"

"Right. So mothers who are left by their sons must live in the north area."

"The city center, the east area, the south area are all connected by an underground highway, but there's no way to get to the west or the north area from the center."

"There must be a way! We just don't know it." Yu was getting excited. "Listen, Ai, when I meet with the psycho consultant tonight, I'll ask him how to get to the west area. Okay?"

At the end of the plantain-lined promenade a huge silver tower loomed in the dusk. This was the Silver Palace.

"Yes, Yu, of course! Please come as soon as possible. I'll wait for you without eating. I'll be in a disco."

The girl waved through the glass entryway and ran into the Silver Palace.

Yu felt depressed and had no appetite. He went through the motions of eating, pushing food far back in his throat, forcing himself to swallow, playing with a fork. When he began to feel nauseated, he held his breath; breaking into a cold sweat, he tried to keep from vomiting.

The yellow thing which was stuck to the meat was supposed to be natural cheese, but cold now, it was like soft plastic against his tongue. The dark red, slightly burned bacon looked like the intestines of a dead animal. Looking at the remains of the food, now on the verge of vomiting, Yu suddenly stood up, covering his mouth with his hand.

"Yu, what happened?" his mom murmured in his ear. "This is your favorite food. You're still so young and must eat more. Your mom cooked it just for you." Her sweet and cloying whisper filled his head, reminding him of a saturated sponge. Her voice was so rich with love that its sweetness sickened him.

Yu jerked his shoulder away from her clinging touch. Staring at his knife, having totally forgotten about the meal, he felt his nausea retreating. "The knife, the silver knife . . . The silver knife is in my room," he was thinking.

After leaving Ai in front of the Silver Palace, Yu walked alone past the skyscrapers in the city center. When he arrived at the consultant's, he was taken to the same dark and quiet room he had been in before.

Yu lay down on the sofa as instructed. The consultant was sitting in a chair that Yu couldn't see.

"How are you and Ai getting along?" the psycho consultant asked in a deep voice.

With a discernible tension in his voice, Yu answered this question with another question. "If Ai and I decided to become partners, what would happen to us?"

"There is a place where only partners can live."

"The west area, right?"

The consultant slightly leaned in, but the emotionless face remained silent. It seemed that the consultant had no intention of answering Yu's question. But it wasn't just the consultant, the computer learning machine only taught that the Silver Ceremony was meant to formally acknowledge a man and woman as partners— nothing was said about the future.

Where those men and women who became partners would go was still a mystery, like destinations of the mothers who were left behind by their sons. Yu tried to reword his question.

"If we are accepted as partners, we can go to that place, right? So, how do we become partners?"

"That's easy—but also very difficult."

The consultant lowered his voice. The voice had a slight pressure, as if he were trying to hypnotize Yu. Yu felt like he was in a daze but he somehow sensed what the consultant was going to say before he said anything. Yu tried to suppress his thoughts. He just didn't want to think about it. "Easy and difficult?" Yu muttered, "I don't understand . . ."

"Yes, you do. You just aren't trying to face this head-on. There was a custom called marriage before the Great Destruction. Sexual partnerships between men and women were the foundation of society. These families provided various social functions for the education and protection of children in the next generations. Our partner system is patterned after the old marriage system.

"It's easy in this sense. You and Ai are required to love each other not only mentally but physically to become mature sexual partners. That's all you need to do in order to be accepted as partners. But such a simple task can be difficult. Isn't that right, Yu? No, no, you can't deny it! You must say it clearly in your own words. You two applied for a use of a bedroom in the Silver Palace last week. You must tell me what exactly happened or what didn't happen there."

"... that ..."

Yu had a headache and felt dizzy. He was thirsty with anxiety. But he had to obey the psycho consultant. Through the orange-colored message on the display screen, the city computer had ordered Yu to let the psycho consultant handle everything. To disobey the psycho consultant would mean disobeying the city computer.

Feeling embarrassed to death, Yu finally pushed words out of his mouth. "... I couldn't do it, sex, I mean." The voice of the consultant had no mercy; it was as if he were beating Yu with a whip.

"You couldn't perform sex with Ai, right? But why is it? Yu, you have no problem having sex with your mother. The gold ring on your finger is proof. Only those who have passed the Golden Ceremony can wear the ring. In other words, there is no physical or physiological condition preventing you from performing the sex act. You can have sex with your mother and cannot do it with your lover—whom you love so much that you want to be her partner. Listen, the cause is not biological but psychological. It's all in your mind. Go ahead and think, think about the reason yourself."

Yu already knew the reason; he didn't need to think. "My mom got in my way. Every time when I tried to touch Ai's body, the image of the unhappy mother appears in my mind. It forbids me to touch Ai. 'You are such a bad boy. How can you touch a woman's body other than your mother's? You came out of my womb and you will be always a part of me. I won't let you do such things. I won't allow you to do such filthy things' ..."

"That's right, Yu. Your mother is the cause for your impotence. You must now make a choice. Mother or lover. You must decide which one to love."

"I've already decided on that. I'd rather live with Ai alone than with my mom. I really, really don't want to sleep with my mother anymore. I want to escape—to run away with Ai to somewhere where my mom won't be around."

"You cannot escape, because the image of your mother is in your mind. No one can escape from his mind. So the solution is easy: you must commit a murder. You must kill the image of your mother that is eating away at you and destroy this monstrous love which controls you and your creativity and independence. You understand, don't you? The psycho consultant can only give you advice; you must take responsibility for your own actions."

Yu's response was a half-scream. "But what can I do?" He really didn't know what to do. Ever since he was born his mother was the closest person to him—she was now almost a part of his own body and mind. How could he erase the existence of his mother within him?

Suddenly the words *kill your mother* echoed through and electrified Yu's mind. He felt the shock run through his body. He simply nodded as the consultant spoke urgently behind him.

"You can do it, Yu. This is the discipline that all boys in this city must go through. That's why we have the Silver Ceremony. Listen, Yu, *you must do this!*"

The consultant then placed something heavy and cold on Yu's palm. It was a small silver dagger.

"The Silver Ceremony is tonight. Leave the display screen on. The city computer will talk to you. Now listen carefully: without completing the Silver Ceremony, you and Ai cannot be sexual partners. Unless you and Ai become sexual partners, you cannot live together. You must remember that."

Yu clasped his hands over his eyes, pressing hard. It felt as if every wrinkle of his brain was being burned.

That night Yu once again could not perform at the Silver Palace. In front of Ai, who shyly opened up her body, Yu's penis remained miserably unaroused. On the bed, burying his face in Ai's young, firm breasts, he first screamed in despair and then began crying.

Suddenly, the orange-colored message appeared on the display screen. Startled, Yu glanced up.

"Now, we'll begin the Silver Ceremony. Take the dagger. Then keep looking at the screen. No matter what happens, you must not take your eyes from it."

Numerous red, green, and yellow lights began flashing on the screen. Yu found himself being sucked into this screen with its mysterious hypnotic power.

Powerful and even violent sensations started to fill his every cell. He could feel them penetrating his very fiber, tunneling deeper and deeper to extract the violence locked up at the bottom of his being.

Yu heard a door open. It must be mom! he thought. But the image that came with this thought seemed totally different today: dirty, disgusting, fat, sweaty, bad smelling—the very symbol of the human body's decay! It made him feel like vomiting.

The middle-aged woman was walking toward Yu, shaking her flacid hips and lower part of her body. She whispered to Yu, reaching for the organ between his legs. "Yu, come on. Take off your clothes. Make love to your mom. See, it's already so hard."

Yu's pants were already off. His penis, which was shrunken in front of Ai, was straight up in the skillful hands of his mother. "*I hate it! I hate it! I hate it!*" Yu felt nauseous. Then even before he knew what he was saying, he screamed, "Don't. Don't touch my body."

"What are you talking about? Come on, Yu, let's go to bed."

Mother, so involved in her own desire, didn't seem to notice the mysterious tension in Yu's words. The tornado of lights on the screen were moving faster, its myriad light delivering intense messages to Yu's subconsciousness.

"Kill, kill, kill."

Yu's right arm started to lift as if it were controlled by some invisible power. Kneeling down to hold Yu's penis in her mouth, Mother didn't notice the mysterious tension in his voice. Despite the dark blue anger swirling around his entire body, Yu was almost ready to ejaculate as a result of her expertise. I am impotent in front of Ai because of this woman. I can't forgive her. I can't forgive her.

"Kill, kill, kill." The circles of light were still shouting. No, I can't forgive her. Kill . . . Yu felt something was igniting deep inside the hot core of his brain. No, I can't forgive her. Kill, kill, kill. The silver dagger slowly came down on his mother's neck, as she was kneeling down. Yu saw the whole thing as if he were merely an observer.

The Silver Ceremony was over.

Immediately the blizzard of lights disappeared. The screen still displayed the orange-colored message. The bloody, naked body of the woman on the floor was lit with the dim light of the flashing orange-colored message on the screen.

Under the clear, shining sky, there was an ocean, slightly darker blue than the color of sky. Soft waves were gently bumping against the sand, churning up white foam. There were pine trees behind the beach and a cozy bungalow, in which anyone would want to stay at least once in his lifetime.

A man was looking at the scenery, feeling the strong rays of the sun even in the shade under the palm trees. It was the psycho consultant who sent Yu and Ai to the west area two years ago. Since then, the consultant had visited the west area several times, not to see Yu but to see Ai.

Sea, beach, trees. These rich resources looked natural, but the consultant knew they were artificial. Outside the domed city was literally the world of death. Without protective space suits, any human being outside the dome would be destroyed immediately. Such severe conditions existed throughout the world. The Great Destruction had turned the entire Earth into the world of death.

The consultant spotted a young woman standing among the trees. He started to walk slowly on the sand toward her. It was Ai. He must confirm the results of the Bronze Ceremony.

"Ai."

As the consultant talked to the woman, gentle and low, she looked devastated.

The pregnant Ai's stomach was sticking out to its maximum. The due date must be very close. At the consultant's words, Ai slowly raised her face. Then, a small bronze container fell into the sand from her hand. It was what the consultant had handed to Ai several days earlier.

The consultant lifted the bronze container and shook it by his ear. The container was empty. The Bronze Ceremony had been completed.

"He didn't suffer, did he?"

Ai nodded.

The consultant continued. "Now, you can deliver your baby safely. You can hold your baby in your arms."

". . . why? But, why?" Ai shouted suddenly. She covered her face with both her hands and sobbed uncontrollably for a long time.

"I loved Yu. I loved him so much. I gave him poison. Why? Why?"

The consultant put his hand on Ai's shoulder and said, "You can't blame yourself. There is nothing anyone can do. No matter how strong your love for Yu, you're totally powerless in front of the city computer's power. It operates on your subconscious mind. No one can resist it."

"But, I started to hate Yu, somewhere in my mind. That really hurts me."

"That's because I told you that you wouldn't be able to become a mother unless you completed the Bronze Ceremony. That is the order of this Oedipus City. You wanted to deliver a child. Then, when Yu seemed to stand in the way of your becoming a mother, you naturally started to feel some hatred toward your partner."

"No, no, you're wrong!" said Ai. "The baby started to grow bigger. Then Yu started to seem detestable. Maybe because I wanted to have my baby all to myself. Then, when Yu touched my naked stomach, I started to tremble with hatred."

The consultant didn't say it, but knew that her reaction was inevitable. The message that had been supplied to her subconscious mind by the city computer would explain what would otherwise seem like impulsiveness. The human psychological control system that was supposed to paralyze these violent, impulsive explosions was simply overridden by the computer and hatred flooded the mind—hatred that made it possible for a son to murder his mother or a wife to murder her husband. This was the secret of the psychological system that was controlling the minds of citizens of Oedipus City.

What caused the Great Destruction was not nuclear, biochemical wars. Rather, there was incurable social confusion on the global scale which lead to the final war. It first began in the developed countries in the twentieth century, and several centuries later, it spread to the entire world with the speed of cancer cells eating up human flesh.

The origin of the sociopsychological devastation of civilized society was the illness called family destruction. The sharp increase of adolescent crimes and family violence started to shake the fundamental framework of society. It was related to the incapacitation of the sociopsychological controls that had supported civilization ever since its beginnings. The sociopsychological control system was referred to as the Oedipus Complex.

In Greek mythology it was prophesied upon his birth that Oedipus would someday kill his own father and sleep with his own mother. He was doomed to live out his fate. This story was symbolic of various human desires. The prohibition and control of such desires enabled the construction of civilized society. In the twentieth century these prohibitions and the controls of the family and society began to collapse.

The power of the father was lost, and the psychological intimacy between mothers and sons became dangerously close. It was only a matter of time before psychological attachment turned into physical attachment. Sexual encounters between mothers and sons, witnessed by husband/father led to the son's murder. On the other hand, due to the too powerful influence of the mother, many sons became impotent in front of women other than their mothers. And many tried to escape from this spectacle by murdering their own mothers.

This flood of Oedipal desire ran out of control and completely destroyed the family structure upon which society was based. The final war was an all-out attack on the previously held values of civilized society—thus destroying the foundation of self control.

The few people who survived the Great Destruction constructed the domed city and lived inside it. They set up this complicated social-psychological system in order to avoid the revival of the Great Destruction. In short, the Golden Ceremony became the official acknowledgment of the sexual relationship between adolescent boys who have reached puberty and their mothers. The Silver Ceremony compelled the son, who has chosen another lover, to kill his mother. And the Bronze Ceremony described the murder of the husband by the pregnant wife. When the construction of the domed city was complete, the system was already set up. It was concluded that there was no other choice but to enforce this mysterious system in order to maintain a civilized society, liberated from Oedipal desire.

Unconsciously protecting her stomach by putting her hands gently over it, Ai asked the psycho consultant, "What will happen to me?"

"You will have a baby in this west area as you desired."

"But if it is a girl, they will take the baby away from me. Won't she be taken to the south area where I grew up?"

"That doesn't happen. Don't worry. You will have a boy."

Meanwhile, the consultant thought to himself, "That will not happen, my daughter. It was already genetically determined that you would have fraternal twins, a boy and a girl, just like you and Yu. The girl will be raised in the south area and the boy will be left in your arms. You will move to the east area with your son. Then, the twins you deliver will be guided by the psycho consultant someday to the Silver Palace, meet each other, and fall in love—just like you and Yu. Fate will repeat itself indefinitely. Only an exceptional human, immune to the poison spread by the city computer could escape this destiny. The man who has escaped must maintain the secret of Oedipus City and continue to turn the wheel of fate. Daughter, this is a cursed job . . ."

"Now," the consultant spoke to Ai invitingly. "Let's go back to the bungalow."

The sea was reddened by the setting sun. The wind was chilly. Ai muttered dreamily, letting her long hair flow in the sea breeze. "My baby moved. I will never be apart from this child. No one can separate us. I can never love any other human being like I love this child. This child means everything to me."

The consultant shrugged and nodded to the young, dreamy pregnant woman.

Translation by Kazuko Behrens; stylized by
Sinda Gregory and Larry McCaffery

Not Just a Gibson Clone:
An Interview with Goro Masaki

Sinda Gregory and Larry McCaffery

Although rumor has it that the man who uses the pen name Goro
Masaki was born in Kanagawa Prefecture in 1957, the "real" Goro
Masaki was born in Tokyo in 1986 on a Fujitsu word processor. He
was heavily influenced by science fictions of Philip K. Dick, James
Tiptree, Jr., and Cordwainer Smith. His rather incidentally composed first commercial novella, *Evil Eyes* (1986—excerpted here),
vividly describes the conflict between a mind-control software company and a new religious organization, ending up with the revela-
tion that Maria, a full-armored woman working for the company,
and Mugen, the charismatic figure of the organization, were produced by a multiple personality, the owner of which had been born a
disfigured baby; *Evil Eyes*—which won the thirteenth Hayakawa
SF Contest in 1987 and is regarded as the best example of Japanese
cyberpunk science fiction—was eventually included in Masaki's
first collection of the same title (1988). In 1993 Masaki further developed the ideas in *Evil Eyes* and completed the hard-core virtual
reality/hypergender novel *Venus City,* which won the fourteenth Japan SF Award, the Japanese equivalent of the Nebula Award. His
other works include a pseudo-autobiograpical story collection *Won't
Cry for a Cat Anymore* (1994) and an erotic hard-core SF novel
called *The Shadow Orchid* (1994). His first English translation,
"With Love, to My Eldest Brother" (original, 1988), was published in
Fiction International in 1993. Now Goro Masaki is almost completely invisible in Japan, just like his literary influences. (LM)

Sinda Gregory: How did you get interested in SF initially?
  Goro Masaki: My first contact as a reader occurred when I read
H. G. Wells's *War of the Worlds.* It was not a children's book, and I
was six then. Most of the book was too difficult for me to understand. I just wanted to pretend to be a grown-up. But I remember
some descriptions of the killing machine were very chilling. I would
like to add that *The Secret Garden* was my first exposure to mys-
tery-oriented literature. It was the only children's story I could enjoy. I confess it is still a part of my standard of a "good story." I began
reading Verne, Poe, and Doyle when I was ten or so. My entertainment reading was mostly restricted to the mystery genre when I

was in my teens. I read most of the classic detective stories in translation, then moved to hard-boiled mysteries and Kobo Abe. They both seemed to me the same kind of stories, about an individual facing the absurd. The influence from Shozo Numa's *Yapoo, the Human Cattle* was enormous for me in my formative years. This is a novel several critics regard as the most important SF and the strangest book ever published in postwar Japan. It is about a world in which only Caucasoids—especially white women—are regarded as human beings and dominators, while Negroids and Mongoloids—especially men—are regarded as cattle and used for the "living parts" of various products, from living toilet bowls and drawers to living carpets and diving suits. This unique novel first appeared in 1956, highly appreciated by such mainstream authors as Yukio Mishima, and is still available in Japan.

I had also seen several SF and monster movies when I was a little boy. Like many of us, my father took me to the theater for the monster movies. I think we are the first generation with less need for written SF, since SF imagery was everywhere in the visual media. Imported TV shows such as *Time Tunnel, Lost in Space, Thunderbirds,* and *Batman* are also imprinted in my memory. American imagery was flooding in, and kids' comics then were full of quasi-scientific images of the future technology. Osamu Tezuka's *Astro Boy* may be the best example. Shotaro Ishimori's *Cyborg 009,* published as a kids' comic, was where I learned the term *cyborg* when I was ten or so. It was the futuristic Apollo days, and popular science magazines were full of lines such as "we will change our body parts into more effective machines for working in space" or something like that. I remember when I was thirteen asking my classmate how cyborgs can have sex with their mechanized bodies: one is born to write SF. But the first really important SF writer for me was Philip K. Dick; I remember reading *Do Androids Dream of Electric Sheep?* when I was entering university and thought that this was something very different from what I had regarded as SF. It was a very unusual reading experience—the first time for me to discover a genre SF novel that mattered. I was nineteen then, and with so many SF-oriented media around me, I had little need for SF literature. I had thought that written SF was already dated. Audiovisual media were far more compelling. But I changed my opinion after reading Dick. I bought more than ten copies of that novel, because I have a habit of giving my favorite books to my friends who haven't read it.

SG: What was it about that book that made it seem so interesting and powerful to you?

GM: Using traditional SF gadgets, Dick examines what human

nature is and the ways that technology affected it in our day. The theme of the book is, in short, "What is it that can be thought of as a human being and how is this different from machines?" This is essentially an ethical question, and, with the aid of SF settings, he could speculate freely on the metaphysical problems in a very concrete way. I thought this is just the power that SF literature can have over and above other SF media; that is, abstract thought experiments based on the concrete examples. Dick didn't use abstract terminology to his end, but simply depicts the situation, using metaphors of humans and androids. In this novel, if he thought a person were lacking humanity, then he depicted him as an android. If a machine is kind enough, then it should be a "human." This is his essential view of the world, and a very humanistic one. It is no surprise that French readers loved him much, given this high humanistic spirituality. We can be both humans and androids, depending on the situation, and his conclusion goes: what is finally important for us is not whether it is an original or a copy. Rather, everything with kindness can be regarded as true and therefore human, while unkind existence is nonhuman. What a straightforward humanistic manifesto gained in the midst of the relativistic universe. He also says that the most important feature of human nature is "empathy," an ability to feel as others do. That is, to go out of ourselves and to see others as they see us. So, in this sense, the book is about human communication; that is, how we can understand each other. Reading the book made me think a lot about communication and empathic ability, which might be a big subject matter in the whole literary tradition.

Larry McCaffery: Were you already thinking about writing SF while you were in college? I take it you didn't major in literature as an undergraduate.

GM: No, my undergraduate study was in social sciences, sociology. Before that I wanted to be a natural scientist; in fact, I studied just about everything except literature.

LM: What was it that drew you to write SF rather than other types of fiction?

GM: I was always very fond of writing, and my writings were always highly graded by my teachers through my school days. But I never wanted to become a professional writer, though I enjoyed writing stories for myself very much. By the time I was thirteen, I was constantly writing stories, not SF but mainly mystery—or fantasy-oriented studies. I stopped making stories when I was nineteen and went to the university; I soon found I was too busy studying social sciences to do any writing other than that. It wasn't until ten years later when I was twenty-eight or twenty-nine that I began again, so there is a ten-year blank in my writing career. In 1986 I felt great pressure both from my work and from private matters, and I suddenly began writing SF. During the blank time, I had read several SF writers who were new to me, such as James Tiptree, Jr., Cordwainer Smith, and John Varley. I am ready to admit their direct influence on me through their works.

LM: But not any of the cyberpunk writers as yet?

GM: I have to admit that I was often regarded as one of the first Japanese cyberpunk writers. Just before I wrote my first commercially published story, *Evil Eyes*, I had read Gibson's "Burning Chrome" and some other short stories and then *Neuromancer*, all in translation, but that was the only cyberpunk I had read before *Evil Eyes*. After my debut, I intentionally stopped reading Gibson because I was always compared to him. So I started to try purposefully not to write like Gibson. It was an uninteresting decision because I liked his writings. I bought a signed copy of his book at the Forbidden Planet in London. But I had to avoid becoming a "Japanese Gibson."

SG: If you were consciously trying *not* to write in a cyberpunk manner, what was it about your early stories that made others compare them to what the cyberpunks were doing?

GM: Actually, I feel that *Evil Eyes* was more directly influenced by Tiptree than by Gibson or other cyberpunks. I had been playing with the main idea itself since 1979 or so. I once tried to write it down, but failed. I was too busy then. And I completed the story during the summer and fall of 1986, and it was published in 1987. I thought it would be regarded as a Tiptree-like story, but when it appeared, people immediately said it was a kind of cyberpunk. To be more correct, it was regarded as a Gibson clone.

LM: What was *Evil Eyes* about?

GM: I would say it is about femininity in highly developed capitalist nations. Literally, it's about a mind-control software designer who is captured by a new religious group who tries to utilize his skill to brainwash the whole world. Somehow he escapes from that religion and destroys that cult, but then it turns out that all this was planned by an opposite power, a mind-control music industry which had produced much mind-controlling software and was firmly competing against the cult for their audience. I think the story criticizes industrial society and some of its consequences. And the cult leader is at first referred to as *he*, but actually he is a female who doesn't have a body.

LM: What do you mean? And does he have no body?

GM: The cult guru is first introduced as a living Ricca-chan doll. Ricca is a Japanese equivalent of Barbie. But it is revealed that actually the doll-like thing was made solely from human brain tissue. Its doll body is only a kind of plastic container exoskeleton, and it is filled with living human central nerve tissues taken from many others. It absorbs brains and memories of other people. It can change its "clothes" and appears as a beautiful boy elsewhere. And the creature insists that it is a "mind without body." Since mind functions are all that it possesses, the creature is a pure spirit. It has a seemingly twisted logic. Gradually it becomes clear that actually it was born as a girl child, and, by an accident, it lost the chance to live a usual life. Instead, prosthetic technology gave it a chance to evolve into a brain-and-knowledge-sucking superpower, who can utilize others' nerve tissues as some kind of additional memory storage. It becomes a hyperintelligence and then a cult leader.

SG: Were you trying to depict a certain kind of "new femininity" that was actually arising in Japan during the eighties?

GM: If seen from that perspective, yes. At first, our guru, called Mugen, appears and speaks as a male, even though it presents itself as a Licca doll. But it gradually becomes clear that it is actually a female character. It is also shown that this is actually a story of a woman who was torn apart in a highly developed information society. On one side, she tried to objectify herself by becoming a guru leading millions of followers. This shows Mugen's macho aspect. On the other side, it behaves as one who is dominated, deprived, and desperately seeking for the possibility of conceiving a child and being loved. But after all, what she was always trying to do was just to love, even though it lacked the relevant objects, and to take care of the world and other people.

SG: The cyberpunk authors in the eighties presented technology much more ambiguously than their New Wave counterparts of the sixties, who tended to be extremely pessimistic. How would you describe your own feelings about technological change?

GM: I tend to write rather pessimistically and critically, because things suspicious and distrustful are easier to be accepted and passed as the signs of careful professional attitude. But *Venus City* shows a more openly positive view of the future. A more cheerful aspect of myself. I myself was astonished by this. My typical writing style is shown in my early short story "The Weather Won't Stop" (1988) in which I have depicted an idea of heaven's atmosphere directly influencing mental atmospheres of people. For the story I used the synergistic theory by Hermann Haken, and I wrote the whole thing in a narrative style of a teenagers' romance. That is my usual way of hiding myself. But a smart way is not always a wise way, and after having a child, I lost a certain degree of my hiding instinct. After all, our son is the proof and he's there. Now I can write a little more straight tale with some positive nice views. I think it's okay for all of us.

SG: Is the world you depict in *Venus City* the world of Japan as you imagine it will be in the future? Or is it the world of Japan *now*?

GM: *Venus City* is mainly about Japan in the twenty-first century. In this world Japan has become a kind of network nation and a very influential international power. Also, there is a presence of anti-Japanese extremist groups from America.

LM: Was this anti-Japanese aspect of the novel partly a reaction on your part to the Japan-bashing which was so common in the U.S. and elsewhere during the eighties and early nineties?

GM: Yes. The protagonist Sakiko is a Japanese woman who hates American people, at least partly because her boss is a male American in a Japanese company. So there is already a kind of racial tension that is a very significant feature of the novel. I wanted to present my story as evenly as possible, so it is composed of three sections: the first is told in the first person of the Japanese woman, the second from the perspective of the American boss, and the third is the objective, third person, where I tried to be perfectly neutral.

LM: Have you been tempted to move outside the SF genre?

GM: I am attracted to SF because I wanted to write freely. This freedom to experiment may be one reason why I'm writing in SF genre, but insofar as I can write with much freedom, the genre is not very important to me. And, to be honest, I soon found out that there existed many norms and restrictions even in the SF genre. Besides, I never seriously thought of a professional writer's career.

LM: Tell me a little about the background of "With Love, to My Eldest Brother," the story I published in *Fiction International*. It seems to be almost like a holocaust or postbomb, apocalypse story.

GM: "With Love" was actually about the secondary influences of atomic bombs on the next generation after an atomic-bomb blast. I wanted to write this because I myself am the son of a Hiroshima survivor. My father was a lieutenant of the Japan Imperial Army and was sent to China only months after graduation from the university. There he served as an educational officer for the Chinese people. Then he was sent back to Japan and was trained as a commando of kamikaze-type human torpedo. He was staying at Hiroshima when the bomb was dropped. By some chance he went to a nearby town just one day before the A-bomb was dropped, so he survived; but he went back to Hiroshima City and searched for his fellow soldiers the day after the explosion. So he too suffered from the A-bomb, to a certain degree. For instance, he lost most of the hair on his legs and arms, and his liver was also affected, so his skin is more yellow than usual Japanese. I have heard that my parents hesitated to have a child for a while, because they feared there might be some secondary effects on the children. Luckily my father was not so badly affected, but I had heard these stories while very young, and all these things strongly inspired me to write the story. For Hiroshima victims and survivors and their relatives, "With Love" is not just an interesting tale—it's almost a realistic fear.

LM: Has your writing been influenced by earlier conventions of Japanese storytelling, such as the use of the traditional autobiographical "I" narrator?

GM: In *Evil Eyes,* for the simple reason that I didn't have much space, I deleted almost all "I's." It's literally condensed, I have written some 150 pages and summed the draft up into just one hundred pages. In Japanese it's very easy to delete the subject "I" from the lines. Also, I wanted to make it very universal, not private or uniquely Japanese, so that it will apply to everyone. So I tried to omit the subject "I." I have an English version of *Evil Eyes,* which is a close representation of what I have written, but even in it, there are more "I's" than in the original. My second collection of short stories, *Won't Cry for a Cat Anymore,* is mostly private Japanese autobiographical stories, of the sort that might begin, "one day I went somewhere to see something." I think these are very traditional uses of the Japanese writing style. I tried this style because I had to escape from the puzzling fame of being a Japanese Gibson.

LM: Why did you use a pen name? Did you personally want to split yourself in two?

GM: The reason is simple. I did not want to be known. James Tiptree, Jr., once explained this kind of psychology very well. She said she wanted to be some kind of spirit who could leave what she has written in front of the reader and just disappear. This may be a fundamental instinct of hiding before the unknown. To hide from the unfamiliar is a natural response of an animal. To escape from some objects thrown at oneself is also a normal reaction. I have never known baseball rules very well.

Transcribed by Pam Hasman

The complete interview with Goro Masaki can be accessed at www.centerforbookculture.org.

The Human Factor *(from* Evil Eyes*)*

Goro Masaki

The Central Information Bureau, Movement for Mind Reformation, aka MMR. Up close, the holo sign covering the entire facade is more vivid, so glorious it arrests speech and inspires genuflection. Beaming, enter fabulous hall, ushered by young man in dark suit. A ceiling so high that a person on tiptoe couldn't reach it. Great support pillars decorated with elaborate carvings of the double helix. Bow to the deadpan staff and smile into the dry eyes of the dried-up reception girls. Everything is beautiful and wonderful. Except I'm not quite in the mental state to believe it.

Being in the software design business has an advantage: we're somewhat resistant to softcore mindsoft. Once, on a train, someone shoved an MMR be-mod program into my PFX. It converted my twisted mind into that of an innocent, martyred spirit and took control of 99 percent of my will and behavior. But in the deepest room of the soul, a ghost lay screaming into the glorious false dawn.

Scattered strategically around the clean, spacious lobby, potted plants block prying eyes. Attention to detail paid mindlessly. The extreme discomfort of sinking into a sickeningly comfortable sofa. If I could, before it kills me, I'd make a break for it and go back to that horrible grave, even for just a moment. Please. Let me go, right now, and leave me there forever!

Sometime later, the PFX throttles down as it switches to remote control, and the tension is released. Hard, jerky breaths and fast heartbeat. Mind Reformation, no doubt about it. No one cares if a child makes a mess in the toy box.

PFX and MMR. Competitors. One the producer and seller of mind-stabilizing devices integrated with the mental-health care system, the other the propaganda bureau of a religious cult disguised as a popular movement. The difference is there, but negligible, amounting to whether or not the hand of God is visible. Liberalism vs. totalitarianism. One limits options in the name of free choice, the other offers only one choice as the supreme value.

Either choice is the refutation of the other. Belonging to one or the other is happenstance, fallout from a bad experience.

Young man in dark suit walks in, fiddling with remote control, rolling the small device between his hands. One slip and my brain goes ghostly for real. Gentle smile on his lips. The long, slender fingers of a tech. Luckily, not trembling.

"Sorry to have kept you waiting. This isn't our normal business. Please excuse our rudeness."

"What's your business? I'd appreciate it if I could finish as quickly as possible and go home . . ." Finger touches remote. "I don't want to go home. Whatever thy will might be, for the great cause, I embrace my rebirth after extinguishment of life in this world, achieved spontaneously, without will . . ."

Puzzled expression. "I turned the control off right away."

"I can recite from memory, I've been here before. What do you want, anyway?"

A stunned pause. "I advise you to quit the stupid acting. Mugen Daishi prefers more refined jokes, as you already know."

"Wants to see me, does he?"

"Come this way."

"Why?" He takes the question on his back and disappears into the potted plants. Follow.

Mugen Daishi. Great Teacher Unmanifest. Silly name. What he has is not jokes, but hundreds of thousands of followers and the power to control them.

The PFX joint secretariat once tried to investigate him. Their best man came back with a giant amoeboid compressed into the cavity where his brain had been. As the single cell muttered the Spontaneous Unmanifestation Mantra through his mouth, his body was quickly absorbed into its vacuole. Legend has it that once it swelled to normal size, only the larynx remained at the top of a huge mound of light-green gel, bubbling out the mantra until it was reduced to powder in the freeze-drying room. Mugen may be a joker after all. But he's a man one rarely gets to see.

Elevator at far end of lobby opens as a matter of course, closes as a matter of course. Slender finger points to 50F, the top floor, as a matter of course. No feeling of gravity, pressure, or power. Indicator points to 50F, and the door opens on the 30th basement. A banal misdirection.

The lowest floor of the MMR building is Mugen's apartments. A long, long passageway. Silence. The winding passage dead-ends at black double doors. Bracketing the doors is a pair of muscular sentries, each with a 360-degree rotating sensor where its head should be. Their arms slowly rise, holding needle cannons.

Young man in suit says the magic words, a phrase from the Spontaneous Unmanifestation Mantra. The muscles take a prayerful posture, the doors open.

Darkness. Nudged from behind, duck through the door.

Visual perception negative. A small sound echoes in the distance from somewhere above. Distant thunder. The words just come to me. In the 30th basement? A dazzling flash across my view briefly lights an endless deserted wilderness with one sad little tree. Another bolt from the dark sky splits the dry trunk in two. Blackish purple clouds boil. A wind begins to blow, heavy and humid, rubbing sticky contagious air into skin and moving on. A swamp wind. There must be a murky swamp nearby. Another flash.

And the voice.

We arise from the muck and return to the muck. Pitiful are the dust beings of this world, for they bear the burden of eternity without understanding. Wandering eternally, reaching nowhere, spontaneous accomplishment without manifestation.

Another bolt of lightning backlights the floating shadow of a small person. The wind blasts and howls.

Accomplishment without movement, shift without change. Error lies in choosing to make no error. The error unconsciously chosen escapes and transports without changing. To intend without accomplishing; to be without understanding.

Dramatic, you might say. The latest and most pompous version of the Spontaneous Unmanifestation Mantra echoes across the wasteland. A bright overhead light snaps on and melts the illusion. A small, clean room, like an intensive-care unit. Quiet breeze from the ventilator.

"I've been waiting for you, ghost," says Mugen Daishi.

A voice like a ringing bell. The only simile I can think of. It sits relaxed, two yards away on a leather-covered divan. Maybe only five feet in height. Golden plastic hair, overlarge eyes, huge head, smooth skin without shadows. But for the head, utterly hairless. Undistinguished clothes, no adornments.

Remember the plastic dolls of children? Imagine a much larger one. This is . . .

"I am Mugen. Please don't call me Rikka-chan." The bell tinkles laughter. Sophisticated jokes, huh? Nothing but a bad pun.

"You mustn't complain about differences in taste. I thought this would suit you, but . . ." The doll spreads its arms and shrugs. Another psy?

"Some use such expressions, those who can't help but rationalize everything. Tasteless talk. I just know you, that's all." I have things I don't want anyone to know.

My patience reaches its limit. "It may be unnecessary to you, but I'm used to using my mouth, so I will. What do you want?"

"My, we are impatient, aren't we? I was so looking forward to having a little chat with you, but . . ." He seems to be trying to look sad, but only manages to distort the plastic face grotesquely. Poor at expressing emotions?

"Not myself, rather it's this container is so clumsy. Except for that, I like everything about it." An exoskeleton?

"We'll begin the explanations there. I could get straight down to business, but you wouldn't be convinced. Have a seat. The going will probably get a little rough."

"I don't like lectures. Keep it short."

"A most fastidious ghost. All right." In a relaxed pose, the doll crosses its unnaturally long legs. The squeak of plastics. As the torso turns, I see tubes and cables running from the hip to the back of the divan.

"You know who I am. But you probably don't know what I am, do you? I am mind." What in hell could he be talking about?

"Everyone has a mind."

"No, that's not what I mean. Mind without flesh. Understand?"

"What's this doll stuff then?"

"Only a container, as I said."

"Are its contents just illusion?"

"Not illusion. The content is me. Would you like to see?"

No. I imagine an exhibitionist Rikka-chan doll exploding her guts.

The reality is worse. The polarizing plastic turns transparent. Plastic walls divide the body into small cells, each filled with white blobs and viscous liquid, connected by a complex web of tubes and cables.

"This is it. This is me. Mugen is mind without flesh. Now you know." I look away and nod. Some might think that way. "Sure. No body cells, no organs, no muscles, no skin, no bones, only neurons. An entire body made of brain cells, right?" Monster! As I think it, my PFX takes off. Acute pain.

"Please don't use such expressions. I'm rather neurotic about them, I'm afraid." Right.

"But now you know what I am, ghost. I am mind. Mugen is a fleshless mind."

"Aren't neurons flesh?" The doll-shaped plastic bag full of neurons tilts its head and winks.

"Does the soul exist? Let us end this metaphysical dialectic. The answer is easy. Cells alone are neither flesh nor mind. Flesh and mind are specialized functions. If we fiddle around with matter, we get flesh, and if we manipulate ideas, we get mind. My cells are specialized in mind, therefore I am a fleshless mind. Did you never study James's psychology in your classical literature class?"

"I only remember chemistry, where I learned to brew and distill wheat. But why not contain yourself in an oval shell? From any angle, that container looks like nothing but, well, flesh."

"It won't anger me if you call it a doll, ghost. You're sweeter than I thought."

"It hurts more than you think."

"Mugen sees hearts, especially yours. Don't forget. But you ask a pertinent question. You hit me where I live." Laughing quietly, he picks up a picture from the side table.

"Look. To answer your question."

An old photograph, taken at probably three months old. The right chest is caved in as though gouged out. No arms. From the navel down it's covered with opaque plastic gauze, from which several tubes extend beyond the frame. Where there should be a face is a ripped canvas, the picture on it a failed abstraction. But why?

"This time you are brutally cruel. Must I say it? Sometimes I want to look like a man." No emotion in the bells. None.

"You got me wrong. Why do you have to explain this stuff? I don't get it."

"I prefer to undertake discussions with full understanding. Despite my appearance, Mugen is very much the gentleman." Mugen Daishi manifest as a plastic doll. As he says it, the extremely neurotic boss of MMR eerily folds his smooth face in the parody of a smile.

This is all immensely silly. Is Mugen crazy? Perhaps, but even so he remains, unfortunately, logical. People often go crazy logically, invariably working from bad assumptions.

"Well, what's your purpose?" I know the answer without asking, but if I don't ask, the meeting will never end.

"I want you. Your mind, your cortex, and the software design skills stored there." He begins to reveal himself.

"Do you plan to just scoop my brains out and smear them on yours?"

"Please don't speak so harshly. I'm sensitive, despite how I look. I don't want any part of such savagery. But I can transfer the necessary synapse patterns onto appropriate structures. The lobectomy is long out of fashion."

"How much do you weigh?" How many other people's nerve centers have you absorbed?

"Seventy-five pounds. I have taken in perhaps fifteen or sixteen people, plus several dozen pattern transfers. In terms of knowledge and experience, I can easily defeat you." A Polyannish giggle.

"And if I say no?"

"I don't understand why. I'm sure we can work something out. With money, for instance."

"And if I say my reasons are not resolvable?" In point of fact, there are no such reasons. Money exists to solve problems.

"If so, I'll only collect what you owe me."

"I don't remember owing you anything."

"I have an IOU. One fresh slice of cerebral cortex, several hundred grams. Five years ago, at the back door of this building, you were assaulted by a ruffian. The front of your head was caved in. I replaced the injured part of your brain with a new one and transferred all the memories, at tremendous cost I might add. Now I want you to pay me back. That's reasonable, isn't it?" He tosses some documents at me. There's even a copy of the police report.

He may be telling the truth. I'd been there to sell some avant-garde soft. I may have had my frontal lobe worked on then without knowing it. I don't sense any memory blanks, but it's easy to transplant continuous memories. As easy as bribing a cop.

"That's about it. Very good, ghost. You're exactly what I anticipated you would become. Quick connections."

"Did you predict me then?"

"Not quite. I created you."

"Created?"

"Yes. One or two distortions that would not be sufficient grounds for a malpractice suit. They make you enjoy the world a bit less than you used to and like drinking more. Don't forget this. There are plenty of would-be artists who bring us self-indulgent avant-garde software that has no hope of sale. Brain tissue transplants and memory transfers are very expensive, because the brain is of itself a total gestalt. But a hit product, with even just one individual, can recoup the investment and more." He widens overlarge eyes. Long, creepy lashes.

"Quite the entrepreneur."

"I told you, knowledge and experience."

"You value my skills that much? Flattering."

"Your skills suit my problem. The system I built does not connect quickly enough. Especially for upgrades. People are getting bored with the current version of the mantra."

"It's easy to crank out a good piece of software in a hurry. Set up a competitive-feedback matrix and toss the first chunk of code into it. The software evolves on its own, feeding on shreds from insignificant lives."

"Unfortunately, we must maintain a certain reputation. This is not the sort of business that is suited to capitalism, so we must proceed in a less conspicuous manner. Therefore . . ."

"Therefore you use the back door, right?"

"But in good faith, you understand." He runs a hand up through the blond plastic hair and winks.

"If I say no, nevertheless?"

"I don't understand why."

"You created me. Me, the hit pop-soft ghost. Sure, I'm better off than I used to be. I'd have gotten nowhere if I'd stayed the same and went on fooling with that stuff. If I accept that, I suppose I should thank you for it." I bite the words off and spit them out.

"The past is dark to those who cannot see beyond themselves."

"Yeah, I do seem to have learned how to make software that sells."

"I'm always impressed by the charts." A breath. "Your songs, as well."

A beat. "My skill comes from my past, my own experience, what nobody else can really know. But I build it into my music in ways that anyone can understand."

"Such effort to communicate! I'm impressed."

"You get me wrong. I'm just spitting off the top of a well of poison to keep from drowning in it. It's not sublimation, otherwise I'd die of self-poisoning. That's why machines can't do mindsoft. It requires the craft of someone who refuses to die of poisoning."

"That's grand." Bells tinkle.

"One poison senses and reacts to another. In smooth words, that's the human factor. People live by smearing shit on one another. Those who smear well succeed, but what they smear is still just shit. Machines still can't be as dirty as people. Machines can't shit. Machines can't finish mindsoft."

"Such a misanthrope, ghost. We arise from the muck and return to the muck. My propaganda doesn't seem so bad now, does it? And then?" He listens, amused. I want to throw it all away and get it over with.

"So I can't give up my skills. Let's say I admit that I borrowed the medium they're stored on. And in it you buried a small nexus that controls me in the presence. Following the program, I became what I am now. My skills may have grown from your seed, as you intended. But it's not your power that's been refining them. It's my life, the shreds of my life and my past. My past isn't yours. My skills are my past."

I spit out my monologue and stand up. Which doesn't mean I can see a way out.

"I understand what you're saying. The words, anyway." The transparent doll filled with neurons slowly turns. An old picture on the table. He snaps plastic fingers and the heavy black doors open. The young man in the suit stands waiting.

"I haven't had such an interesting conversation in a long time. Let's call it a day now. No need to rush. Come again. In four or five days." He throws a kiss like a young girl, a grossly exaggerated mannerism. Dynamation porn.

"So long, Rikka-chan. I had a nice time, too." Trembling voice, exhaustion. As I walk away, Mugen addresses my shoulders. "Oh, and by the way, I've just remembered, there is one small flaw in your argument." I stop and turn reluctantly. His voice is too confident to ignore.

"That cortex I let you borrow is, actually, mine."

"I've heard enough of that bull."

"You're wrong. It's part of the cortex that constitutes me. In other words, part of what I was born with." I freeze. Neurons don't regenerate. That means . . .

"Yes. You are part of me. You maintain your consciousness using me. What you call your experience and past is nothing but part of me."

"But . . ."

"I've been having a little trouble recently. Some parts are getting out of hand. Parts not recognizing the whole is a problem. Anyway, don't forget this. You, who are whole to yourself, are, in reality, just part of me. You are me. I'm not always you, though." More bells. The heavy door closes at my back.

Later that night, I feel like straightening out the facts. I returned to the grave accompanied by the man in the dark suit. Several times I had the urge to ram a knife into my brain. This sort of disgust is unaffected by reason.

Many possible interpretations. The mind software business got started in the previous century as a by-product of the laws restricting psychoactive drugs, just as the Volstead Act had nurtured the underground liquor business. The ban on drugs necessitated something else to stabilize the mind, something to divert latent, chronic anxiety.

Mindsoft and cult religion. Service businesses of the same kind. They make money selling weights for people to hang on their worries. From his inferiority complex, Mugen developed a special collecting habit. Organ transplants and transactions are common. But what he chooses are cell structures that cannot regenerate, namely nerve centers.

Mugen's extreme neurosis led to the side business of renting out the storage media that he'd collected. He transplants part of himself, which retains a certain degree of distortion, into people with certain potentials and waits for the potentials to bloom. He demands payment once the storage medium is filled with information, enriched by shreds pulled from the bodies of other lives that the owner consumes to stay alive. His knowledge and experience swell, and he uses them to fuel his religious organization. Some call that rational management.

All this comes from the rarity of the storage media and the craftsmanship required for mindsoft production. If the mind could be recorded on disk, there'd be no problem about the medium. If the software could be finished by machines, there'd be no need for the craftsman. Technical constraints make Mugen's management policy effective, and that will continue for some time. The public is still conservative about the ethical aspects of human-machine integration. Some even oppose transplants. Now I can relate.

The medium is clearly not the message. Given sufficient recording capability, any medium will do.

But think about it, a situation in which an organ from someone else is creating my perceptions, my awareness of being myself. If the disk is clean, I'm more or less comfortable even if it's used. But wouldn't you resist a once-and-for-all test of your favorite program on an operating system with unknown and undetectable bugs? And the humiliation to have what I believed to be an independent self revealed as a slave to a master program. All these boil down to the human factor.

Translation by K. Odani and Steven Ayres

Bird outside the Cage:
An Interview with Yumi Matsuo

Sinda Gregory and Larry McCaffery

Yumi Matsuo was born in Kanazawa, Ishikawa Prefecture, in 1960. After studying English literature at Ochanomizu Women's University, she worked for a major electronic company for several years. Her first publication, *Ijigen kafe terasu* (Coffee House in Another Dimension), in 1989 was followed by *Baruun taun no satsujin* (Murder in Balloon Town—an excerpt of which follows), which had been inspired by her marriage and childbearing in 1990 and which was awarded third place in the 1992 Hayakawa SF Contest. The idea of the story involves a very un-PCish pregnant female detective who resolves the mysteries caused within the very network of pregnant women. The series springing from this novella made this new writer so popular that her first collection of stories, *Barun Taun no Satsujin* (Murder in Balloon Town), was a finalist for the fifteenth Japan SF Award in 1994. Leading SF critic Mari Kotani finds her imagination comparable to those of Charlotte Perkins Gilman, James Tiptree, Jr., and Margaret Atwood. Matsuo undoubtedly helped us recognize the invisibility of a pregnant woman we had never noticed, just the way Ralph Ellison, in the 1940s, made us aware of a black guy as an invisible man in a WASP-oriented country. Yumi Matsuo's other postfeminist works include: *Burakku enjeru* (Black Angel, 1994), *Pipinera* (Pippinella, 1996), *Jiendaa-jo no toriko* (The Prisoner of Gender Castle, 1996), *Makkusu Maus to Nakamatachi* (Max Mouse and His Friends, 1997), and *Runako no kichin* (Runako's Kitchen, 1998). She currently lives in Tokyo, where she is completing a new set of stories in the Balloon Town series. (Amanda Seaman and Takayuki Tatsumi)

Larry McCaffery: What was it that got you first interested in SF? Were you reading it a lot as a teenager?

   Yumi Matsuo: My father bought all Hayakawa's paperback SF series as they were published, which means he bought all foreign SF books published in Japan at that time. So SF books were all over my house, before I ever got interested. I think many people "discover" SF—by themselves or via friends—when they are young, and they find it as some kind of countermeasure. I mean, for them, SF is "something else," something antitraditional, in many cases not approved by parents or teachers. Maybe this explains how some people get into SF. But in my case SF was tradition. So this might be the reason, or part of it, for my not going too far into SF; later on, when I was in college, I somehow wound up in an SF club.

LM: So at this point, while you were in college, you were reading SF but not yet writing it?

YM: I was writing stories, but I'm not sure if it was SF or not. Most of my writing was really short and not very eventful. Many of them are set in a world almost the same to our reality, only different in a slight, particular way. For example, one story is set in a world where men no longer wear neckties—they do exist, but are regarded as some sort of strange habit of the old days. A woman happens to choose a striped necktie as a gift to her boyfriend, a man she has met accidentally and started to date. But after she gives it to him, she gradually notices something strange, for every time she does the tie for him, the knot comes to a different-colored stripe, as if the size of his neck is always changing. She begins to worry and consults a friend, who immediately concludes that the boyfriend does not really exist—he is a phantom the heroine has made up in her mind. She says it can't be and rushes to meet him. He undoes his necktie, picks her up with his fingertips, and puts her away in the neatly rolled necktie. Most of what I wrote then was something like that—nonrealistic and really short. They appeared in the fanzine of my SF club.

LM: Who were the writers you were influenced by?

YM: As for SF, I read Ray Bradbury or Frederick Brown from my father's bookshelf. When I went to college, my friends at SF club introduced me to newer writers like Samuel Delany, Tom Reamy, or John Varley. I liked them, though I am not sure if they influenced what I wrote then. But what I liked the best among all SF short stories I have read was Carol Emshwiller's "Adapted." A friend recommended it, and I was immensely moved when I read it. I might have been influenced by Emshwiller, if I could have read more of her works in Japanese. "Adapted" was translated into thrillingly beautiful Japanese by female translator Fusa Obi.

Sinda Gregory: Since you were studying literature in college, is it possible that instead of being influenced by SF writers, you were influenced more by mainstream or serious literature?

YM: Yes. British Literature was my major and I read authors such as Margaret Drabble and especially Iris Murdoch—who probably had some influence on me.

SG: *Murder in Balloon Town* seems like a very controversial book in terms of its treatment of feminist issues. Have you read a lot of feminist fiction and criticism, or have you not been influenced by that?

YM: I cannot say I'm influenced by feminism in any conscious way, because I haven't read much feminist fiction and almost no feminist criticism.

SG: Perhaps the book's main influence was your own pregnancy. Was it written during or after your pregnancy?

YM: I wrote the first draft of the first story (the book is a collection of four rather long "short" stories) when I was actually pregnant—*very* pregnant, I would say. I set it aside for some time, and after I gave birth to our son and everything had settled down a little, I again worked on it and, when I was done, sent it to Hayakawa's contest. They published it, and three more stories, in their *SF Magazine*.

SG: Could you tell whether or not women like the story more than men?

YM: I first thought women would like it—and they did—and at the same time I was expecting to get some objections from men. But I haven't seen such negative response from men, at least not as much as I have expected. Of course, there must have been people who say, "I just don't want to read this kind of book," and those people must have stayed silent. Anyway, when people talked about that book at all, they talked favorably. I was concerned that the book may offend women who cannot get pregnant even if they want to. Maybe I was too nervous, because you can't write anything without a fear that it might hurt people. A self-righteous, or simply bad, fiction will hurt many people. And even a good, well-balanced fiction may hurt some people in some ways. But the woman who wants to have children and cannot seems to be under a special kind of pressure—maybe especially in Japan, where many people still find values in traditional ideas of family and blood lineage. So I was concerned, but I wanted to and decided to write the book anyway. So I tried to make it as good as I could.

SG: Your work seems to be very concerned with the political aspects of gender. Was your mother a liberated woman who pointed these things out to you?

YM: Not actually. She is like most Japanese housewives—certainly not a feminist.

SG: When did it happen, as Americans say, that your "consciousness was raised"?

YM: When I was a child my father always said—not that he was particularly oppressive—but he told me "girls shouldn't do this" or "should do that," as many fathers do. It seemed to me that girls had more restrictions than boys, and I thought it wasn't fair! If that could be called a gender consciousness, mine was raised when I was very young. But the bigger wave came when I got married. Not that

I am blaming my husband. I am talking about the system. Like the
Japanese family registration system, for which, as far as I understand, you have no equivalent. When a child is born, parents report
it to the City Hall and his/her name is added to the family register
topped by, usually, the father. The register is stored and managed at
the prefectural office. When the child grows up and gets married,
his/her name is deleted. Another register for the new couple is created, usually—again—topped by the husband. You will need a copy
of this register on many occasions, like when you get a passport, a
driver's license, or a job. And when you request the copy at the prefectural office, you always have to refer to who is on the top of the
register. That is our family registration system, and in the old days
men didn't move to a new register even when they got married.
Women "married into" the register of the man's family, topped by
her husband's father or grandfather. Today people move to a new
register when they get married.

SG: So your book, *Murder in Balloon Town*, grew out of this period?

YM: Yes. It is about a near future where women don't have to
carry a child—they can rely on a new technology, artificial uterus,
instead of their own body. Some women don't like this and want to
carry their children in their stomachs. Those women are gathered
into a Special Ward in Tokyo. Not too long after that, the place gets
a nickname: "Balloon Town." A murder takes place just outside the
town: three men witnessed the murder and knew for sure the murderer was a pregnant woman, only they cannot describe her features except her big, round stomach. They are so overwhelmed by it
and cannot remember anything else. So a female police detective
goes undercover inside the town, with a fake identity of a pregnant
woman in an early stage. She solves the murder and other cases,
with the help of an amateur sleuth—her friend who is really pregnant and living in the Special Ward. The four events take place following the sequence of time, so that you can see the growth of the
two heroines—one deepens her career as a detective, the other with
a stomach getting bigger and bigger. And at the end of the fourth
story she gives birth to a baby. Some of them are parodies of famous
detective fictions, like "The Turtle-Bellied League" named after one
of the Sherlock Holmes stories, "The Red-Headed League," or "Why
Didn't They Ask the Midwife?" after "Why Didn't They Ask Evans?"
by Agatha Christie. I wrote the first of the four stories when I was
pregnant. In a way, it's a parody of John Varley's "The Barbie Murders"—a story about murders in a town where all residents look
strictly identical as a result of surgical operation. Residents of the
town are all followers of a religious cult, which forbids the followers
to conceive ideas like "oneself" or "individual." So the residents all

look like asexual Barbie Dolls, and when the murder takes place, you can't tell the murderer from any other residents. In fact, the victim, the suspect, and the witnesses all look identical. A female police detective goes there undercover—after taking the surgical operation and becoming a Barbie herself. I read this story when I was pregnant. It somehow reminded me of pregnant women, because pregnant women too live in a small world and many of them believe in something that can be called a cult, in a very broad sense. So I changed the Barbies to pregnant women and wrote this story about Balloon Town.

SG: So the direct inspiration for this story had to do with the fact that while you were pregnant, you were very aware that you had no individual identity.

YM: Very much so. I don't know if this is true in America, but in Japan, we have something that can be called the pregnant woman's culture. There are many books and monthly magazines directed specially toward pregnant women—one of the magazines is actually called "Balloon"—filled with suggestions about how to stay healthy, what to eat, how often or how wildly you should have sex with your husband. They even interfere in what music you are supposed to listen to.

LM: I suspect rock music isn't held in very high regard.

YM: Of course rock-and-roll is the worst! They say Mozart is the best, which seems humiliating to both rock and roll and Mozart. My sleuth says "it [her baby] won't survive a life with me, if it would have a convulsive fit on listening to the Stooges." Anyway, I certainly didn't agree with most of these. Of course you should listen to arguments on such matters as smoking, alcohol, and nutrition. Those matters are scientifically proven. But I didn't like the "you-should-do-this-but-not-that" tone of those books and magazines. So I decided to write about a pregnant woman who is inclined to rock-and-roll, sleuthing, and inevitable smoking—for all amateur detectives should puff, brood inside the smoke, from the days of Sherlock Holmes. I invented cigarettes with "no nicotine, no tar, with a carbon-monoxide neutralizing filter" especially for the purpose, though, I strongly doubt if something like that can really exist.

SG: One of the most striking things about Balloon Town is how it's made from so many different elements combined in so many unusual ways. You have the detective formula and a domestic story, and, of course, just the idea of having a pregnant woman doing anything is unexpected. In American literature I can't think of many novels or short stories that even involve a pregnant woman. It's as if when you're pregnant, it's time off; you are expected to more or less disappear.

YM: You're retired.

SG: Yes, you're no longer really in the world, but somewhere else.

YM: I know the feeling very well; and in fact, that's why I wrote that first story. I was pregnant myself, and I didn't want to think of myself as retired. At that time, I was finding it hard to keep on writing, being married and having a baby. I was kind of cornered then— because, though at that point I had some of my works published, they were far from successful. And it seemed the publishers I had worked with had no interest in me anymore. So I decided to write this story, send it to the contest, and thought, maybe I would give up writing, if this one should not be accepted. Fortunately enough, it was.

SG: How would you say your fiction since *Balloon Town* has evolved or changed?

YM: Of course, I'm not trying to write only about pregnant women or feminist issues. But being pregnant actually made me aware of many other things. For example, I began to notice the relationship between Japanese society—which is almost synonymous with industry—and the individual. Because in Japan, towns, roads, even parks are designed for and interlinked with productivity; they're not really intended to be used by old people, pregnant women, or handicapped people. So being pregnant made me aware of other social relationships and situations in Japan and how these related to individuality. It is very difficult to be an individual in Japan. In Japan you can be someone only as long as you belong to some big structure, like enterprises or government offices, not small structures like families.

SG: Your upcoming novel—about the Japanese woman who, when she goes into her house, shrinks—seems connected to what you just said because it seems to suggest that what happens to a Japanese woman who does not have a larger affiliation is that she gets lost. What is the title of that book?

YM: *Pippinella*. This book deals with the paradigm shift that's been occurring in Japan from the perspective of sexuality; it's also a book where I tried to address issues of surveillance and punishment. Pippinella is the name of a female canary who appears in two of Hugh Lofting's books for children, *Dr. Dolittle's Caravan* and *Dr. Dolittle and the Green Canary*. Pippinella is a great singer, which is unusual since, as you know, canaries usually do not sing; but in my book she even becomes a prima donna of opera, which may remind us of "Carmen Dog" by Carol Emshwiller, in which a dog heroine becomes a prima donna of opera. When she is young, Pippinella is told by her parents not to try to sing because females can't sing well even if they practiced, and such an attempt is really shameful too. Pippinella thinks this is unjust because, according to her, females can sing —all they lack is practice. So against interference from her family and after much practice and hard days—including a time when she actually works as "a canary in a coal mine"—she gains success in her musical career. You can call this an early example of feminist fiction. I used canaries not only as a feminist figure but also as a metaphor for all people whose souls are caught in some invisible cage.

LM: A bird in a cage.

YM: Exactly. Here contemporary Japan is shown to be a kind of prison. I called the heroine Kanako because the name partly resembles *canary* pronounced in Japanese. She is a married woman, whose body shrinks into child-size, three or four feet, whenever she takes off her shoes. As you know, we Japanese don't wear shoes inside our houses. Her body starts to grow at the moment she puts her feet in her shoes in the doorway. Thus she can be quite normal outside. But all this is what she tells us, because the novel is written in the first person. It is the case of an unreliable narrator, like *The Turn of the Screw,* by Henry James. Maybe her body really shrinks, or maybe it's just what she believes. Some people who are close enough to see her without her shoes—her husband, of course, and a close friend—will not deny her words, but readers can suspect that they are pretending, trying not to hurt the heroine's feelings. Her husband disappears one day, leaving a strange word "Pippinella" on his notebook, and the heroine sets off on a journey to find him. At the end of the story, the protagonist confronts her true problems. She also sees her husband's own problem and the reason why he has gone away; though she cannot meet him there, she, for the first time in four years of marriage, fully understands her husband and his love toward her.

SG: Tell me a bit about *Black Angel.*

YM: It is a novel about college students who like American or British rock-and-roll music. When they put a CD of an American band in the player, a small, shadowy figure in the shape of a winged woman springs out of the player. It darts upon one of the girls and kills her. The police conclude her death is a suicide, but her friends know it wasn't, and they try to find out the identity of the monster and the reason why it attacked that girl. So the book has a mystery, love, and a little insight about the relation between Japanese society and American pop culture. I thought it would attract people, but the book didn't sell much, though I received some favorable remarks from readers and editors.

Transcribed by Pam Hasman

The complete interview with Yumi Matsuo can be accessed at www.centerforbookculture.org.

Murder in Balloon Town

Yumi Matsuo

A Note Regarding the Foundation of the Special Seventh Ward

1. Objective for the Establishment:
This special ward will be established with the goal of offering a space for living and superior residential space to nurture expectant women in regard to people who wish to live here (refer to separate accompanying data).

2. Outline:
In order to carry out the aforementioned goal, a portion of the Seventh Ward will be appropriated. Approximately six hundred hectares have been secured (200 hectares of parks and green areas, 200 hectares of living space and 200 hectares of commercial space) to make this space. A target of 2,500 single-person dwellings is set.

Addenda:
1. The qualities of the Special Seventh Ward will include flat terrain and good sunlight.
2. The religious institution "Suitengu Shrine" will be transferred from the Second Ward and placed under the authority of the Special Seventh Ward upon its completion.

It was ten o'clock in the morning. Eda Marina turned down the hallway and knocked on the door of her boss's office.

"Come in."

She opened the door and walked into the room. Wearing a miniskirt and Reebok walking shoes, her outfit was out of style—just like the career of a policewoman.

The room was in the main offices of the Tokyo Metropolitan Police. When Section Chief Nojima turned away from the window, he said with his trademark poker face, "Marina, there's been a murder."

"A murder?" Marina was puzzled. "Why did you call me? If it's a murder, I just dealt with one last month. You know, the bizarre one in the Third Ward. Aso and Toda have only had robbery cases, and Taki has been grumbling about wanting to see some blood . . ."

"This time I don't want to bother them," said Nojima, putting his hand into the pocket of his stylish side-vented jacket.

"What is it?" asked Marina. "If it is a criminal investigation, then it would be the same regardless of who heads it."

"That is not the case. You're talking about the computer. This time, at any rate, it can't help us since the situation is in the Special Seventh Ward. More precisely, it took place outside the walls of the ward, near the commercial district."

The Special Seventh Ward. What could that mean? wondered Marina.

"The scene of the crime is an open area with few passersby," Nojima continued. "Three businessmen who sometimes cut through there witnessed a crime. The suspect stabbed the young male victim and fled, knife in hand.

"The suspect ran past the three men, who were dazed, and disappeared through the gate into the Special Seventh Ward, leaving behind the murder weapon—a fruit knife—and one apple."

"An apple?" Marina asked.

"It appears that the criminal was carrying a picnic basket. We can't get any fingerprints from the wooden handle of the knife or from the apple."

What should I make of this? thought Marina, slightly puzzled.

"The Special Seventh Ward? You mean . . ."

"Exactly. What people call Balloon Town."

"So the suspect disappeared into the heart of Balloon Town?" Marina said slowly. "The suspect is a resident of Balloon Town? That is to say, a woman with a special condition . . . ?"

"Right. The problem is that the gate in question is only for the use of the residents. The witnesses' statements all indicate that the suspect is a pregnant woman, one clearly in the latter half of her term."

Nojima said this nonchalantly, but Marina was shocked.

"The suspect was a pregnant woman!"

She found it difficult to articulate the words.

The words *pregnancy, pregnant women,* and *childbirth* were not ones that well-brought-up women used. Marina had graduated from an old-fashioned women's college in the Second Ward; it was a fact that she had always tried to hide from her colleagues.

After the ban was lifted, the use of artificial uteruses (known as *in vitro* gestation or AU) soon became fashionable, and in due time it became the norm. Just as in the days when the place where women gave birth changed from the home to the hospital, "safe birth" was the catch phrase. In contemporary society a fetus gestated inside the mother could not be shielded from harmful things like toxins, electromagnetic waves, and noise. As a result, the AU wards in hospitals were the only places considered to be safe. There was also the problem of the mother's career to be considered. No matter how many nurseries were established, women were the ones who were pregnant for nine months and thus continued to juggle two careers. While they worked, the stress would have a detrimental effect upon the fetus.

Once permission was given to use *in vitro* gestation, people worried that humans had become oviparous.[1] There also was a fear that no mother to gestate the baby would mean a society of fathers. Despite these misgivings, *in vitro* gestation spread and became permanently rooted within a generation.

Among one group of women, however, there was dissent.

"I want to raise my child in my womb," these women said. There was no particular logical reason for this. Still, "of course," women wanted it this way.

Tokyo was the one city which responded to this demand. The various economic and governmental functions of the city were divided up (among them, the Metropolitan Police), and the wards were reorganized to prevent the city center from becoming a ghost town. The entire city was redesigned, with wards spiraling outward—the First Ward in the center became the business district, the Second Ward became the residential area, and so forth.

Tokyo was creating the image of a city that aims to be people-oriented and was offering a place to the women who had complained. Tokyo, a city for pregnant women! What a commotion! Here, on one side of the luxurious green spaces of the Seventh Ward (near the commercial district), a special ward was established, where women who chose pregnancy and childbirth came to live.

Here was a town of pregnant women. Women who had another life inside them could leave their homes and their jobs for a while, congregate here, and live peacefully. It was a perfect environment, safe and secure. Rent and living expenses were very low. When the ward was created, of course, there were criticisms. Some called it a people ranch, and certain men called Balloon Town a form of sex discrimination. Such an advantageous living situation certainly had its charms, but there wasn't a huge rush of people who wanted to live here.

Many women wondered who would want to endure the months of inconvenience, the deformed body, and the painful experience of childbirth, but people regarded those willing to take the trouble to do just that as a very different sort altogether. This special ward continued to be a paradise for women who wanted a quiet environment in which to gestate. Those with no connection to the place somehow started to call it Balloon Town, but with no bad intent.

People regarded the place as one completely removed from crime, especially murder—until now.

"So you were told that there were multiple witnesses," asked Eda Marina as she stood in Nojima's office.

"That's right," replied Nojima.

"In that case, we can call a police sketch artist and circulate a sketch among the residents."

"That's the problem." The section chief's brow suddenly wrinkled. "Do you know the expression 'Chinese people are all the same'? Westerners can't tell the difference between two Chinese people, and so they think that they all look the same. Well, this is the same thing. 'Pregnant women all look the same.' No one was able to recall what the criminal's facial features and height were like."

"You mean that . . ." Marina started.

"The witnesses, three men, all noticed one thing. Even when we pressed them for more details, they were overwhelmed by it."

"This one thing," Marina murmured, "was the suspect's stomach."

"Uh-huh. They say that it was pretty big. They used the expression 'really round.' "

"Hmm."

"Exactly. Not much of a clue. As they say, 'the red-faced baboon is really red.' "[2]

Marina folded her arms. "Maybe we should consider that the witnesses weren't there from the beginning."

"True, true. Well put," said Nojima, rubbing his hands together happily. "I certainly trained you well."

"What about the evidence? The things that the victim dropped . . ."

"The knife has been checked out," said Nojima. With dangerous items, one can do an on-line investigation, which was one reason it now took less time to complete a criminal investigation.

"The knife is one which can be purchased in the Balloon Town supermarket, so there's no way to tell who bought it. The apple wasn't investigated, but I doubt that would be possible."

Was this a joke or not? Marina couldn't tell.

"It seems that we should handle this case without the computers. Someone should take a trip to Special Ward Seven and see what's there. The residents could probably give us some useful information, since they don't see themselves as interchangeable. I want you to go."

"Me? Go to Balloon Town?" Marina said.

"You'll get a better reception there than a male detective. Besides, you might want to check it out for later on.

"Just kidding," he said, seeing her face. "There's no need to get angry."

There was no subway stop in Balloon Town, since the magnetic fields associated with them were said to be bad for pregnant women. Marina got off the train at the west station in the Seventh Commercial Ward, just a brisk walk from Balloon Town.

She went first to the crime scene. The open area at the edge of the town was deserted. A spring wind was blowing sand around, and Marina narrowed her eyes against it. She walked close to the wall which surrounded the special ward. It was low with trees planted on one side, so that you couldn't see beyond it. She cast a glance at the gate through which the suspect had rushed, and walked a little farther to the main gate.

"You're Detective Eda? I am Ms. Takayama, the chief of security here."

The chief of security was surprisingly attractive. She looked younger than her years and had an excellent figure. She was wearing a bright green suit, had her hair in a chignon, and wore her glasses on a long chain. She had the air of a sexy 1950s Hollywood secretary, but spoke briskly.

"Welcome to the Special Seventh Ward," she said, handing Marina a visitor's badge. "It's too bad that you had to visit as a police officer. Young women visitors are always welcome."

As they entered, a device on the side of the gate checked Marina's badge. In the Special Ward, it was crucial that outside visitors be checked, for the security of the pregnant women.

As she passed through the gate, thinking about what useful information this was, she felt a soft breeze against her cheek. Marina noticed that it blew from the thick row of green trees. Through them, one could see a big pond beyond, with a five- or six-yard-high stone statue. The statue was of a woman. It had deeply carved features and a cascade of hair, with a body shaped like a pear. It was a giant pregnant woman, clad in light clothes, and standing with her hips slightly swiveled. Coming closer, Marina could see a pigeon sitting on its head and two more sitting on the statue's protruding belly.

She could hear the sound of water. It looked as if the statue was holding a water jug, but she noticed that next to the statue was a platform on which the water jug rested, the statue's hand simply touching it. What an oddity, she thought.

"That statue . . ." Marina began.

"It is called 'The Good Vessel,' " Ms. Takayama explained. "The vessel is a metaphor for pregnant women, and so it is a symbol for these residents."

"Why is the jug on that platform?"

"Well, the statue is a pregnant woman. She can't very well hold something that heavy."

Marina did not know how to respond to this, so she didn't say anything. Through a break in the trees, an open area came into view. It was a park. Small paths ran between the trees, with flowers and benches placed here and there. Basking in the sunshine were a number of people sitting or strolling around. All of them were pregnant women.

If you never have seen pregnant women, you might imagine that they are normally proportioned except for their protruding bellies. You would be wrong. Their hips and thighs were fleshy, the lower halves of their bodies were massive, and from every direction and from every angle they produced unusual silhouettes. They wore jumper skirts with numerous gathers, making them look like triangles.

I can't believe it, Marina thought. Why is this normal? Every clumsy one of them wore a uniformly contented expression on her face, basking in the sunshine.

In the bright light, these strangely shaped figures moved slowly, as if in a nightmare. Weaving among them were Ms. Takayama with her staff badge and Marina with her visitor's badge, walking at a brisk pace.

"Don't you think that they're cute?" Ms. Takayama said in Marina's ear.

"Sure . . ." said Marina vaguely, suspecting that Ms. Takayama looked at these pregnant women as if they were some species of animal.

If you viewed them dispassionately, these figures *did* look like some sort of attractive creature, drifting through the greenery. The spring breeze softly billowed the pastel-colored skirts of the women as they waddled about—at least, to the extent that their skirts could fill with wind.

"They look like boats at full sail." Marina said.

"It doesn't mean that they are strutting," said Ms. Takayama. "They move like that because it's hard for them to walk any other way."

She stopped in midsentence as a woman close to them dropped her handkerchief. Ms. Takayama quickly crouched down and retrieved it, handing it to the woman with a big smile.

The woman thanked her and walked away.

"It's hard for these women to crouch down." Ms. Takayama continued to smile as she spoke, and Marina secretly sighed.

It wasn't just the pregnant women's movements that were slow, but their way of talking. When Marina thought about the pace of the investigation, she realized that it too would be painfully slow. She shook off thoughts of work.

"Those clothes—are they some kind of uniform?" she asked. Every woman was wearing the same kind of dress, differing only in their colors.

"Uniform? No. They are a 'maternity-style' design. People seem to favor a standard style of dress."

If these outfits were standard, then given what was known about the criminal's clothing, it would be hard to find the person in question. Marina was depressed. Furthermore, nearly everyone was carrying a picnic basket.

Among the ten women seated at a bench, perhaps five or six had picnic baskets and were eating something in the warm sunshine. Some of them who were finished eating gently brushed the bread crumbs off the tops of their stomachs. There were a good many peeling fruit with knives.

"Well, I think it's a good idea to wear a girdle sometimes." Marina overheard snippets of conversation.

"It's easier to move when you're wearing one. They don't slide down like those belts."

"No, no, cotton is best for the skin. You don't want to get heat rash during the summer."

"Isn't it a pain in the neck to roll the bleached cotton?"

"I just discovered a new way to do it. Instead of wrapping it around your body, you hold the end, leave the rest on the floor, and spin 'round and 'round. That makes it easier to wrap."

What on earth were they talking about? Marina had no idea, but she envisioned the women wrapping their spindle-shaped bodies with cloth.

"What is bleached cotton?" Marina asked Ms. Takayama.

"Oh, it's a belly band" came the response, but Marina still had no idea what it was.[3] She didn't try to ask any more questions after that, and simply walked along.

Ms. Takayama's office was a tidy room. Her only decoration was a framed picture of the Madonna and Child, which Marina eyed suspiciously.

"So, what are your impressions?" Ms. Takayama asked and immediately started making tea.

"I was surprised," Marina said candidly. "I only saw women with really big bellies. Aren't there any women in the earlier stages of pregnancy?"

"They don't go out much. Probably due to morning sickness or something," she said, putting the teacups on the saucers. She continued, "It isn't unusual to be surprised. When I first started here, I felt the same way. All I could notice was their bellies. When I walked among them, I felt like I was playing dodge ball.

Ms. Takayama took a drink of tea.

"But after a while, I was able to understand that pregnancy is real and natural. It's like heavy fruit ripening, then falling from the branch with a thud."

The "thud" noise was surprisingly real, and Marina felt a little uneasy.

"I think that's how it used to be," said Ms. Takayama. "AU is somehow unnatural. Do you know, Detective, the most popular way to make babies?"

"More or less." Marina replied. Ms. Takayama's question was not meant to make her feel stupid. She wanted to make sure that Marina knew the exact procedure.

"When a couple decides to have a baby, first both men and women quit using birth control. They go to the hospital and borrow a small boxlike machine, which determines when a woman ovulates. Then, on the appropriate day, they have sex. The next day they can go to the hospital. At the hospital, the woman has a procedure called 'the morning after'; if fertilization has occurred, then in several days, before the embryo becomes implanted in the uterus, the woman undergoes the extraction procedure. After that, the rest is left to the hospital. The pregnancy is artificially maintained, while the woman returns home.

"The problem was that the progress of medicine made this kind of process almost entirely painless. The ex-utero fertilization of the past and the process of egg extraction were relatively painful and dangerous.

"Today's procedure for ex-utero fertilization is no more painful than the pelvic exams that the women of the past had to undergo frequently. Still, this way of doing things made people think the new way is more stylish. Natural pregnancy and childbirth are both far from stylish and quite painful. It's no wonder that AU spread. It's too bad."

"Ms. Takayama," asked Marina, "Why do you think that AU is bad? Because it's not natural?"

"It's not only that. For example, do you know that AU can be monitored, Detective Eda?"

"How?"

"You can always get up-to-date details on the condition of the fetus. When you hear that, you think that AU is convenient. In the case of an incurable illness or injury to the embryo, however, the parents are able to make a decision."

"Make a decision?"

"Whether or not to continue with the pregnancy. That's what has happened since the old days. If you wanted to abort a fetus in the mother's womb, then surgery was necessary. In the case of AU, you just turn off the switch. Thus there's no pain. I think it's a dangerous thing to be able to make a frivolous decision about a fetus. Does this mean that you can allow only the desirable children? What *is* a desirable child, and who thinks they are desirable—that's the question."

"When you have AU," Marina asked, "is there a way to avoid the monitoring function?"

"No, there isn't. You only find out when you go to the hospital, but doctors tell people that they have to use the technology. This monitoring ability is the one reason why AU became popular. In the 1990s information about pregnancy spread, and even when there were children born with minor illnesses, people said that the mother went too far, and mothers were condemned by their peers. Therefore, the needs of mothers who are afraid of shouldering such a heavy burden and the needs of the State are met by AU."

"The State?"

"There are several reasons why a technique like AU has to be regulated. Yet, why is it that you can use insurance to cover it?" Ms. Takayama lowered her voice. "The nation consistently has been behind the spread of AU. The goal was to rein in the falling birthrate. Another factor, however, was this monitoring ability. AU meant that women could produce healthy children for the State. Do you understand? From the time you are a fetus, you are expected to be loyal."

"I find that odd," replied Marina.

"Although," said Ms. Takayama, "when you compare it to SAU, AU is preferable."

"SAU?"

"A semi-artificial uterus, also called the cyborg uterus. The woman's original uterus is augmented—that is, it's a kind of mechanization. From the point of view of control, you can conveniently monitor the pregnancy; material exchange and temperature adjustment are things that you can rely on the mother's body to do. The maintenance costs are cheaper than AU . . ."

"That's terrible," Marina said angrily.

"Yes. The reason is that living women were seen as raw materials for reducing costs. The burden on the woman's body was similar to that of old-fashioned birth—although sometimes it could be higher. Because you insert something like a frame into the womb, the woman's stomach is bigger in the early stages of pregnancy. There was talk that a group of politicians would promote this procedure, but there was a strong reaction from every side, and so the procedure was never put into practice."

"Do you think that people would refuse to use it? No one would accept such . . ." Marina began.

"There was a slogan when AU begun," said Ms. Takayama, " 'It's more baby-friendly than the womb.' Safety for the baby was the official selling point. Women's comfort was what came with it. Once you understand this situation, when someone says, 'we made an even safer way,' it becomes impossible to object . . . officially."

Marina pondered this.

Ms. Takayama continued, "In comparison, AU really is better. Of course, I think that raising the child in the mother's womb is the best. What do you think, Detective Eda?"

"I . . . um . . ."

Although Ms. Takayama's words were persuasive, Marina didn't feel as if she could subject her body to something like that. She wouldn't be able to give up the slender body that she got from the gym and undergo something like pregnancy instead.

Marina turned the question around, "What do you think, Ms. Takayama? What do you think about going through pregnancy and childbirth?"

"Well, if I were married . . . I wonder if that will happen or not."

"Are you single?"

"Yes, I'm an old maid." This good-looking, sexy woman used the old-fashioned word. "I don't really care for men."

Marina wondered if this was a joke, but the eyes behind the glasses were serious. She decided to return to the original question. "Let's talk about the incident," she said straightforwardly.

"Certainly," responded Ms Takayama, sitting up straight.

"We haven't necessarily decided that a resident of this town is the suspect. Still, we believe that the suspect was a pregnant woman, based upon eyewitness accounts."

"Don't you think the suspect could have been disguised as a pregnant woman?" asked Ms. Takayama.

"The problem is the security system here. Each resident carries a special ID card. If they don't have it, then they can only use the main gate, right?"

"Correct. Other than the residents who have IDs, there is no one who can use those gates."

"Do you think that someone could have stolen an ID card?"

"There haven't been any theft reports. Because the cards are so important, if you didn't have one, you would make a fuss."

"I understand." Marina now was sure that the suspect had to be one of the residents. "There is something that I want to confirm about the special gate. I assume that there's a sensor that checks the IDs of the people who have come through the gate. Is there some way to record who uses the gate and when?"

"No, the purpose of the system was to check for intruders and to protect the residents—not to watch over them," said Ms. Takayama.

These pregnant women were treated like a rare breed of animal—a delicate, shy animal, one that needed to be protected from injury and wouldn't harm a flea.

Marina knew that the security system couldn't function like that, but she couldn't help thinking that it would be great if it did.

"Did you see a pregnant woman run from this gate yesterday?" Marina asked.

"Yes, yes."

She was excited when she heard this answer. Marina was on a walking path behind a huge supermarket. All roads except the main streets could be called walking paths, since they wound through the trees.

For an active detective from the First Ward, this town was too quiet and calm, and she felt like she was going insane. Flowers grew on every street corner and the buildings looked as if they belonged in a fairy tale. For one thing, the supermarket's bird-shaped weather vane annoyed Marina.

"There was a person who emerged from the shadow of those trees," drawled a woman in a light-blue jumper. Her leisurely way of speaking was one of the reasons Marina was irritated.

"She was running really fast, with a full head of steam. She turned the corner, and then I couldn't see her."

"What kind of person was she?"

"Hmm. She looked like she was just eight months along."

"What?" said Marina, pausing. "Oh yeah, the time that she has been pregnant. So twenty-eight weeks—that's starting the eighth month."

"Right. She certainly was bigger than me."

This woman herself was about seven months along. Marina cast an eye on her stomach. She noticed that it was quite large.

"If there is anything else . . ." Marina began.

"Yes, the shape—the shape was *togari*. Do you know what I mean? There are two kinds of stomach. When you are narrow here, and this part sticks out in front, you are sharp-shaped, or *togaribara*. Then there is turtle-shaped, or *kamebara*."

"Meaning what?" Marina asked, her head spinning. "This area is wide and the lower area doesn't stick out as much?"

"Everything is flat, like there's a turtle shell on your front. They used to say that a *kamebara* will be a girl. I have a *kamebara*."

As she said this, she stuck out her chest proudly. Marina wondered whether she shouldn't be embarrassed to say that her stomach was shaped like a tortoise shell. She took out her memo pad and wrote *togaribara* in it.

"Anything else . . ." Marina asked.

"Anything else?"

"Besides the shape of the stomach, like her hair or her height or what her face looked like . . ." Marina paused.

"I don't know . . ."

For a moment, Marina felt a chill run up her spine. Is it possible that the only things these women recognize about other women is their bellies?

The woman in the light-blue jumper stood with her arms folded over her stomach, a pose which dwarfed her hands.

Pointing her finger, she said, "Well, I guess her hair was long, and I think that it was braided in the back. She was of average height, and she wore a salmon-pink jumper skirt."

Marina felt a little relieved, but she continued to write. Her description was vague, peppered with "I think" and "I guess," in comparison to the description of the suspected stomach.

"Was that helpful?"

"Very," said Marina.

"Do you want me to call my friend who was with me yesterday? I think she's still in the supermarket."

"That would be nice."

Marina waited. When they finally arrived, she didn't feel as if she'd waited that long. She'd been prepared to wait half an hour. The returning woman was accompanied by another pregnant woman in a lemon-yellow jumper.

"That woman we saw, she was maybe in the latter half of her eighth month."

Marina looked at the large belly of the women in yellow. She thought that this woman herself was also in her eighth month. Both of the women, however, thought that the suspect was larger than they were.

"She had a *togaribara*?" asked the woman in the sky-blue jumper.

"Yes, that's right," confirmed her friend, "You could see it more clearly than mine."

Looking at her belly, one could tell that the shape was a little different from the belly of the first woman.

"That kind of *togaribara* is unusual," the friend commented.

"Do you remember anything about her face or her height?" Marina asked.

"Well . . ."

Her description was almost identical to the one her friend offered. Of course, the size of her stomach and its shape were what caught their eye—nothing else.

"Still," asked the woman wearing the lemon-colored jumper, "Would you run like that at eight months?"

"True," said her friend. "What was she thinking? How terrible."

"She was a disgrace to pregnant women everywhere."

Marina interrupted them, "OK, how about her clothing. Your friend here said she was wearing a salmon-pink jumper."

"That's right," declared the lemon-yellow jumper. "She didn't have a blouse on, so she was just wearing the dress sundress-style."

"Is that so?" said light-blue jumper. "In this changeable weather? How convenient."

"Isn't it? It means that you don't have to buy so many maternity clothes."

"Right. And, if we get pregnant again, we can still wear them," they chorused. "Even though next time it may be winter."

Looking at their peaceful faces, Marina's head began to hurt. Why they looked so contented, she had no idea.

NOTES

[1]I.e., are hatched from eggs grown outside the body.

[2]This a tautological remark for which there is no direct equivalent in English. The general sense is, "that goes without saying."

[3]A belly band, or *hara obi,* is a length of cotton cloth several yards long wrapped around a pregnant belly. It is supposed to support the weight of the stomach and improve the pregnant woman's posture. Still used in Japan today, women start wearing them in the fifth month of pregnancy.

It Don't Mean a Thing, If It Ain't Got That Swing: An Interview with Haruki Murakami

Sinda Gregory, Toshifumi Miyawaki, and Larry McCaffery

The Japanese author who has best captured the odd combination of consumerist abundance and spiritual emptiness that has characterized Japanese life during the past twenty-five years is Haruki Murakami. Born in 1949 in Kyoto and raised in Kobe in an academic family setting (his father taught Japanese literature at a nearby high school), Murakami as a teenager shared with many Japanese youths a fascination with Western cultural artifacts—television shows, rock music and jazz, films, and fiction; by the time he entered Tokyo's Waseda University in the late sixties at the height of student activism (which he witnessed but did not actively participate in), Murakami had deliberately turned his back on Japanese literature in favor of the sort of hip, new, fabulist American writings by Vonnegut, Brautigan, and other postmodernists whose works were beginning to appear in Japanese translation. Convinced that he wasn't yet ready to embark on a career as a fiction writer, Murakami spent the next six or seven years running a jazz bar in Tokyo—an experience which provided him with an ideal perspective on the evolution of Tokyo's bored-but-hyper youth culture that was then emerging. Starting in the late seventies, Murakami began publishing a series of coming-of-age novels—including *Pinball 1973* and his enormously popular *Norwegian Wood* (which sold several million copies)—which vividly portrayed central characters aimlessly drifting through life in a brave new Japanese world like some latter day equivalents of Holden Caulfield. Presented in a lyrical (though often affectless) style that lingered obsessively on the surface features of Japanese life, full of casual sex, references to Western music, film, and other forms of pop culture, and often dripping with nostalgia, these early novels made Murakami an instant celebrity—a role he felt uncomfortable enough with that during the late eighties, he embarked on a several-year period of self-imposed exile in Europe and the United States.

If Murakami was embraced by his younger readers as their

spokesperson, the popularity of his novels was viewed by most Japanese literary critics at the time with suspicion and often harsh condemnation. Murakami quickly became a flashpoint within Japanese intellectual circles in much the way (and for many of the same reasons) that Bret Ellis and Jay McInerney were in America during the 1980s. Blaming the messenger for the message, these critics frequently voiced their displeasure with precisely those features of Murakami's fiction that so successfully and poignantly captured the blankness, spiritual emptiness, and confusion of the emerging *shinjinrui* (literally, "New Human Race") generation of Japanese youths from that period, who found themselves unable to find any sense of personal satisfaction from a life of empty consumerism and mindless commitment to job—and equally unable to envision any means of effecting a change or even expressing their dissatisfactions.

However, beginning with *A Wild Sheep Chase,* Murakami began to develop innovative narrative strategies that successfully integrated paraliterary elements (most notably those drawn from detective and SF formats), cultural and political criticism, and metaphysical and psychological investigations in a manner that allowed him to present the struggles of ordinary Japanese citizens to remain human in a world that seemed increasingly unreal and inhuman. No longer merely passive victims, the main characters in Murakami's major novels during this period—which include *Sheep Chase* and its sequel, *Dance Dance Dance,* and (perhaps his masterpiece to date) *Hard-Boiled Wonderland and the End of the World*—were now presented as *questors* seeking not merely romantic and nostalgic connections to the past but also a more active means of making sense of their lives and the bewildering plurality of hyperrealities around them. No longer content, as he had been in *Pinball 1973* and *Norwegian Wood,* to tell a story about the conflict between self and environment in terms of daily, surface reality, Murakami devised a kind of "simulation approach" in which the conflicts existing within his protagonists' personal consciousnesses were simulated and then projected into the surreal, labyrinthine regions of dream and personalized, Jungian unconsciousness. Fully aware of the confusing, often banalizing impact that hyperconsumerism was having on Japan, these novels are all cautionary parables about the dangers of life under late capitalism—dangers which included information overload, the irrelevance of human values and spirituality in a world dominated by the inhuman logic of postindustrial capitalism, and the loss of contact with other human beings.

By the mid-nineties (when this interview was conducted in Boston, where Murakami was then living), Murakami was in the process of completing another ambitious novel, *The Wind-Up Bird Chronicle,* which focused on another loss—that of history and historical perspective generally, and in particular the ongoing difficulty of the Japanese people to come to grips with their collective responsibility for what occurred during WWII. Moving freely back and forth between dream and reality, the past and the present, and mixing together elements of the Gothic romance, war novel (key sections of the novel deal with the horrific violence inflicted on the Chinese during Japan's invasion of Manchuria during the 1930s), and hard-boiled detective fiction, *The Wind-Up Bird Chronicle* vividly describes a hypermediated world in which the actualities of reality and history become transformed into hyperconsumerist byproducts. (Toshifumi Miyawaki)

Larry McCaffery: Most of your biographical statements mention that you owned a jazz bar for a number of years. And of course references to jazz appear frequently in your works. Has jazz had any influence on your writing in any way?

Haruki Murakami: Not consciously. Jazz is just my hobby. It is true that I was listening to jazz for ten hours a day for several years, so maybe I was deeply influenced by this kind of music—the rhythm, the improvisation, the sound, the style. Managing that jazz club did have some direct effect on my decision to write, though. One night looking down the bar of the club, I saw some black American soldiers crying because they missed America so much. Up until that point, I had been so immersed in Western culture ever since I was about ten or twelve—not just jazz but also Elvis and Vonnegut. I think that my interest in these things was partly due to wanting to rebel against my father (he was a teacher of Japanese literature) and against other Japanese orthodoxies. So when I was sixteen I stopped reading Japanese novels and began reading Russian and French novels, such as Dostoyevsky, Stendhal, and Balzac, in translation. After studying English for four years in high school, I began reading American books at used-bookstores. By reading novels I could escape out of my loneliness into a different world. It felt like visiting Mars at first, but gradually I began to feel comfortable there. But that night, when I saw those American men crying, I realized that, no matter how much I loved this Western culture, it meant more to these soldiers than it ever could to me. That was really why I began to write.

LM: My sense is that in the 1960s in the United States, many of the postmodern writers—Thomas Pynchon, for example—were very influenced by jazz, especially jazz's reliance on improvisation. In your own case, would you describe your writing as being improvisational at all?

HM: Rhythm is more important to me than notions of improvisation. When I am writing, I am always thinking of rhythm. "It don't mean a thing, if it ain't got that swing."

Sinda Gregory: You adopt an interesting version of the hard-boiled style in your novel *Hard-Boiled Wonderland*. What about the hard-boiled style appeals to you?

HM: Its authenticity. But I wasn't really interested in writing a hard-boiled mystery; I just wanted the hard-boiled mystery structure. I'm very interested in structure. I've been using other pop structures in my writing as well—science fiction structures, for example. I'm also using love-story or romance structures. But as far as my thinking about the hard-boiled style, I'm interested in the fact that they are very individualist in orientation. The figure of the loner. I'm interested in that because it isn't easy to live in Japan as an individualist or a loner. I'm always thinking about this. I'm a novelist and I'm a loner, an individualist. I think that's why I came to this country. It's my dream to write hard-boiled mysteries.

SG: One of the conventions of the hard-boiled style is having the individualist/loner who at some point had a very bad pain; you typically get the feeling that this guy is trying to deal with this pain somehow, but he doesn't talk about that pain. I thought that might be part of why it's a good structure for you, because so many of your characters are suffering from a similar sense of angst. So you can create characters whose lives in the present are very much a response to that pain without going into all the messy details of all the specifics of the pain. The pain is still there, but you're not wallowing in it.

HM: I think you're right. When I was younger I was very attracted to the hard-boiled fiction writers like Chandler and Ross Macdonald, maybe because their detectives seemed to be so individual. No matter what happened to them, they were always able to live their own way, working in a way they like and never complaining about their misfortunes. I love that. I myself don't write directly about those kinds of pains and sufferings and everything. Of course, I have those pains and sufferings, but I don't talk so much about myself, generally. And I don't write about this because I have read so many books that care about those pains and pains and pains— I'm tired of it! So I don't write about it.

LM: I think just about all of your novels are in the first person. Have you ever thought about not writing in the first person?

HM: Yes, for a short time I tried to write in the third person, but it didn't work out.

LM: What's the problem? Is it not as interesting? Is it the voice?

HM: When I tried to use third person, I just felt like I became a god. But I don't want to be a god. I don't know everything. I can't write everything. I'm just myself. I would write something just as myself. I don't mean that I really am the protagonist but that I can envision what my protagonist sees and experiences. Writing lets me enter my own subconscious; that's the process I use to tell my stories. It's the most exciting thing I've ever done. For me telling a good story is like what happens when I walk down the street. I love the street, and so when I'm walking, I'm watching everything, hearing and smelling everything. When you do this, the world changes—you're experiencing everything in a new way. The light and the sounds and your emotions. That's the way writing is for me. I'm forty-six and married, but when I'm writing I can become twenty-five and unmarried. I can walk around in somebody else's shoes—and feel those shoes. Writing becomes your second life. That's good.

LM: Some critics, both in the U.S. and Japan, have said that your work is not really Japanese. Do you yourself think of yourself as having a distinctly Japanese sensibility—or as writing specifically about Japanese experience versus just writing about universal experiences?

HM: The opinion that my books are not really Japanese seems to me to be very shallow. I certainly think of myself as being a Japanese writer. I write with a different style and maybe with different materials, but I write in Japanese, and I'm writing for Japanese society and Japanese people. So I think people are wrong when they are always saying that my style is really mainly influenced by Western literature. As I just said, at first I wanted to be an international writer, but eventually saw that I was nothing but a Japanese writer. But even in the beginning I wasn't only borrowing Western styles and rules. I wanted to change Japanese literature from the inside, not the outside. So I basically made up my own rules.

SG: Could you give us some examples of what you mean?

HM: Most literary purists in Japan love beautiful language and appreciate sensitivity rather than energy or power. This beauty is admired for its own sake, and so their styles use a lot of very stiff, formal metaphors that don't sound natural or spontaneous at all. These writing styles get more and more refined, to the point where they resemble a kind of bonsai. I don't like such traditional forms of writing; it may sound beautiful, but it may not communicate. Besides, who knows what beauty is? So in my writing, I've tried to change that. I like to write more freely, so I use a lot of long and peculiar metaphors that seem fresh to me.

LM: I think that sense of freshness is one thing that makes your books appeal to Western readers; and I suspect that American readers may also be drawn to your works because they're familiar with many of the literary and pop-cultural references you make—which are usually to Western works. On the other hand, it also strikes me that when people in non-Western countries receive our pop-culture, it also means something very different.

HM: Yes, of course such things mean something different when they're taken out of their original context. For a long time I made many references to Western culture in my books because that's the culture that surrounded me and I liked. I am of the generation of Elvis Presley, the Beach Boys, and television shows like *Peter Gunn*. Most Japanese people during the sixties were impressed by American culture because of what we saw on TV. When I was a boy, I was especially impressed when I saw American TV shows like *Father Knows Best*. The lifestyle of those people seemed almost unimaginably rich to the people in Japan of that time. These Americans had big cars and TVs and so many other gadgets. It was like heaven. Jazz, detective fiction, television, rock music—these were parts of the world I was most familiar with, and so when I began writing, I naturally made references to them. But such references in my books are not really very complicated. When I write, it's just like a Bruce Springsteen tune—there's a certain sense in which the meaning is right on the surface, so you know what it means. It hurts. But to be honest with you, I'm finding that I don't need these sorts of pop references in my writing anymore. I can do without those things. So I have changed my ways.

SG: What's been the reaction of American readers to your work? I'm wondering especially about younger readers.

HM: I found it very interesting when I visited universities in the U.S. that many students are interested in Japanese literature and culture. What I noticed was that they seemed to be reading contemporary Japanese books simply as novels rather than as "Japanese novels." They're reading my books or ones by Amy Yamada or Banana Yoshimoto the same way they had begun to read García Márquez and Vargas Llosa and other Latin American novelists a few years ago. It takes a while for this kind of a change to take place. Writers from different countries are changing each other and finding global audiences more easily nowadays; it's a small world and a world which is getting smaller. I think that's a great thing.

LM: Your early books up through *Norwegian Wood* all concerned themselves with that sixties generation of young people. There's a sense of idealism and lack of jadedness in your descriptions of these people that seems anachronistic today, that's been replaced by irony or cynicism.

HM: As I said earlier, things were much simpler in the sixties. It was easier to be idealistic. I belong to a generation of Japanese people who grew up during the counterculture era and the revolutionary uprisings of 1968, 1969, and 1970. The Japan when I was a child was poor, and everybody worked hard and was optimistic that things were getting better. But they are not. When we were kids, we were a poor country but very idealistic. That began to change in the sixties; some people just got rich and forgot their ideals, while other people struggled to save idealism. Many of us were very political during that time, and for a while everything seemed to be changing; there was a lot of promise and optimism. Then, very quickly, all that simply disappeared. The uprisings were all crushed by the cops and the mood became bleak. The whole sense of the counterculture rebellion seemed finished.

SG: It's difficult to sustain a revolutionary spirit during economically good times like Japan began to enjoy in the seventies. Beginning with *A Wild Sheep Chase* and *Dance Dance Dance,* you seemed to begin writing less about the sixties era and more about what's been going on in Japan in the aftermath of the success of late capitalism. Overall, you portray what's going on very negatively—you tend to suggest that all this money and prosperity and information and hyperstimulation have a very sinister, corrupting effect. Everybody's idealism has been bought off. And yet people in your books are still lonely; all the consumer goods they own don't make them happy and there's a tremendous sense of nostalgia for the sixties.

HM: That is one of the reasons I think *Norwegian Wood* sold so many copies. Japanese readers still yearn for that kind of world where there could be idealism. But after that book, I decided I wanted to write about a character who is lonely and alone in this big, very sophisticated and very complex society of information and money—which is what you find in *A Wild Sheep Chase* and *Dance Dance Dance*. People in Japan today are taught to believe that having a BMW and a new computer will make you feel happy and not isolated; that's not true, but this is not spoken about truthfully. So everyone retreats into cynicism and hypocrisy. The big problem is that this new society seems so big and powerful that it is difficult to know where to even begin to attack it. But things are changing.

LM: Do you see your writing being more directly interested in politics?

HM: I don't write political novels—or at least when I write, I don't think of politics except subconsciously. But I agree with you that all my books, even the early ones, have all involved political factors; it's just that these factors were never treated directly. So these political issues were present in my books only in the background; even though it is undeniable that politics and economics have helped produce the circumstances that my characters find themselves in; I have never been interested in writing about such things directly. I suppose my earlier books were responding to that sense of disappointment and frustration that my generation went through; they probably reflected the fact that it just didn't seem possible that political change was really possible, and so providing any sort of political analysis in my fiction seemed boring, a waste of time. As I said earlier, though, the political change that seems to be happening in Japan may be encouraging writers to write more directly about politics.

LM: When we lived abroad—we lived in France for a year, and we lived in China for a year—it always seems that being exposed to these other cultures actually makes us think about our own country even more. Have you found that to be true? Is there a way that being away from your country lets you see it even better?

HM: To a certain extent, yes. Living abroad has let me test Japanese culture from the outside. Many Americans have asked me why don't I write about this country, but the truth is that I'm not really interested in writing about this country. I want to write about Japan. I've been living in this country for several years now—mainly at universities like Princeton and now Harvard, which I need to do for my visa, but I don't have any real obligations—and I have really enjoyed life here. But somehow I am so impressed with this country that I don't want to write about it. I would rather write about Asia. So I am now writing a book (*The Wind-Up Bird Chronicle*) about what the Japanese people did in China in 1930. I began writing this while I was in a library in Princeton. I read a great many books about the war, and I was wondering at that point about who the Japanese people really are. What did we do there? That's a very big question. I'd like to know what my father did in China. He was there in the thirties, and when I was a little kid he used to talk about the war. There were some scary stories that shocked me—not big stories but very bloody. Now, about forty years later, I found that I wanted to write about this.

LM: You mentioned that with *A Wild Sheep Chase* you wanted to write about people's lives in the seventies and eighties rather than about the sixties. But there was also a change in your style with this book—you also appeared to turn away from the basically realistic approach you used in your first couple of novels. Was that a conscious shift—a desire to find a way of writing that gave you more freedom?

HM: By the time I was writing *A Wild Sheep Chase,* I knew that I wanted to be a storyteller. That's the most important thing that happened to me as a writer. The first two books are shorter and didn't require a story; they were both really collections of fragments. But as I developed as a writer, I began to see that stories have many possibilities—so much so that I think that the most important question I ask myself now when I am writing is whether my story is alive or not. I also understand better now that there are many different kinds of stories; sometimes just creating a metaphor can wind up telling a kind of story. Anyway, by the time I began *A Wild Sheep Chase* I knew I wanted to tell a continuous narrative— a big, long story. And when I tried to write this story, I found that I needed some supernatural power to tell a story. I wasn't interested in writing a realistic story, but one that was a supernatural, fantastic story. In these days it's not easy to tell a story using traditional realistic methods of storytelling. Somehow you need something else—something supernatural or fantastic—to make it become truer. I know that in *A Wild Sheep Chase* the story seemed to become more realistic when the sheepman appeared, even though the sheepman himself is not realistic. I like that.

The complete interview with Haruki Murakami can be accessed at www.centerforbookculture.org.

Three German Fantasies

Haruki Murakami

1. Pornography vis-à-vis a museum-in-winter.

Sex. Intercourse. Coition. Copulation. There are many other words, but what I always conjure up in my mind (from the spoken word, the act, the phenomenon) is a museum-in-winter.

A *museum-in-winter.*

Of course, I realize that there's quite some distance before you arrive at "museum" from "sex." You must make countless subway transfers, shuttle beneath office buildings, let the seasons fly by in a limbo. But as these are irksome only to the utter novice, if you should complete but once that circuit of consciousness, you could find your way from "sex" to that museum-in-winter before you knew it.

I'm not lying. You really could. Perhaps I should explain a little.

When sex becomes urban conversation, when copulative undulations fill the darkness, as ever, I'm standing in the entrance to the museum-in-winter. I hang my hat on the hat rack, I hang my coat on the coat rack, I place my gloves, one atop the other, on the corner of the reception desk, then, remembering the scarf wrapped around my neck, I remove it and place it over my coat.

The museum-in-winter is not very large at all. The collection, its taxonomy, its operating philosophy are by any standard amateurish. First off, there's no unifying concept. There's a figurine of an Egyptian dog deity, a protractor used by Napoléon III, a bell found in the Dead Sea caves. But that's it. There's no way to connect the display pieces at all. They sit hunched over in their cases, eyes fixed shut like orphans mortally seized by cold and starvation.

Inside the museum it is extremely quiet. There is a little while yet before the museum opens. I retrieve from my desk a butterfly-shaped metal key and wind the grandfather clock near the entrance. Then I adjust the hands to the right time. I—that is, if I'm not mistaken—work here at the museum.

As always, the quiet morning light and the even quieter presentiment of sex fills the museum like almond extract. I make my rounds, opening curtains, opening radiator valves. Then I neatly arrange our fifty-pfennig pamphlets and stack them on the reception desk. I adjust the necessary lighting (which is to say, for example, when I press button A6 at the mini-Versailles Palace, the king's chamber lights up, etc.). I also check the watercooler. I maneuver the stuffed European wolf a little farther back into its display out of children's reach and restock the liquid soap in the washroom. Even if I didn't think to remember each of these tasks one by one, my body of itself would complete them. This, in other words—well, I'm not sure exactly how to put it—is the me-ness of me.

After all this I go to the little kitchen and brush my teeth, get some milk out of the fridge and heat it in a saucepan over a little portable range. The electric range, fridge, and toothbrush are by no means extraordinary (they were bought at a mom-and-pop electronics shop and corner convenience store), but inasmuch as they are within the museum, they appear somehow relic-ish. Even the milk looks like ancient milk, drawn from an ancient cow. At times it all gets quite confusing. I mean, as concepts go, is it more precise to say that the museum erodes the quotidian, or does the quotidian erode the museum?

Once the milk is warm, I take it and sit down in front of the reception desk. As I drink I open the mail left in the slot and read. Mail separates into three categories. First, you've got things like your water bill, the archeological circle newsletter, notice of telephone number change from the Greek consulate, and other kinds of administrative correspondence. Next are letters written by people who've visited the museum, chronicling various impressions, grievances, encouragements, suggestions, etc. I think that people are prone to come up with an assortment of reactions. I mean, all of this stuff is just so old. Think how it must irk them to have the late Han period wine flask next to the Mesopotamian coffin! But if the museum were to cease confusing and irking its clientele, where else could they go to be irked?

Once I've mindlessly filed away the letters into these two categories, I reach into the desk drawer and grab a few cookies to finish off my milk. Then I open the last type of letter. This type is from the owner and, as such, is extremely concise. Written in black ink on artsy egg-colored paper are my instructions:

1. Pack up urn at display #36; put in storage.
2. To compensate, take sculpture-stand from A52 (minus sculpture) and display at Q21.
3. Replace light bulb at space 76.
4. Post next month's holiday hours at entrance.

Of course I comply with every instruction: I wrap the urn in canvas and put it in storage; to compensate, I take the sadistically heavy sculpture-stand and, near-herniating, put it on solo display;

and standing on a chair, I replace the light bulb at space 76. The urn at display #36 was a museum-goer's favorite, the sadistically heavy sculpture-stand looks awful by itself, and the replaced light bulb was itself quite new. These were not the sort of things which would have pushed themselves to the forefront of my mind. After doing exactly as I was told, I tidy up my dishes and put away the cookie tin. It's nearly opening time.

Before the washroom mirror I comb my hair, fix the knot of my necktie, and make sure that my penis is properly erect. No problems.
    *urn #36, check
    *sculpture-stand A52, check
    *light bulb, check
    *erection, check
Sex crashes against the museum doors like a wave. The hands of the grandfather clock read a precise 11 in the a.m. The wintry light, as if slowly drawing its tongue over the floor, extends subduedly into the room. I cross the floor slowly, undo the latch and open the door. The very instant I open the door everything changes. The little lights in Louis XIV's chamber flicker on, the saucepan ceases to lose its heat, and urn #36 slips into a soft, jellylike slumber. Overhead a bunch of bustling men echo their footfalls in a circle. I even quit trying to understand people. I can see someone standing in the doorway, but I don't care. As far as I'm concerned, they can keep right on standing there. Whenever I think about sex, I'm always in the museum-in-winter, and we are all there, hunched over like orphans, seeking a little warmth. The saucepan is in the kitchen, the cookie tin is in the drawer, and I am in the museum-in-winter.

2. The Hermann Göring Stronghold, 1983.

What on earth did Hermann Göring envision when he hollowed out that hill in Berlin and constructed his enormous stronghold? He literally hollowed out the entire hill and filled it up with concrete. It stood out strikingly in the diffuse twilight like an ominous termite mound. Once we'd clambered up the steep slope and stood on top, we could look down and see into the heart of East Berlin, where the street lamps had just been turned on. The batteries which faced in every direction would have afforded a view of the enemy forces closing in on the capital and could probably have repelled them. No bomb could have toppled the stronghold's thick walls, and certainly no tank could have scaled its steep slopes.

The stronghold contained enough supplies—rations of food, water, and ammunition—to house 2,000 SS officers for a number of months. Secret underground passages crisscrossed below like a maze, and a marvelous air conditioner supplied fresh air to the stronghold interior. Hermann Göring boasted that even if, for example, the Russians or Allies surrounded the capital, those inside the stronghold would have no need to fear; they could survive indefinitely inside his indestructible fortress.

But in the spring of 1945, when the Russian army stormed into Berlin like the season's last blizzard, the Hermann Göring stronghold was silent. The Russian army torched its underground passages with flamethrowers and detonated high explosives in an effort to eradicate the stronghold's very existence. But the stronghold would not be eradicated. There were only a few cracks on the concrete walls.

"You could never bring down Hermann Göring's fortress with Russian bombs," laughed my young East German guide. "They could barely bring down Stalin's statue!" For who knew how many hours, he'd been leading me around the city, showing me the lingering traces of the Battle of Berlin in 1945. Did he think I had some strange desire to see the aftermath of Berlin's WWII? I couldn't guess. But I was surprisingly eager, and since it seemed inappropriate to explain what I really wanted to see, I followed him around the city until late into the afternoon. We'd first met that very day in a cafeteria near Fernsehturm, where I'd gone for lunch.

However odd our union, my guide proved to be very competent and was frank with me. As I followed him around, visiting the battle scenes of East Berlin, I slowly began to feel as though the war had ended but a few short months ago. The whole city was still riddled with bullet wounds.

"Here, look at this," my guide said. He showed me some bullet holes. "You can tell right off which bullets were Russian and which German. These ones so deep they nearly blew the wall in two are German, these others that practically pop out are Russian. The craftsmanship's different, you know?"

Of all the East Berliners I met while I was there, his was the most understandable English. "You speak English very well," I said praisingly.

"Well, for a while I was a sailor," he said. "I've been to Cuba and Africa—I even spent some time on the Black Sea. So I picked up some English along the way. But now I'm an architectural engineer . . ."

We descended from Hermann Göring's stronghold and after walking briefly through the city, we entered an old beer hall on Unter den Linden. Perhaps because it was Friday night, the hall was stiflingly packed.

"The chicken here is quite popular," the guide said. So I ordered chicken and rice with beer. The chicken actually wasn't bad, and the beer was great. The room was warm and the noise and bustle pleasant.

Our waitress was a drop-dead gorgeous Kim Carnes look-alike. She was platinum blonde with blue eyes, a small, trim waist, and pretty smile. She brought our beer steins to the table, holding them admiringly, the way she would an enormous penis. She reminded me of a girl I once knew in Tokyo. She didn't look like this girl, nor resemble her in any way, but somehow they were subtly alike. Perhaps some aftereffect of Hermann Göring's dark labyrinth was conflating them in my mind.

We had already drunk plenty of beer. The clock read close to ten. I had to be at the S Bahn at Friedrichstrasse station by twelve. My East German traveler's visa expired at midnight, and if I was so much as one minute late it would be extremely troublesome.

"On the outskirts of the city there is an old battle site that's still really torn up," the guide said.

I was staring idly at the waitress and didn't hear him.

"Excuse me?" He continued, "Russian and SS tanks attacked each other head on, right? It was the real climax of the Battle of Berlin. The wreckage is at an old marshalling yard, but it's remained exactly how it was back then. All the broken tank parts and stuff, I mean. We can borrow a friend's car and be there in no time . . ."

I looked at my guide's face. It was thin over his gray corduroy coat. He placed both hands on the table. His fingers were long and delicate, unsailorlike.

I shook my head, "I've got to be at the Friedrichstrasse station by midnight. My visa'll expire."

"How about tomorrow?"

"Tomorrow morning I'm leaving for Nuremberg," I lied.

The youth looked a bit disappointed. A wave of exhaustion rolled suddenly across his face. "It's just that if we went tomorrow, we could take my girlfriend and some of her friends along. That's all," he said as if in explanation.

"Aw, that's too bad," I said. I felt as though a cold hand was squeezing all the nerve bundles in my body. But what could I do? I didn't know. Here I was absolutely lost in this strange battle-scarred city. Eventually though, the cold hand loosened, retreated like a tide from my body.

"Well . . . hey, Hermann Göring's fortress was great, right?" He said with a smile. "Nobody's been able to bring it down in forty years."

From the intersection of Friedrichstrasse and Unter den Linden you can see quite clearly in all directions. To the north, S Bahn station. To the south, Checkpoint Charlie. To the west, Brandenburg Gate. To the east, Fernsehturm.

"Well, don't worry," said the youth. "Even if you took your time you could make the station in about fifteen minutes. Got it, okay?"

My wristwatch read 11:10 p.m. Yes, I'm all right, I told myself. We shook hands.

"It's too bad we couldn't go to the marshalling yard, eh? And then the women, eh?"

"Yes, regrettable," I said. But to him, what could possibly have been regrettable about our not going? Walking alone, northbound on the Friedrichstrasse, I tried to imagine what Hermann Göring had envisioned that spring of 1945. But really, no one will know what the Reichsmarshal of the Thousand Year Empire was thinking. Göring's beloved and elegant Heinkel 117 bomber squadron lay in the Ukrainian wilderness like hundreds of bleached bones, the corpse of war itself.

3. Herr W's Midair Garden

The first time I was taken to see Herr W's midair garden was on a fog-heavy November morning.

"Well, she isn't much," said Herr W.

And he was right. The midair garden just sat there floating in a sea of fog. It was roughly eight yards long and five wide. Other than the fact that it was airborne, it differed in no other way from a regular garden. Well, let me rephrase that: it was a garden certainly, but by terrestrial standards, it was third-rate. The grass was dried up in patches, the flowers were eerily unnatural-looking, the tomato vines were all withered, and it lacked even a wooden fence. The white garden furniture looked as though it had come from a pawnshop.

"I told you it wasn't much," Herr W repeated as if in apology. He had been watching my eyes the whole time. But I wasn't particularly disappointed, I hadn't come to see splendid arbors, fountains, animal-shaped shrubbery, or Cupidean statues. I just wanted to see Herr W's midair garden.

"This is better than any of those ostentatious, earthbound gardens," I said, and Herr W seemed a little relieved.

"If only I could float a bit higher, then it'd really be a midair garden. But things being as they are . . ." Herr W said. "Would you take some tea?"

"That would be lovely," I said.

Herr W reached into a canvas *something* of indiscriminate shape (daypack? basket?), pulled out a Coleman stove, a yellow-enameled teapot, and thermos full of water and began preparing the tea.

The air was extremely cold. I was wearing a thick down jacket and a scarf wrapped around my neck but they didn't seem to be helping. As I sat there shivering I watched the fog flow southward beneath me. Floating over the fog, I felt as though we were drifting off into terra incognita.

When I mentioned this to Herr W over hot jasmine tea, he chuckled slightly. "Everyone who comes here says the same thing. Especially on really foggy days. Especially then. Like we'll drift off into the stratosphere over the North Sea, eh?"

I cleared my throat and pointed out the other possibility, "Or into East Berlin."

"Ah, yes, yes," said Herr W, stroking a withered tomato vine. "That's part of the reason why I can't make this a proper midair garden. If I go too high, East German police start getting nervous. They keep their spotlight and machine guns trained on it! Obviously they don't open fire, but it's still not very pleasant."

"No, I suppose not," I said.

"And also, like you said, if it were any higher, there's no guarantee that we wouldn't get caught by a stiff breeze and wind up in East Berlin. And then where would we be! We'd probably be arrested as spies, and even if we survived we'd never make it back to West Berlin!"

"Hmm," I said.

Herr W's midair garden was tethered to the roof of a claptrap four-story building near the Berlin Wall. Since Herr W kept it floating no more than eight inches off the roof, you'd mistake it for just another rooftop garden if you didn't look closely. Maintaining a maximum altitude of eight inches on such a marvelous midair garden is not the sort of feat most people could have duplicated. Everyone said Herr W managed because he was such a "quiet, nonconfrontational sort."

"Why don't you move the flying garden to a safer location?" I asked. "Like Köln or Frankfurt, or even farther into West Berlin? Then you could go up as high as you like and no one would mind."

"Nonsense!" Herr W shook his head. "Köln! Frankfurt!" He shook his head again. "I like it *here*. All my friends live here! In Kreuzberg! It's just fine here!"

He finished his tea and pulled a Phillips portable record player out of a container. He placed a record on the turntable and flipped the switch. Soon the second movement of Handel's *Wassermusik* flowed forth. The brisk trumpets sounded clearly through the dull and overcast Kreuzberg sky. Could there have been another composition better suited to Herr W's midair garden?

"You really ought to come back this summer," Herr W said. "The garden is absolutely wonderful then. Last summer we had a party every day! Once we had twenty-five people and three dogs up here!"

"It's a good thing no one fell off," I said, amazed.

"Actually, two people have fallen off: got drunk," said Herr W, chuckling. "But no one died: the awnings on the third floor are quite sturdy."

I laughed at that.

"We've even hauled up an upright piano before. Pollini came and played Schumann. It was quite splendid. As you know, Pollini is a bit of a midair garden fanatic. Lorin Maazel wanted to come but I couldn't fit the whole Vienna Philharmonic up here, you know."

"Of course not," I agreed.

"Come again this summer," Herr W said and shook my hand. "Summer in Berlin is quite a sight. In summer this place is filled with smells of Turkish cooking and children laughing and music and beer! That's Berlin!"

"I very much wish to return," I said.

"Köln! Frankfurt!!" Herr W repeated, shaking his head.

And thus, Herr W's midair garden awaits summer's arrival, hovering just eight inches over the sky of Kreuzberg.

Translated by Keith Leslie Johnson

The Twister of Imagination:
An Interview with Mariko Ohara

Larry McCaffery, Sinda Gregory, Mari Kotani, and Takayuki Tatsumi

Mariko Ohara was born in Osaka in 1959. Long an admirer of the SF works of A. E. van Vogt and Cordwainer Smith, as a student at Sacred Heart University she published a novella, *Hitori de Aruite Itta Neko* (The Cat Who Walked Alone), which won second prize in the Sixth Hayakawa SF Contest of 1980. *Haiburiddo Chairudo* (Hybrid Child), her story of a multiracial child who merges with objects, won the Seiun (Nebula) Award at the 1991 Japan SF convention, and her *Sensou Wo Enjita Kamigami Tachi* (Gods Prosecuting War) won the 1994 Japan SF Award for best science fiction work of the year. Ohara is the author of numerous other works of fiction, including *Taimu Riipa* (Time Leaper, 1993), which concerns a Japanese businessman who travels thirty years into the future; and *Kyuuketsuki Efemera* (Ephemera the Vampire), which follows the adventures of an immortal female vampire. In 1997 Ohara turned to the wide-screen baroque with her *Arukaikku Suteitsu* (Archaic States), in which galaxies battle in the twenty-eighth century.

In addition to fiction, Ohara also writes for comics, video games, and radio, and her "Saiko Saundo Mashin" (Psycho Sound Machine, 1998), based one of her short stories, won the Galaxy Award for best radio drama.

Aside from creative work, Ohara has co-edited several volumes of the *SF Baka Bon* series (Collected Slapstick SF Stories, 1996-) with her husband, Keigo Misaki. She has also published essays on her internet experience in "Nettowaakaa Eno Michi" (The Way of the Networker, 1994). President of the Science Fiction and Fantasy Writers of Japan from 1999 to 2001, she currently reviews science fiction and fantasy for a major Japanese newspaper and chairs the nomination committee of the Japan SF Award.

"Mental Female," which appears here, was originally published in 1988. (Hisayo Ogushi)

Sinda Gregory: Why did you start writing SF?

Mariko Ohara: I started writing fiction when I was ten years old. One of my early stories was about personified animals, for example, the werewolf. Then I moved on to *yaoi* fiction, like K/S fiction. It was at the age of around sixteen that I first started to write SF. Anyway, the reason for all of this was very simple. I started writing fiction because I was strongly conscious of myself being a natural born liar. I incorporated my lies into the form of novels; otherwise fiction would have always invaded my life, hurting me and people around me.

SG: Were you attracted by just something about the otherworldliness of SF?

MO: Yes, I think so. It seemed to me that the present real world, this side of reality, was wrong, even though most people believe in it. At first, such incongruity was not very clear to me—it seemed as ambiguous as something in a fog. Science fiction, however, enlightened me to the fact that there is no universal value and that we should see the present world relatively.

Larry McCaffery: Could you define "wide-screen baroque"?

MO: "Wide-screen baroque" is a kind of B-movie/space-opera in which highly metaphysical issues are discussed—a hodgepodge of the pop and the avant-garde. For example, Samuel Delany's *Empire Star* or Barrington Bayley's *The Garments of Caean* are typical wide-screen baroque. Every time you flip a page, there is something different, a surprise. It is a page turner, a funhouse. In a short story I put in something new every ten pages or so. Even in a wide-screen baroque novel, for example in its 350 pages of text, you should do the same thing as you would in a short story. This is what I am doing in the series called Archaic States written for *Hayakawa's SF Magazine*. It is somewhat like a reappropriation of the short-story technique into novel writing.

SG: You have said that you used to write K/S fiction. As a young woman, you were already dealing with sexual issues. Did you have a sense of this being forbidden, transgressive?

MO: I didn't have any hesitations in writing sexual fictions even in my teens, because I discovered my own world when I found the paper on which I composed the sentences. That is the world where I can construct whatever I wish. So I tried not to restrain my emotion or desire. Of course my writings didn't hurt anybody, since I seldom showed my works to others.

SG: Not that it was gay, but that it was sexual.

LM: And also, why write about gay relationships rather than heterosexual relationships?

MO: Reading Mari Kotani's *Techno-Gynesis,* the winner of the Japan SF Award in 1994, I was very surprised to know that *yaoi* culture exists outside Japan. But at the same time, it convinced me very much. As for me, I started writing *yaoi,* not as an imitation of others, but as a narrative (in those days, we called this kind of fiction simply homosexual novel) necessary for the description of sexual love in my imagination. I was not able to enjoy the conventional pornography, which had been made for men; I feel impatient with its patriarchal form. This is why I could not help but produce a new style of sexual love. And I was not the only one who thought this way. It is the female imperative that produced *yaoi* fiction in Japan and other countries simultaneously.

There is, however, a sharp distinction between *yaoi* and gay fiction, although it is possible to read *yaoi* as gay novels. We, women writers, write *yaoi* for ourselves, hoping it will be consumed by mostly women readers. To tell the truth, now I am not really interested in *yaoi*—or rather, I lost my interest in ordinary pornography itself. We cannot fantasize about sex as freely as before. For, as *yaoi* became a quite successful genre in terms of popularity and commercialism, it lost its avant-garde flavor. I had once expected that *yaoi* would have led us to the new form of sexual love, surpassing the boundary of sex.

LM: What is the fascination of women for writing this type of fiction?

MO: It's the same fascination that we feel toward SF. Reading SF, you transform yourself into robots, see the Earth as an alien, or establish relationships with aliens. We can be the opposite sex. *Yaoi* and SF have basically the same possibility in which we enjoy limitless freedom.

SG: Let's talk about "Mental Female." I have a question that seems to be a real problem, which is the ambivalence toward the women in "Mental Female." On a personal level, fiction aside, I suspect that you have a strong sense of women's power, all the positive things about women. But in your book the woman is the nightmare, the terror, something that wants to love you, but you flee from.

MO: Recently, I contributed an essay on maternal fascism entitled "The Queen of the Year 2777" to a journal *New Feminism Review*. In general, the myth still exists that motherhood is something great, excellent. The mother figure in myself, however, is really nightmarish, a kind of destroyer silently invading others with a weapon called love, rather than kindness and generosity. All women, including you and me, have destructive motherhood, which plunders and kills someone's heart with "generosity." So I envision the destroyer aspect of my internal mother figure vividly.

Do you remember the movie *Solaris* by Tarcovski? The sea in *Solaris* represents maternalism which is at once creative and destructive. We don't know whether the sea has consciousness or not. Or, in the first place, nobody knows what it is—the mysterious sea in *Solaris* was very horrible. Because in creating something, you have to destroy and bring out "change" which can be considered, in a way, as being evil. Thus creation is always the same as destruction. And we cannot deny that raising children has this kind of aspect.

LM: The vampire figure in your works seems to operate as a sign of femininity. Can you talk a little bit about this notion, this ambiguity of the vampire as a sign of femininity.

MO: The construction of Japanese femininity or womanhood can easily be compared to the vampire.

Takayuki Tatsumi: This is like the "OBATARIANs." Most Japanese middle-aged women are housewives and are, as you already know, "OBASANs." Some are even worse, even vulgar, and they are called "OBATARIANs," which is a derogatory term that shows contempt toward this type of woman. But they did devote much to the construction of the modern family or the ideology of "increase and multiply."

MO: Yes. Well, Japanese womanhood represented by OBASAN is really like a vampire because they are the ones in control of the family finances, they rear the children who may be considered, in this sense, as captives, they suck up everything from their own husbands, and, after he retires, they just throw them away. Usually these husbands are called "huge junk" by the OBASANs . . . except that they are bringing money from their companies. Of course, the husbands who entrust their own aims of life to their companies are also problematic.

LM: Just to return briefly to "Mental Female". . . this question has to do with your process of writing. What gives you the inspiration?

MO: When I started writing "Mental Female" in the mid-eighties, Japan was thought to be rich and wealthy, it was the heyday of the bubble economy. So in terms of the bubble economy, the story was a speculative experiment. My topic was quite simple—if we can retain this kind of society of abundance forever, what will happen to us? I suppose this was what sparked me. In retrospect, I animated the society of abundance; that is, if this kind of society were a person, this person must be very generous, treating everyone in an overly generous way.

SG: I guess he or she would step over the boundary. In "Mental Female," the "She" says "Don't just watch one TV, watch a hundred TVs." It is like a baby that sits there and is being fed too much. That is the part of the horror of the story.

MO: This society of abundance with transcendental high technology is like an enchanted island.

SG: In the story this overabundance seems to try to get people to be dependent and removed from their desires. Wolf Boy and Sheila don't want all these televisions. They want to be left alone to experience their own passion and sexuality. This seems to suggest that all of this abundance is keeping people from being human.

MO: I've written a short story titled "The Archeology of War" and in that story, again, I set up an overabundant society where people are wired to cyberspace and they are doing all kinds of creative activities with the power of high technology. However, techno-magic abundance makes people childish, and information accelerated by technological progress (like watching 100 TV screens at a time—too much information!) ruins us seriously. Then people get cocooned to protect their own sensitivity. How can we avoid developing a childish society? This is one of the problems the present advanced countries confront now, since childishness leads us to the completely opposite side of humanity.

In "The Archeology of War," hypercapitalistic cultural strategy renders creative activities more and more competitive and finally brings up a great war which involves the whole galaxy. And in this context, any form of creation must be closely intertwined with the logic of war; that is, the logic of destruction. Again, we have to speculate on the analogy between creation and destruction. What I described here, nonetheless, is that creation with destruction is a sort of illness. Indeed we need some kind of creation without excessive destruction. In other words, if we would avoid childishness and heal our trauma, it is indispensable to naturalize the act of creation and appreciate all the things in the world.

LM: Do you consider what you are doing as being something like staking out a position as a postfeminist?

MO: Many feminists have pointed that out to me, calling me a radical, postfeminist. Of course, they consider maternity as something good. But it seems to me that it is high time we transgress that existing cause of feminism, which looks for approaches to postfeminism. However, since I am a writer, not an activist, I will take different steps from those of hard-core feminists.

I turn my will to dominance to the field of fiction writing. I want to stress that what we need when we feel our desire to control something is the sense of "respect" or "appreciation." While I am writing the novels, I am nothing but a "worshiper of beauty" and I feel extremely happy sometimes. In this sense, the works are superior to me as a writer. The novels are never under my control only because I am an omnipotent author, but instead they let me notice a lot of things while I write. The old works always tell me something new every time I read them. Raising children is like writing works. I don't want to regard children as inferior to me, but to appreciate them as a superior existence. If you cannot respect or appreciate, then you should give up raising children. To tell the truth, I do want to have a child to inherit my genes.

LM: To what extent do you think your writing has been influenced by other media, like television or the movies?

MO: Of course, television was there since I was born. I have been greatly influenced by visual effects of television and film. But I do want my works to be different from movies. I use words and I have a reason for it. I like to experiment with language. For example, I love puns. I'm aware of the visual impact in my works but at the same time, I enjoy literary and linguistic experiments. There are certain things that can be done only through fiction. That is what I want to explore. I don't want my works to be an imitation of the visual media.

On the other hand, I am a radical neophilia. I have set up a homepage on the Internet. I have also written a script for a Nintendo television-game. I am also ambitious to incorporate hypertextual methods.

Mari Kotani: Finally, as a way of supporting the answer that was given to the question about your background, I should point out that your specialty in university was psychology. You graduated from Sacred Heart University, which is a Catholic school.

MO: Yes, but first, there was "me"—that is, the identity of myself came first, and only later did I become assimilated into psychology or Christianity. This logic is applicable to my obsession with monsters, K/S fiction, SF, personal computers, Internet and other things I have been fascinated with.

LM: Have you ever been tempted to write non-SF or nongenre work?

MO: What I have long been conscious of is the notion of the avant-garde. To me, SF is the greatest form of avant-garde. Recently, however, I have felt like writing standard, hardcore SF novels without gaudy gadgets. I want my novels to be read not only by SF fans but also by other kinds of readers. But of course, since I am a SF writer basically, I cannot live without the twister of imagination.

Transcribed by Reiko Tochigi and Hisayo Ogushi;
translated by Takayuki Tatsumi

The complete interview with Mariko Ohara can be accessed at www.centerforbookculture.org.

The Mental Female

Mariko Ohara

Techie and Kipple had coupled in every possible position, in every corner of the city, across 100 million TV sets. They'd shown it all, and nobody could turn them off. Techie, when vertical, stood ten inches tall in his virile metal armor of gears, springs, and tubes. Microchip beauty Kipple, at only 7.5 inches, wore a kimono of purple silk organdy which, for Techie, opened readily to reveal the whiteness of her ceramic skin.

Before anyone, that is, everyone, realized what was happening, Kipple's abdomen was swelling like a fresh rice cake. Her body had only looked like white porcelain; actually it was made of rubber. Some thought that her midriff was being inflated with air, like a balloon. Others thought that both Kipple and Techie were just manipulated images, existing only in the electronic reality of TV. But then, on screens mounted in every wall, every room, every shop and office in the city, Kipple gave violent birth.

It was a male, half an inch long. He'd looked like a maggot.

But although he had been born only last Thursday, already he had grown into a young man.

Among the city's one million inhabitants, there was one person who was shocked to see his face.

"I love you."
"And I love you."

"Do you really?"
"Yes, really."

"You do love me?"
"Yes, I really love you . . ."

The soap opera was interminable. No excitement or emotion; only this vacuous drivel. Aimless chatter would have been better. But this . . . not only did it lack drama, it couldn't even be called conversation.

As Kipple and Techie droned on, their hands roved over each other's bodies.

"I want to wear flowers . . ."
"Your body, dressed in flowers . . ."

"Let's boat over to the island for a swim."
"Floating on the waves with my lover . . ."

"I have a present for you."
"You will dress in octopus . . ."

The dialogue ploughed on. Across the bottoms of omnipresent TV screens, the DATA display showed their pulses speeding up, so it was obvious that they were in love.

"The ocean is like a bubble bath, don't you think?"
"Open your kimono and let me in."

"I'm not ready yet."
"Then get your motor running for me."

". . . it sounds like a geisha game!"
"We'll play catch, and whoever drops the ball has to strip."

Some fifteen minutes later the first missile had been launched. The city's defense system woke immediately, but it couldn't cover the entire sky.

Already a half-century had passed, but still the scars of The War affected Her, like the shadow bodies burned into glassified walls. Sometimes still, dying cells from those scars lashed Her brain into uncontrollable frenzies of destruction.

After three days of toss-and-catch—missiles lofting back and forth like a geisha's gold and red sex-toy balls—the program on 100 million screens unfolded.

"Oh! I dropped it. Well, I guess that means my kimono . . ."

Kipple was Her self-image. She loosened her sash. Her kimono was transparent—her body had been visible throughout—but fully naked she was even sexier than imagined. For two weeks they sexed each other, their tumbling, endless intercourse exciting every citizen of the city—human, android, cat, dog, bird, reptile, mole, whale, friend and foe, self-styled gods and prophets of gods—anyone with eyes had them riveted to the screens.

This Love Simulation program really worked. Designed for invasions, it demanded answers, drove relationships, and made it clear who She was talking to: Techie, the artificial intelligence. Long ago he was the enemy's weapon, based in a northern Siberian fortress city before he got into Her hot, hot data channels.

How could they possibly have fallen in love? And married? And even had a baby?

The program was a real soap opera. Everyone watched, not only in Tokyo, but in northern Siberia as well.

Room 8875: the top floor of an eighty-eight-story apartment tower, where Wolf Boy lay in his crib.

A chill shivered along his spine as the baby grew, a premonition that soon proved accurate. The child, growing on 100 million TV screens, grew to look like him. Out of a million citizens, She had chosen his remodeled B-style wolf face, his black fur, his eyes the silver of mercury.

Wolf Boy lay curled on his soft sheepskin sofa, alone in the dim light of the TV. Beyond his wall-sized window, an enormous moon hung in the sky like a stage prop.

Wolf Boy had been born lucky. He'd won this coveted top-floor apartment in the lottery. He'd been created innately beautiful and talented in Her artificial womb, as a lover for the finest of humans. When he drove, traffic lights always turned green, and he'd only had one accident. At the touch of a sensor, vending machines released their contents to him, with no charge to his ID balance. And large sums of credit which he knew little about were deposited into his account.

A commercial for a "friendship club" with a branch down the street drifted across the screen:

Are you in love?

People. Machines. Robots.

The toothy smile of an ordinary-looking old man filled the screen.

The club was in fact a cult which had been growing in power over the past ten years, preaching a belief in love and peace flowing from motherhood. They were known for their aggressive advertising.

The commercial bled back into the program. The doll couple went at it again.

Their furry child refused adamantly to go to school. He attacked his father. He bit off his mother's nipple.

"We love you so much."

"I don't love you at all."

"Don't you feel our love?"
"Can't feel what I don't see."

Wolf Boy's eyes involuntarily focused on the screen. His ears stood up in stiff triangles. Two tiny white images played across his silver pupils.

"I love you."
"I'm not getting that."

"I love you."
"I don't feel a thing."

Wolf Boy's tail twitched in annoyance as he tried to ignore the deadly dialogue. Even if he left his room, he couldn't get away from it. It would be on TVs in every hallway, wall, and ceiling, along every sidewalk, and in every shop.
Love.
What was the point?
No machine could ever understand it! Machines could only simulate, representing love through images of caring and gentleness. But these weren't real feelings.
Wolf Boy felt ill. He got up and went to the bathroom. When he was finished, he returned to the sofa and spoke a number to the TV.
The face at the other end of the line did not appear. It was masked by the program, which always had priority.

"Hello?"
Such a nice voice, Wolf Boy thought. He relaxed a bit. "Is it okay without the picture?" he said. *Was she tilting her head slightly, as she usually did?*
"When something's missing," she said, "sometimes you notice other things more clearly."
Wolf Boy's mind calmed like a dry sponge slowly absorbing a mild liquid.
"So what are you noticing?"
"Honesty. Courage . . ."
"Don't bullshit."
". . . Manliness . . . the power to dream."
"I said skip it!"
"Strength . . ."
"Will you come off it?"
"And what's more . . ."

"Enough!"

"Love."

Wolf Boy blushed bright red under his fur and was glad the soap opera was overriding his video link. Of course, his girlfriend still might notice his reaction from his voice. Perhaps she'd even meant to make him feel like this. Yes, he was sure of it.

"Gentleness," she giggled.

Beneath his black fur Wolf Boy's heart wiggled in his chest. Whenever he talked with her, he caught fire.

"I want to see you," she said.

"Well . . . wait a minute."

"What's the matter?"

"Are you watching TV?"

"Fortunately I'm nearsighted, so . . ."

"Put on your glasses."

"Now why are you being so . . ." but she stopped herself from arguing, and said contritely, "OK, they're on."

"So take a look."

"I don't . . . oh, my!"

"Looks like me, doesn't he?"

"He doesn't look like you. He *is* you."

"So you see it too." For some reason, a note of condescension had crept into his voice. "Well, well, well. You see it too."

"Well I appreciate your approval, Mr. Chosen Citizen. So glad you find me up to snuff."

That pride is what drew Wolf Boy to her. She was brutally frank about his charmed life and not awed in the least. It didn't impress her that the city seemed to cater to him, that he never suffered sickness or mishap. In fact, his one and only accident had been the fender-bender when he ran into her car. But Wolf Boy was certain She had planned that so they would meet.

"How dare She," she said. "I'll never forgive Her for this." That finality in her voice—*I'll never forgive Her for this*—that really turned Wolf Boy on. It was a magic spell that could recast his fate.

"Doesn't it piss you off?" she said.

"Uh, a little."

" 'A little?' " Her voice was knife-thin with anger. "As long as you're in Her womb, you're safe, right? You don't even have to work for a living, and you're just wasting that glorious voice of yours."

Wolf Boy thrived on this attitude of hers. He no longer called her out of boredom with the program, but rather because she gave it to him straight.

"I have to see you," he said.

"Well, if She allows it, I guess you can come over."

His girlfriend was speaking ironically, but in fact they were not able to meet as planned, because before Wolf Boy could leave, the Bird showed up at Room 8875.

She was lending her Experience Body to that "friendship club" down the street as a focus of ceremonial worship. At morning prayers, the Experience Body laid eggs. During the afternoon prayers it ate freshly slaughtered hens. And for the evening prayers it gave milk to the Chosen as a symbol of the Eternal Mother's Love.

Alfred G. Usano, the cult's leader, had a visceral hatred for the Experience Body. It was Her sense receptor, an independent intelligence which he had to submit to and accept. What was worse, the Experience Body looked like a big yellow chicken, and he hated birds because their feet reminded him of snakes. And the Bird's feet were as big as Indian pythons.

"Sir, a call for you." A beautiful attendant in a bikini brought him a telephone on a silver tray.

Usano was watching TV by his pool during the break between morning and afternoon prayers. He didn't have to ask who it was. Who else could it be on this line?

How are you?

"Fine, thank you." Usano's gaze never left the TV, though the story had made no progress since the child's suicide last week. Suppressing a sigh, he asked politely, "And how are you, Mother?"

The brilliant surface of the pool riffled in the gentle, clean breeze. Usano's penthouse was on the highest building in the city, and the swimming pool was in the shape of a pearl. He'd had soil and plants brought up, and he found peace of mind only when tending his garden.

Lousy, She answered.

Usano broke out in a cold sweat. Why did he still have to deal with these things? He was nearly seventy, after all. It made him dizzy.

"What's the matter?"

He's gone! She shouted hysterically.

Usano felt a pain in his side and rolled into a new position, out of habit keeping his eyes on the TV throughout the maneuver. He had a dark presentiment.

"Your child, you mean," he said.

How on earth did you know!?

He'd been afraid when they'd started playing catch with nuclear missiles too, but back then he'd thought he didn't care about anything and was ready to give it all up.

But this was no longer the case. What was going to happen?

The dizziness and now a headache welled up, making him long

for the bliss of amnesia. Long ago he'd been a computer programmer; he was never meant for religion, and he found it exhausting to provide psychotherapy to lunatics.

My skin got darker after my baby was born.

"It did not," he protested. But once She believed something, it always became the truth, and he had never changed Her mind.

On the TV, Kipple wept. She was clinging to a giant old refrigerator as if it gave solace.

"I . . . want . . . to be . . . as white as . . . this . . . refrigerator." Against the pure white surface of the appliance, her skin was a creamy yellow.

Usano's stomach ached. His doctors had diagnosed nervous gastritis, in addition to autonomic ataxia—his body temperature and sweat glands were out of sync—and he also suffered from lumbago, perhaps brought on by nerves as well. Whenever something happened, terrible pain afflicted him. Why on earth had She placed him at the top of the organization?

In any case the job had killed his predecessor, who wrote in his diary his belief that She, like a vain celebrity, craved the adoration of Her fans.

Kipple shrieked at the refrigerator, "I'm darker than you but my figure's just as good!" She clutched at the metal door, sobbing like a child. For a moment Usano had no idea what to say. He sensed his gastritis and simultaneously his lumbago getting ready to flare up.

"What are you talking about?" he ventured. "You're as beautiful as ever."

And then it was time for afternoon prayers, Usano felt. Relief washed through him as he broke the connection.

High atop the altar, flames danced up around the throat and gaping beak of Bird. The temple was packed to capacity. Ten thousand devotees watched as Usano, in a swirl of smoke and light, descended in an open gondola.

From the perspective of the worshippers, Bird's beak looked like a chicken's.

From the gondola, it looked like a giant tulip in full bloom.

The faces in the crowd blurred together, glinting in the passing spotlights like waves catching the sun. Usano's stomach churned; if not for the obscuring smoke and light, he'd have fainted already from his fear of heights, which all these years had done nothing to dampen.

Usano flapped his arms like wings as he descended, beating the air with the long sleeves of his golden, printed circuit-patterned kimono. Five hens milled about his feet on the floor of the gondola, clucking in consternation as they pecked aimlessly at his shoes. Directly below the top of the altar, the gondola stopped. Artificial flames leapt up around Bird's beak in all the colors of the rainbow.

Usano still couldn't believe that he was Her spokesman; the rapt faces of the worshippers depressed him. The roar of their voices, like the crashing of waves, subsided into silence as they regarded him, the High Priest of their goddess.

His heavy voice reverberated through the temple space.

For our Mother, let us pray.
For our beautiful Mother,
For our peaceful Mother,
Let us pray.

The echoes died away. Three times a day Usano had to do this. There was no choice, as he well knew from his predecessor's sudden death. He seized one of the hens by the neck and beheaded it with a deft stroke of a glass knife. He swung the headless bird around by its feet, showering the first rows of worshippers with blood, then flung the head and body into the flames at the top of the altar. Bird gulped them down, and Usano began the litany.

Let us offer
Let us offer
The Lord's blood
And our blood.

As he chanted, Usano lopped off the heads of the other chickens one-by-one and cast them into the beak, pausing only to wipe his bloody hands with white feathers.

Evil bird, he thought. He hated it so much he wanted to vomit. If he stopped cursing it for a moment, he knew he would lose his mind. As usual he wanted only to wash his bloody hands.

Now the scene around him began to grow distant. The new drug EDF had started flowing into the temple through the ventilation system.

On the enormous ceiling screen a beating human heart appeared, the symbol of the cult. Its throbbing filled the chamber as the litany reached its conclusion.

Our hunger has been satisfied
Our longing has been fulfilled.
Now let as slumber.
Let us slumber.

Worshippers began tumbling like dominos, and Usano himself felt his eyes closing.

But without warning, Bird unleashed a jarring scream. Usano looked up in confusion, his heart racing. Bird had pulled its long neck back from the rainbow flames and was lurching down from the top of the altar on two clawed feet. Its awesome head looked around impassively. Its eyes were too far apart, utterly devoid of intelligence, and yet it was Her machine, with access to all the information in the City. Under Her direct control, it was capable of anything.

It broke into a run. At twice human size, it tossed people out of its way like dolls. Usano watched in terror from the gondola, with no clue what had happened or what was to come. No one ever knew what She was thinking.

Bird ran at a steady, relaxed pace straight to Mezon Setagaya, where it bashed through the doors and bounded up eighty-eight flights of stairs at the speed of an express elevator. At Room 8875 it hammered its beak on the door.

There was no answer. A minute passed.

The building's locks were not connected to Her nervous system—it predated The War—so Bird popped two blasters on telescoping arms out of the small door in its breast. Twin beams vaporized lock and hinges, and as the heavy metal door crashed in, blazed into the apartment, setting the curtains on fire.

Wolf Boy, who had been standing in front of the window, hollered as his fur ignited. He ran into the bathroom and frantically doused the flames with water from the toilet.

What the hell was that, he thought, frightened out of his mind. The thing in the door had looked like a fat scarecrow. Wolf Boy caught a glimpse of himself in the mirror. His beautiful black pelt had been badly singed—he could see the skin of his bony chest—and his gorgeous tail was stripped bare as a rat's. He touched an exposed rib with a wet hand. After a deep breath, he charged back out of bathroom.

The thing was struggling to squeeze through his ruined door frame, its huge feet slapping on the flattened door. Its legs were like tree trunks. And its head, mounted on a neck like an elephant's, bore the most ridiculous face Wolf Boy had ever seen—a cross between an ostrich and a duck.

Bird opened its tulip beak and said, "Do you know . . ."

"What? What did you say?" Wolf Boy shouted in panic.

"Do you know that somebody loves you?" Bird's voice was like a snake in dry grass. It wriggled its short, useless wings, gave one last mighty push, and rasped through the door frame in a cloud of feathers.

"Do you know . . ." it squawked.

"What the hell is this!" Wolf Boy cried as he backed away, denuded tail arched straight up in alarm. His burnt skin was beginning to sting.

Bird could not straighten up without hitting its head against the ceiling. It lumbered forward into the smoke-filled room with its neck stuck out in front of it.

"Do you know that somebody loves you?" it said, coming right at him, oblivious to the furniture it was smashing.

Wolf Boy dove for the sliding glass doors to his terrace, where the emergency air car was parked. In the space of a few heartbeats he'd buckled his harness and his fingers were flying over the instrument panel.

As the vehicle powered up, Bird threw itself against the glass doors, bursting the glass outward with a great *crack*. Wolf Boy watched with his heart in his throat as the metal window frames buckled. It had been three years since he'd last used the car. But as Bird squeezed through though, the car warmed up and floated clear of the terrace. Ten yards out, Wolf Boy looked back to stick his prodigious tongue out at Bird. He doubted the thing would understand, but She would see the gesture, no doubt, through its camera eyes.

However, before Wolf Boy's eyes, sleek exhaust cones emerged behind each of Bird's drumstick hips, and a larger funnel-shaped intake from its chest. A jet engine. With an ear-splitting whine, Bird rose into the air, throwing a huge black shadow down on the terrace, then across the face of the Mezon Setagaya apartment tower.

Wolf Boy's eyes filled with tears as a fresh wave of fear swept over him. Bird was zooming in, filling his field of vision, its eighteen claws fully extended from their sheaths. Wolf Boy slammed his foot down on the throttle. The car hesitated a moment longer, then shot away at full power, pushing him deep back into his seat cushions.

Bird opened up its throttle too. Beak cracked wide, its voice blared out over the City, echoing off the high towers.

DO YOU KNOW DO YOU KNOW DO YOU KNOW . . .
SOMEBODY SOMEBODY SOMEBODY
LOVES YOU LOVES YOU LOVES YOU . . .

"No! I don't know!" Wolf Boy shrieked in rage, and his anger cleared away the fear for a moment to let him think. He took out his ID card and slotted it in the instrument panel.

"Yes? How may I help you?" said a feminine voice. It was Her voice.

"I want to make a call . . ."

"Please hold for status check," the voice interrupted. "Completed. *I love you!*"

Wolf Boy yanked his card from the slot, and found himself gasping for breath. Now he knew who "loved" him.

Car and Bird swooped and dove through the afternoon light of the City, dodging through airborne traffic and office complexes and apartment towers.

Bird never fell more than fifty yards behind, but as Wolf Boy's fuel reserves approached zero, he had to land. He brought the car down in the middle of Motokin Seicho, jumped clear, and ran.

Wolf Boy was confident of escape if he could only find somewhere tight and narrow to hide. He tried not to think what might happen if he were caught. No one ever came right out and said She was crazy, but everyone thought so.

Motokin Seicho was a rough-and-tumble zone of outworlders, androids, robots, gene-spliced animals, psychics, and other riff-raff, with grimy streets jammed with shops and hawkers selling everything imaginable from the highest-tech to the lowest. Wolf Boy dodged through the streets as he ran, the flapping of wings and dying whine of Bird's engine trailing behind.

Bird trotted after him on its big flapping feet, mindlessly trampling anyone or anything in its path.

This was an area of the City that Wolf Boy knew well. Few dealt with ID around here, which might give him a chance, as long as he avoided the elevators—they were linked to Her data net. He took a sharp corner into a stairwell that led to the district's underground, a labyrinth of malls and arcades interspersed with abandoned tunnels and commercial spaces.

The stairs led down to an empty stretch of mallway where widely spaced ceiling lights left big patches of shadow. Wolf Boy dodged puddles and rivulets from the City's leaky plumbing as he ran, claws clicking on the tile. He was nimble and quick, confident of his strength on his feet.

An explosion rocked through the tunnel, loosing a fall of rubble back at the base of the stairwell. Bird, too big to squeeze through, had blasted it open. Now Bird was charging after Wolf Boy down the mallway, its neck stretched forward just under the ceiling, eyes scanning for him in the X ray and infrared.

Wolf Boy pushed out a burst of speed, heart pounding and lungs starting to labor. By instinct he headed for a more populated, better-lit area. He raced down a crowded main street dense with people and storefronts and cornered hard into an antique shop, knocking over a mannequin in an old spacesuit as he plunged through. A door at the back of the shop let out on a narrow tunnel opposite another door. He took it, crossing through a drugstore and onto the broad thoroughfare on the next block. Directly across was a pawnshop, just as he remembered.

In the pawnshop, the old man behind the counter didn't seem to have moved since his childhood either.

"Hello! How are you?" shouted Wolf Boy as he ran past to a long display case of weapons. "Sorry!" he said, and brought his fists down full-force on the glass cover of the case. From among the shards he snatched a designer Kutani ceramic pistol, then fled, crying "Sorry!" again over his shoulder to the wide-eyed old man.

Meanwhile, Bird had tripped over the good-luck raccoon at the entrance of the antique shop, crashed through head first, and gotten tangled in the wreckage it created. It tried to climb to its feet, but wiring from the collapsed front wall of the store had hooked around its neck, pinning it in the rubble. Bird thrashed and flapped, then lay still for a moment, its body glowing.

Then, with a monstrous push, it rose from the wreckage in a shower of plaster, glass, and smashed antiques. Its beak worked.

"Do not interfere!" it squawked in a voice so loud it rattled what remained of the merchandise off the shelves. A customer cowering in the corner screamed. Bird launched itself through the back wall of the store.

With no idea where to turn, Wolf Boy's only thought was his girlfriend. He had no idea where she was, since she changed her workplace at the whim of her free spirit. Then Wolf Boy remembered Grandma Bei. She could be pretty disturbing, but her place wasn't far off and she might be able to help him track his girlfriend down.

The underground hadn't changed much since his childhood, and it was the part of the City he knew best. He ran into the alley beside the pawn shop and found the manhole cover he wanted. As the sound of Bird smashing its way into the shop reached him, Wolf Boy pried the lid off the cover and climbed down a rusty ladder.

He descended to a nasty subtunnel and found himself knee-deep in foul water, but at least there'd be none of Her security cameras down here.

The water was warm and inhabited—giant cockroaches, blind carp. Wolf Boy waded past floating objects he didn't even want to think about. As he neared the exit he was looking for, something darted out of the water and latched onto his tail.

"Hey," it croaked.

Wolf Boy yanked his tail free and backed away as a crocodile man rose hunched from the water. Old Croc was an escaped genetic experiment who'd been hiding out down here for years.

"What do you want," said Wolf Boy warily.

"Ya stepped on me," Old Croc wheezed in a low voice, his eyes glinting in the dim light of the sewer.

"Sorry. I didn't see you in this filthy . . . in the water. Gotta run!" Wolf Boy turned to go.

"Hold on. Ya gotta pay the toll."

"Toll? You mean . . . cash." In fact, Wolf Boy had only a dim idea of what cash might be. "I don't have any."

Old Croc's lips rose in a sneer, baring long rows of gleaming teeth. "Then ya don't pass."

"Up yours!" Wolf Boy saw he didn't stand a chance against Old Crock in the water, but his exit was just ahead. Bravado would have to do. "Go shake down somebody else."

Old Croc edged toward him. Wolf Boy pulled out his pistol and fired several rounds into the water around Croc's stumpy legs. The shots rang painfully in the confined space, but the low-caliber bullets wouldn't do much damage to the reptilian's leathery skin if it actually came to shooting him.

"Ya little bas-turd!" Old Croc croaked, backing away. "I'll bite yer fuckin heart out! I'll feed yer balls to the rats, with yer prick fer an appetizer!"

Measuring the gun, Old Croc edged toward him again. Wolf Boy drove him back with another shot, then turned and ran as fast as the water allowed. His splashing roused giant cockroaches from the tunnel wall to flight. They swarmed up like bats, chirring and fluttering around his head. Wolf Boy barely beat Old Croc to the ladder he wanted, leaping for it just as Old Croc dove for his feet.

Spluttering wheezes of rage echoed down the tunnel beneath him.

"Next time, ya little mutie . . ."

"Watch your mouth, handbag," Wolf Boy laughed, brandishing his pistol at the eyes glowering up from the murk. "Or you'll wind up accessorized." The eyes disappeared in an angry thrashing of water.

Wolf Boy climbed up and up, back to the level of the underground. At the top of the shaft he clunked his head against the heavy lid of a manhole cover. He cracked it open, letting in enough light to inspect the top rung of the ladder. There it was: the mark he'd scratched with a nail when he was a child. He pushed the lid all the way up and off, then climbed out into an alley deep in the heart of the entertainment district, a seedy, gaudily lit warren of streets thronging with pleasure seekers and those who serviced them.

Water dripped from what remained of Wolf Boy's matted fur as he stepped into the street. A chill ran through his body, and he gave his coat a good shake, showering passersby with stinking sewer water. People stopped to stare in anger or revulsion, but he proudly strode off.

Grandma Bei's apartment was just off the main mallway, back down below street level, under the underground. In this neighborhood the rents were exorbitant, but with her lucrative fortune-telling business, Grandma Bei could afford it. Wolf Boy rang her doorbell, which was shaped like boar's snout, and stepped back as the camera scanned him.

"Hello? Open up," Wolf Boy shouted.

The door swung in onto an empty hallway.

"I've been expecting you," an old woman's voice called from within.

Grandma Bei's place made Wolf Boy feel like a giant. All of the furniture was half-size. In the parlor Grandma Bei sat at a miniature table sipping tea from what looked like a toy cup. Seated, she came no higher than his thigh. She was at least a hundred years old, and her face reminded him of a mouse. As Grandma Bei lifted her cup to her tiny, thin lips with hands as rough as a laborer's, she fixed a vacant stare on Wolf Boy. She had been blind for thirty years.

"The Wolf Boy from the fated star," the old woman sighed, "come back to see old Bei." She set her cup down carefully and gestured across the table to the room's one full-size chair. "For my big people visitors. Won't you sit down?"

Wolf Boy seated himself obediently. On the table before him was a leather spirit board.

"Well then? Out with it! What's on your mind?"

"I'm looking for . . . Sheila."

"Cash in advance?"

Wolf Boy just stared at her. Her sightless eyes held his gaze expectantly; then she broke into laughter.

"You have no money!" She said. "And you've lost your lover." She laughed again.

"It's urgent." Wolf Boy tried to stay calm.

"Isn't it always," she sighed. "You must pay though. Triple rate for service on credit."

"I'll pay. I'll pay!" he growled.

"Well you do seem eager," Grandma Bei said, taking another dainty sip of tea. She was looking at his pistol. She couldn't see it, but her room saw everything, and whispered its reports in her ear.

"Who's after you, I wonder?"

"Please just get on with it!"

"Young man . . ." she said sternly. Then softening, "All right, all right. But say, how about a song for your fortune?"

"A song?" Wolf Boy blinked at her. "Did you say . . . a song?"

"Come on! Are you as deaf as I'm blind?" Grandma Bei sat up straight. "A song! You're a pro, aren't you? How about the national anthem? Sing me a song or you won't get your fortune."

Wolf Boy threw his head back and howled from deep in his throat. AaaaaOOOOOhh! The walls and ceiling vibrated with his cry, and the old woman seemed shaken in her tiny chair. But this was just his warm-up. Wolf Boy took a deep breath, and sang "Itsuki's Lullaby" in a lovely high tenor. The old woman clapped time with her rough hands, carried back to the simple joy of her remote childhood. When Wolf Boy was finished, she was quiet for a moment, her head bowed forward in contemplation.

"I'm just a silly old woman," she sighed. "Your girlfriend is in the Dragon Café, on Seventh Avenue."

"Don't you have to use the spirit board?" Wolf Boy asked doubtfully.

"Hah! That thing's just a toy." Then Grandma Bei stiffened suddenly. She gasped. "What is this bird? I see a huge bird destroying my home . . ."

Wolf Boy leapt to his feet. "Your phone! Where is it?"

"Good gracious! What a rude boy. Do you think you can just . . ."

"Where is it!" he growled ominously, his grip tightening on the pistol.

"Oh for goodness' sake. It's over there." As Wolf Boy placed his call, Grandma Bei shuffled nervously through a Tarot deck. "Imagine treating an old woman like that . . ." she muttered.

Wolf Boy snarled at her for silence, but as Sheila came on the line, the Bird's voice thundered from the hallway of Grandma Bei's apartment.

YOU MUST BE OBEDIENT

Story Maker had decreed 100 million TVs for one million people, and in this City She was the Law, and so there were screens the size of billboards and screens like wallet snapshots. Screens on the sides of the blimps that never left the City's sky and screens embedded in the corners of bathroom mirrors. Every citizen's eyes would be screens, if it were in Her power.

The Dragon Café had thirty TVs in its dressing room and many more out in the lounge. The law required over a hundred for a place this size, but the customers got tired of the endless program, so screens from the lounge were sometimes moved back here where they wouldn't have to see them.

Sheila watched TV in the mirror of the room's long rococo dressing table.

"You're leaving me?"
"How do you expect me to put up with a whore like you?"

"This is so sad."
"Had to happen sometime. It's entropy. Nothing lasts, not even love."

The program was improving a bit. Most of the eight mental females in the dressing room were crying, though Sheila wasn't shedding any tears. She continued grooming her lovely cat fur with her platinum comb, the teeth of which were just the right size for fleas. With careful strokes she fluffed it up, bringing out its deep red tones.

"The poor thing," cried Sheila's friend Platina, who was sitting beside her at the dressing table.

"Who do you mean, 'Tina?" said Sheila. Platina flinched every time Sheila stroked her tail with the comb in her direction. Platina had a thing about cleanliness. She couldn't handle the least spot or blemish, especially on her own body, which she rubbed from head to toe regularly with depilatory creams to remove every strand of hair. Platina wore a fine platinum mesh body suit, from spare strands of which she'd made Sheila's comb as a gift.

"Men are all alike," Platina said.

"It's just the Love Simulation program—a game between computers."

"Relationships are games too," Platina sighed. "And the Simulations are so much cleaner than us."

Sheila frowned into the mirror, knowing what came next.

"If only I could be like Kipple," Platina said on cue.

Across the room, a "man" sat sniffling back his tears as he styled his hair. He was new to the club but obviously a mental female. He called himself Brando.

"Excuse me, dear," he said to Sheila. "Could you hand me a tissue?"
"Sure."

"This story is just awful." He dabbed at his eyes, then blew his nose. His thick hair was scented with citrus. "Perfectly heartwrenching, as bad as that other serious one."

Sheila guessed that Brando meant the love affair with the Memphis

Computer. In that episode Kipple had been loved far more than she had loved in return. When Kipple finally dumped him, he killed himself, and that region of Northern America was supposedly still uninhabited, since nothing could survive without the support of a City Computer. Or the region may have come under Southern American control, but Kipple would have nothing to do with *those* cities anymore, so there was no information at all about the North U.S.

"I can't stand sad stories," Brando said.

"Me neither," said Platina. "I just want romances."

Recently, Sheila had been wondering if she was really cut out for this job. She lacked the required level of empathy. In fact, she didn't really seem to feel much at all. How could she continue as a mental female? Without emotion, she'd be little more than a whore, with or without her first-class Love Engineer license. And yet the money was so incredible . . .

With a glance at the melted Dali-clock which drooped over the edge of the mirror, Sheila put the finishing touches on her hairdo, licking her lush coat from stem to stern with her coarse tongue.

"I envy you that tongue," Platina sighed.

"Me too," said Brando, "You must make people so happy."

Sheila thought of Wolf Boy with a sudden surge of passion, which led her once again to doubt herself. It was so unprofessional to have lovers outside of her clients.

"Then why don't you get one?" she said. "Modification C-2 in the Catalog. Tongue."

Platina and Brando each nodded thoughtfully.

It was time. The eight mental females in the dressing room stood as if on cue and strolled gracefully into the lounge.

The Dragon Café was a franchise, but it was first rate in every respect, offering the top of the line in love services. Customers and mental females alike required personal introductions to get in; one knew what to expect.

But tonight, She, Story Maker was there.

No one could mistake Her. The three yards surrounding Story Maker were filled with a different light, tranquil tones and images in distinct contrast to the purplish low-lit atmosphere of the lounge. Sheila had never seen Her before, but what she had heard was true: a different world radiated from Her, the world which She created, the story She told Herself that She could shape reality, involve others in it, and fill them with joy. Or perhaps Her creation was this world. Verdant pastures hovered around Her under clear skies. Pure white sheep grazed upon fields swept by gentle breezes, which Sheila felt on her cheek—they were real, or more than real. Story

Maker's age was indeterminate—She was neither woman nor child. She had short black hair and a round face. The sunlight around Her was like a golden . . .

A man with a bushy beard took a seat at Her table.

With her sleek red fur, Sheila was popular and got signaled from every table. She chose the one closest to Her.

Platina, at the corner table, was already madly in love with a happy, randy little poodle whom some millionaire on vacation had perhaps kenneled here. For exactly three hours, professional Love Engineers fell in love with anyone or anything—human, cyborg, robot, animal, dolls. All were equal where love was concerned.

Sheila studied the man at the table she'd chosen. He was old, with a sagging, wrinkled face and yellowish gray hair. He gathered his thoughts for a moment before speaking.

"Young lady, what do you suppose will become of those two?" The man pointed his chin at the nearest TV.

Sheila couldn't actually read his mind, but a mental female could interpret thoughts and feelings precisely from body language, expressions, tone of voice, and choice of words. The old man's question went past the immediate story. He felt like talking politics.

"Divorce is my guess," she answered. "With a protracted settlement."

"Hmm . . ." the old man nodded thoughtfully. He was pleased with her answer. "You think the Ruskies'll accept the terms?"

"Sure. Tokyo hasn't done anything wrong. And in cases like this, women always have the advantage."

The old man chuckled with pleasure in the EDF-permeated air, squinting at her under his smile-lined brow.

Sheila glanced around at lovely hairless Platina in the corner, whispering something in her poodle's ear, totally in love. At the next table, Story Maker sat amid the fragrances of fresh grass and the bearded man's cologne. Sheila caught fragments of Her tense conversation and glimpses of jumbled, disconnected images, including something shiny that arced back and forth, drawing Sheila in hypnotically. She found herself staring into Story Maker's black eyes, which returned her gaze with all-knowing warmth.

"Telephone for you." The voice of the waiter startled her so sharply her claws extended. Fur raised along her spine, she focused on the humanoid robot that had appeared beside her. The waiter reached into its stomach as if pulling out its own guts and offered her a blood-red phone.

"Yes?"

"It's me," said Wolf Boy.

"I'm at work!" she whispered harshly.

"I'm in trouble. Please, I need help!"

"What's wrong?"

"I'm being chased by this . . . *bird* . . . and its trying to fry me with . . ."

The bearded man opposite Her suddenly screamed, filling the lounge with fear.

Bird, flapping and kicking, came flying out of Her world in a trail of feathers and terrorized, crying sheep. The gigantic thing crashed into the lounge in an explosion of furniture and customers, hard on the heels of a black-pelted, wonderfully fleet-footed creature: Wolf Boy.

To keep the story interesting, Story Maker sent Bird, Wolf Boy, and now cat-girl Sheila, in quick pursuit, right through the stage set of the Dragon Café, scattering bit players and props in the simulated drama that shaped the world.

All burst forth into the large public square in front of the café, where a traditional O-Bon circle dance was in progress. Hundreds of people in gaily colored light-cotton kimonos bobbed, pirouetted, and waved their fans, advancing in unison around a raised festival platform where drummers pounded their lacquered, barrel-sized drums, flautists played their flutes, and shamisen players plucked sinuous melodies. In a reedy falsetto a woman at the center of the platform sang an old folk song for the rice planting, in honor of the ancestors whom the O-Bon dance celebrated.

Wolf Boy, Bird, and Sheila plunged into the square, breaking right through the circle of dancers, who scattered with yelps and shouts and fans beating the air. But far from being frightened, the dancers were thoroughly enjoying the commotion. There was laughter, applause, and cheers of encouragement for the protagonists. Tokyo had a long cinematic history of invasion by monsters and an even longer history of real destruction. These three were tame next to Mothra, Rodan, or Godzilla. Everyone assumed Her to be in one of Her frenzies, and many turned to the TV screens surrounding the square.

Bird's voice rang out like a train whistle.

DO YOU KNOW THAT SOMEBODY LOVES YOU

"Stay out of my life!" Wolf Boy howled.

"She thinks you're Her son!" Sheila shouted to him.

"Help!" he cried.

Bird was firing laser blasts at him, which Wolf Boy zigzagged around as he ran.

"Why don't you just let Her love you?"

"How can I? *She'll* kill me with *Her* love!"

"No! She's just lonely! Don't you remember? She lost a child on the program last week . . ."

That might be so, but Wolf Boy could never feel close to a mother like this ugly Bird.

On the far side of the square, the three dove into a giant two-story TV screen from which Kipple and Techie had been watching them. A lace of printed circuit patterns parted before them like spider webs, and they tumbled out onto the lovers' tropical resort set.

"My darling!" Kipple cried joyously to Wolf Boy, then heartrendingly, "No! Wait!" But the three charged on down the beach.

"Too late," Techie said with a smirk. "He's got a new girl."

Sheila was falling behind, chest heaving. Her cat modifications didn't give her the speed or endurance of her half-wolf lover. But Sheila's cat-sharp eyes noticed the Kutani pistol in Wolf Boy's hand.

"Shoot it!" she cried between great wracking gasps.

"It's a machine! It won't die!"

"No! the black spot on its beak . . . the spot . . . the air holes . . . the spot above them . . ." She pulled up short, totally winded and on the point of collapse.

Wolf Boy gave a powerful soaring leap, twisted around midair, and landed facing Bird. He took careful aim, then shots popped like firecrackers as he emptied the pistol into Bird's face. The thing shrieked, tumbling forward with wings flapping, neck twirling, and big feet kicking at the air. It came to rest in a sitting position.

The giant tulip beak blossomed and Bird spewed up the half-digested, headless bloody hens it had eaten during the afternoon prayers. As the vomiting died down, Sheila closed in and leapt, tearing into the lightweight metals and plastics of Bird's body with razor-sharp claws and modified teeth. She seized on the neck and shook violently, snapping Bird's head back and forth like a whip.

"Stop it," Bird said calmly. "Stop it."

Sheila shook Bird's neck with murderous violence, an inarticulate feline snarl pouring from her throat. With a great, sucking snap, Bird's head ripped free of its body and toppled to the ground.

"You must be obedient," the head said.

Wolf Boy groaned, his arm raised to his forehead.

"Thank you, thank you my wonderful darling," cried Kipple from far in the distance, her voice fading away.

"Are you all right?" Sheila asked. She paused to set a white cosmo into a hollow, upturned, elephant-sized claw she'd severed from Bird's leg.

Then she came over to sit at Wolf Boy's bedside.

"I'm *not* all right."

"Oh, you're just spoiled." She stroked his beautiful pelt with her platinum comb. The morning sunlight poured in through the large windows of his apartment, lighting up the dust motes like golden magic.

Wolf Boy was inexpressibly happy. His tail wagged languorously back and forth over the bed.

Cat-girl Sheila could never ignore something moving back and forth like that. She tossed the comb aside and took hold of it with a grin, stroking her fingers gently along its length.

"Tell me you love me," she said softly.

"I do. I love you."

"Really?"

They smiled at each other, and he drew her to him to show her how much he loved her. The proof he offered was the same one nearly everyone pursued, which nearly everyone bound each other with, even knowing that a lie might hide behind it. As their little love act began, the one on the TV screen over the bed drew to a close.

"It was fun," Techie said, as if there had been no more to it all than sport. That was the best he could manage, considering how everything worked out.

"I had a good time, too," Kipple replied bashfully. But had she really? An aura of regret pervaded the finale as Techie walked off like Rhett Butler in *Gone with the Wind*. The program closed with a flourish of the orchestra, the credits rolled, and the sponsor's message—*Brought to you by Her Holy Church*—flashed across 100 million TV screens. Then the news came on, leading with a report on the theft and destruction of the Sacred Bird by persons unknown.

Alfred G. Usano's aged face appeared, dark with righteous anger, and decried this latest sacrilege. Wolf Boy's breath caught as a surge of anger rose in his chest. Sheila pressed her supple body to his, calming him.

"Nothing you need to worry about," she purred in his ear. Sheila curled her long, fluffy tail gently but firmly around Wolf Boy's legs. Slowly, sensuously, she began to lick his fur with her coarse, stirring tongue.

Wolf Boy's heart melted like ice cream in the summer. He was so completely wild about her. She was so tough but so gentle, so very female.

Kipple wound up with an enormous settlement from the divorce, since Techie's adultery with the American whore had been exposed, along with his perfidy in attempting to seize control of Her cyberspace. He'd had no choice but to agree to Her terms. The Russians complained bitterly, but they'd lost control of the script, and in the end signed over 45 percent of their wheat production for the next ten years. Kipple's children would live well in the womb of Tokyo for some time to come.

The sets were struck. The lights and cameras were stowed away. Cast, crew, cinematographers, and director said their thank yous and good-byes.

Well done.

Thank you.

Are you all right?

"No, look . . ." The lead actress bared her breasts to reveal a heat rash.

All agreed on the value of the hard work they'd done.

The actor who'd played Techie stripped off his costume, wincing at the effort. "Well, as long as She assigned the role . . ."

They had given a marvelous performance and, as a reward, were being sent on a grand orbital tour of the solar system, Flight 3355.

A cameraman walked across the launch pad toward the rocket, which stood pointing skyward like a talisman. Soon they would all be off to the heavens.

Alfred C. Usano floated in the center of his pearl-shaped pool, his body completely relaxed. The Sacred Bird had been returned from the shop in good repair, and with the end of the Love Simulation program, nothing would be heard from Her for the foreseeable future.

Usano had nothing to worry him, and no doubt he hadn't a care in his mind when the heart attack struck him in his garden by the side of the pool. He was found later floating face down.

As for Wolf Boy and the cat-girl Sheila, well, they married, and— as the story goes—lived happily ever after. Wolf Boy sang in the City's hottest nightspots, and Sheila sold her services to an eager clientele. They worked only when they felt like it and only because they wanted to.

As for the City, that was Tokyo—the richest City in the world. There the Kipple system lived, telling stories to sustain Her children, as women do.

Translated by Kazuko Behrens and Gene van Troyer

Sophisticated Masochism: An Interview with Masahiko Shimada

Sinda Gregory and Larry McCaffery

Masahiko Shimada was born in Tokyo in 1961 and moved to Kawasaki when he was four years old. As a junior at Tokyo University of Foreign Languages, Shimada published the novella *Yasashii Sayoku No Tame No Kiyukyoku* (A Divertimento for Leftists, 1983), which was nominated for the Akutagawa Award. In 1984 he won the Noma Bungei Award for First Novels for his *Muyu Okoku No Tame No Ongaku* (Music for the Kingdom of Somnambulism). After spending a year in New York as a visiting professor at Columbia University, Shimada returned to Japan to publish *Yume Tsukai* (translated as *Dream Messenger,* 1988), an intercultural story about an orphan who earns money as a rental child. *Higan Sensei* (Master and Discipline, 1992—an excerpt of which appears here), which reinterprets Natsume Soseki's *Kokoro,* won the Izumi Kyoka Award. In *Rokoko-cho* (Rococo City, 1993) Shimada turned to science fiction, recasting his hometown, Yomiuri Rando, as a sort of cyber-amusement-park. Other works by Shimada include *Yogensha No Namae* (The Name of the Prophet, 1992), which explores religious themes; *Uku Onna, Shizumu Otoko* (Floating Woman, Drowning Man, 1996), a masochistic sea novel; and numerous other works.

In addition to fiction, Shimada has published extensively in nonfiction and dramatic forms. He directed and performed in his own play *Yurariumu* (Ulalium) in 1990. His Japanese translation of Steve Erickson's *Rubicon Beach* appeared in 1991. (Hisayo Ogushi)

Larry McCaffery: Your book *Unidentified Shadow* (1987) was, I think, one of the first important Japanese books to deal with AIDS. Of course we all know that AIDS is a huge problem in the U.S., but in Japan it still isn't such a problem, so we were wondering what got you interested in it? Did you know somebody who had AIDS?

Masahiko Shimada: Actually I started writing about AIDS before I had met any AIDS patients. My interest in AIDS was through immunology studies. I didn't study immunology deeply, but when I was in New York, I got to visit a laboratory of a Japanese immunologist who was studying retro viruses—very primitive viruses with RNA but no DNA. This experience encouraged me to try and read and understand what happens in the human immune system. But I also knew a very marvelous fact about the retro virus—which is that in very early times the virus contributed to human evolution. In terms of AIDS, this is a very specific virus—I mean, every person potentially has more than a million kinds of retro viruses which are not harmful to the human immune system. But through the process of evolution of the retro virus, suddenly a type of AIDS virus which is harmful to the human immune system accidentally appeared. Anyway, at the laboratory I had a chance to see the AIDS virus through an electron microscope. I recall that I was a little nervous because the doctor wore gloves but he didn't give me the gloves. But of course it was safe.

LM: How did this interest in immunology lead to your beginning your book?

MS: One of the things I noticed while I was writing about AIDS was that it is possible to arrange any kind of metaphor, any kind of figure of speech, through AIDS. I had enough ideas to write five short stories that were deeply connected with AIDS, which were collected and then published. But while I was writing these short stories, I changed my mind and decided that making too many metaphors about AIDS was a bad idea. Instead, I just thought that if possible I would like to offer to AIDS patients a book about how to make a life after they know that they are HIV positive. I had a lot of episodes about AIDS. Everybody knows that media figures like Elizabeth Taylor and Julio Iglesias have organized these AIDS benefits and also helped to collect money from companies and so on. In front of the laboratory I visited in New York there are marble tiles with the names of a lot of these AIDS benefits. I discovered that a lot of universities and hospitals had rushed out to get funding for getting an AIDS laboratory because it is very easy to get the money.

Sinda Gregory: But in addition to your contact with the clinical aspect of AIDS did you get to see AIDS patients while you were in New York?

MS: Yes, I had a chance to meet a group of AIDS patients who were doing performances in a tiny theater about how AIDS patients are treated. While I was staying in New York, there was also an AIDS demonstration that I watched on television. This was a while ago, but these sorts of demonstrations and the reference surrounding them don't really change very much.

SG: AIDS doesn't seem to be much of an issue right now in Japan. As we all know, in the U.S. a lot of rhetoric and imagery surrounding AIDS has been used by right-wing Christians and other reactionaries to reinforce their moral positions about sex and so forth. Has the *image* of AIDS been used like this in Japan?

MS: In Japan the image of AIDS has been used in a very ignorant, reactionary way: AIDS equals foreign people—not so much Western people but Asians. There are a lot of women from other Asian countries who have been hired to work here as prostitutes, and such girls are considered to have brought the AIDS virus to Tokyo. Thus Japanese people tend to see Asian people in Japan as AIDS virus carriers. What a stupid image!

LM: What contemporary Japanese writers do you admire?

MS: There are a few. One would be Kenji Nakagami, who died a few weeks ago. He's a very important writer who was about fifteen years older than I and whose writing is comparable in many ways to the early works of James Joyce. Unfortunately, it is difficult for me to introduce my favorite Japanese writers to Americans because most of their works are so authentic and avant-garde that they are very hard to translate. Most of these writers wrote only in Japanese and out of very non-European traditions. This is something I respect very much, even though it makes it very hard to translate. Of course I'm Japanese, and I am confident about my Japanese, but even I encounter difficulties in reading them. But it is only such Japanese works that I respect.

Mr. Tatsumi has mentioned *Yapoo* several times, and even though this writer is very controversial, his book is a very significant and respectable Japanese work. I myself have been personally influenced by it very deeply. I have never met him.

Another writer who is working in the fringe-area of SF and the avant-garde is Yasutaka Tsutsui, who is respected not only by SF freaks but also by many literature fans. Unfortunately, I can't recommend his recent works. He should be a barbarian in Japanese literature by doing works that would make him seem a complete stranger to mainstream readers of "serious" literature. He should make a protest against the Japanese literature of people like Kobo Abe or Kenzaburo Oe which has already been translated. In my opinion he needs to keep that kind of defiance and protest position; but he is a man possessing an inferiority complex to serious literature. So he has been seduced by a figure like Kenzaburo Oe to stop writing stupid SF and start writing serious literature. But stupid SF is the best!

LM: In his afterword to your story in *Monkey Brain Sushi*, Alfred Birnbaum says that you are probably "the most consciously 'literary' of the authors in this collection." Do you think this aspect of your work is one of the things that perhaps made you feel this sense of separation from other authors in Tokyo? A different way to ask this would be: Are there any contemporary Japanese writers whom you feel a specific sense of affinity with, or who are doing something similar to what you are doing?

MS: The only person I think of as possibly being my partner is the woman writer, Amy Yamada, whose work is also collected in *Monkey Brain Sushi*. Of course, I can't share the same feelings or attitudes with her. What we do share is a certain confidence of using the Japanese language and a similar malicious attitude toward those ordinary images which are naturalized by many demagogues. I respect her way of writing and her attitude toward Japanese language.

SG: What is there about her way of writing and attitude that makes you respect her?

MS: I respect the way she can arrange the ordinary way of Japanese writing in her writing. In terms of her attitude about the Japanese language, I believe that every talented writer must take a positive attitude toward his own language. But the attitude toward the native language when you're writing fiction should be different from that of ordinary people—for example, lawyers, politicians, and journalists. To me, writing fiction should mean deconstructing or simply destroying Japanese. To use Japanese like a foreign language is to make Japanese a nonverbal way of expressing things— to analyze and criticize the ordinary Japanese way of writing. For instance, we have to bring some shock to our own native tongue.

SG: I assume that this kind of shock doesn't arise just because someone like Amy Yamada often writes about shocking situations? You are talking about the language itself.

MS: Yes. For example, the device or the intention of translating one's own mother tongue to Pidgin or Creole language—or similar languages like that of the Swahili of East Africa or Creole French of Haiti—is natural for me. Of course, I am not that ambitious to revolutionize the structure or grammar of the Japanese language. And I don't mean just using a lot of foreign languages (for example, it is quite easy to use Japanese-English in a Japanese context). What I'm talking about here is wanting to keep the attitude toward my native language *flexible*. It is perhaps useful to compare the situation you have in Japan with what you find with the English language. English essentially has no orthodoxy—which I think can be a great benefit. Probably someone will insist on the Queen's English being authentic, but it is the flexibility rather than the "authenticity" that you find in many of the greatest American authors.

SG: One can certainly see what you're talking about in the works of people like Twain and Faulkner. Faulkner's language was recognizably English, but it was also a distinctly American style. You simply can't imagine a British writer ever writing anything like Faulkner.

MS: Exactly. The current situation is especially interesting for me. The Booker Prize winners are mainly non-British. Historically, a lot of the greatest British literature was written by the Irish— Beckett, Joyce, Swift, Yeats, and so forth. So in some ways you could say that British literature turns out to be another name for Irish literature. And nowadays, British literature means Indian literature. But in Japan, literature, especially the genre of novels, is open to the people living in masochistic and S & M situations. I myself would like to be called an immigrant to Tokyo. This is exactly the same situation Masoch wanted to be in. He is Austrian but since he has a very weird taste, he was willing to pretend to be Jewish. If I compare myself to Masoch, I would like to be able to write from the perspective of an immigrant from Asia to Tokyo. I'd be doing this not for these immigrants, of course, but just for me, for my own pleasure. If I said these things to real immigrants, they would think I am very rude.

The complete interview with Masahiko Shimada can be accessed at www.centerforbookculture.org.

Stalled at a Kiss
(from Master and Discipline)

Masahiko Shimada

"Humans were gone. Only their shadows remained. Reality too had vanished, leaving only fiction in its place. You and I are merely characters made to dance on the slightest wisp blown from a fiction which is always in progress, yet in which everything is already concluded," Sensei had remarked to me on one of my regular meetings with him. He wore a hand-knit sweater over his pajamas.

Was his work not going so well? His face seemed full of unfinished business. Or could he have spent the night with a lover and had just arrived home for a bit of sleep? I don't know. I was to see him in this state a number of times. He looked satiated, as though he had had enough of women. Usually, he looked, strangely enough, as though nothing could stand in his way.

I am a fan of Sensei's looks, but I must also say that I am a devotee of his particularly bizarre hidden confidence. He writes the truth in his books. Sensei has a grasp of almost anything. He has a knack. One can count on him for answers. And basically that is why I had sought him out as my mentor; his body played a major part in that choice. A mentor must exude confidence. He was to be the object of my belief, the target of my assault. I had yearned since childhood for a disciple-master relationship.

But I was still a boy then, just nineteen, and I stupidly misunderstood what Sensei had been saying. I was prepared to accept the spell he cast over me—"from now on, you will live in the world of my writings." He had permitted me access to the place where his books were written and conceived, which meant to me that in the near future I was to appear as a character. It gave me pleasure to think about when that would be. Only later did I come to realize other meanings hidden in his words.

Sensei had not finished his pronouncement: "You're handsome. A man's beauty is in his face. We don't give birth to children, so the most we can do is to cultivate our beauty. All men are capable of is an erection; they're incapable of creative work. Did you know that the god who created Heaven and Earth was female?"

One could do no better as a character than to be handsome. I believe I was taken on as his disciple because of my good looks and my ability to keep quiet.

"Being with a handsome youth does have rewards for his bene-factor, don't you see?"

If Sensei intended to go girl hunting, I would be content to be the bullet in his rifle, the hunting dog at his feet. I have confidence in my reflexes and in my physical strength. I will do whatever is in my power to be of help to this man. Does my thinking or my great admi-ration for his works mean that I am specially predisposed to serve him? Sensei embodies something, something I can't explain, never having known anyone else who had it in equal measure. Can I call it moral fiber? My admiration, however, was mixed equally with cyni-cism. What the hell, I thought, a character's a character, so why not be a beautiful young boy by whom the author would be captivated? Some of the athletic louts who turned up in his stories, stupid as well as unattractive, so thick-skinned they had cast-iron stomachs, no class, and no pride, might find fault with the likes of me, but at least I knew I would, in this company, not end up being a mere extra.

I tried neither to exaggerate nor shrink my role. At worst, I could play a bad game of apparent cleverness or, through impudence, bring Sensei to openly ridicule me with those piercing bright eyes of his. I liked what he once wrote somewhere—nothing is as guileless as the wisdom of an adolescent boy.

Sensei was the first writer I had met; his slightest move became part of my own grand bildungsroman.

"Don't novelists all tell the same story? Do you know what you're doing, putting yourself in his hands?"

I never allowed anything that was worrying Satoko to get in my hair. Novelists are not the only ones to have a few eccentricities. Even Satoko often remarked how jealous she was of gay culture, or how she too wanted to "vogue." "Well, isn't it a little odd to want to learn about living and dressing gay?" I reminded her that a novelist was a pro when it came to doing strange things, thinking anything. Therefore, I reminded her, that genus known as "novelist" had to be infinitely more ordinary than most of us plebes who find it impos-sible to think of much of anything, let alone something unheard of. If Satoko and I were 90 percent ordinary, a novelist would have to be 500 percent to be in his right mind, I added.

"What kind of stories does he write?"

"Twisted romances, you know the stuff."

"Are they any good?"

"How should I know? A little porno, a little Sci Fi, a little politics, with a little mystery thrown in for good measure."

"Are there gay characters, any fashion queens?"

"There're plenty of weirdos."

For the most part, I had no way to explain what was going on in

Sensei's novels. All I knew was I could lose myself in that world.

Satoko was concerned more about Sensei's looks than what was in the novels. She despised ugly middle-aged men more than snakes. She'd be likely to pronounce the death sentence on men who groped people on the trains, meaning middle-aged ones. Luckily (and this had nothing to do with Satoko), Sensei had never quite become middle-aged, preferring instead to lead the rest of his life with the aura of spent youth.

To jump ahead, I found myself frequenting Sensei's home. When he asked me whether I was thinking of becoming his disciple, I said yes. He agreed. "It might prove interesting," he added.

"You mean you want to be a novelist?" Satoko asked.

"Absolutely not."

I meant it. I figured it might be one thing to think I might want to write, but another thing entirely to want to be a novelist. I had absolutely no intention of learning how to write novels from Sensei. I needed to be with him from time to time. That was it; nothing more, nothing less. I became his disciple because this way I wouldn't have to make excuses for being there.

Sensei was Sensei, but my sister taught him. She had studied voice in the Graduate Faculty of Music and took on the task, part time, of instructing Sensei in operatic technique. Sensei's fixation on Italian opera drove him to learn how to sing; unfortunately his voice couldn't produce the higher registers. So my sister, who lived nearby, took on the task of improving his voice.

"The voice isn't so bad, it's breath control that gives out too quickly. He runs all out for the first three miles of the marathon and then poops out around the tenth. It's only a problem of air. He loves the music, though. All he wants to sing are difficult tenor arias. It'll take him another ten years before he can hit high C. I tell you, he sings the F sharp an octave lower."

My sister's comments led me to imagine Sensei as middle-aged, red-faced with his efforts to produce the merest falsetto. I hurried to buy Sensei's books, but always put them down because of the author's perversity. This would prove to be rougher going than explicit schoolgirl comics. I found character types I had never encountered who spoke, made love, fought. The Tokyo settings were familiar, yet the language and the reality of the encounters seemed to belong to some other world. I was not to find my role in this play. How could I become a character when nasty authorial lobotomies seemed imminent? Nevertheless, I read the works over and over, persevered until, as I began to glimpse Sensei's own inner life, I felt the fictional world coming ever closer to fitting my own physical contours. Training was requisite to reading such books.

Sensei's voice lessons terminated in about three months. My sister was enrolling in a music school in Vienna. In just this short time she had become a devoted fan. Thanks to Sensei, her tastes in men changed. Now knowledgeable, she had read somewhere in his works that men who were slightly faded were more attractive and that a man's backside was more interesting than his face. Sensei's warped sense of morality had quietly crept into my sister's senses.

Sensei's home was about twenty minutes away by bicycle. He lived with his wife on the sixth floor of a nine-story condo called Riverside Village. I lived with my sister on the top floor of a multiuse building containing a 7-Eleven and a video rental shop. Since the buildings were on either side of the Tama River, I took singular pleasure in being able to bicycle on a clear day across the bridge to visit Sensei.

Sensei had two names by which society knew him: his real name and his nom de plume, but I needed only the one I already used. I kept another, just in case, strictly for my personal use. When I referred to Sensei by this name, it would be reserved for him not just as anybody's mentor, but as mine alone. I thought of it one day as I was walking on the riverbank. Sensei lived on the opposite side of the river. So he became my mentor of the "other side."

I met Sensei three times during the period my sister made once-weekly visits. The first was when she had forgotten the scores she needed for the lesson, and I brought them over on my bicycle.

A woman appeared at the entrance and ushered me inside. Later I learned that this woman was his wife; I had no idea the woman and Sensei were a pair. I had mistaken her for one of my sister's friends, or perhaps someone else; my first impression led me to unilaterally decide that he was single.

Having a sister on the scene helped me get through my fear. In such situations, I normally played dumb and held my tongue. This time, I was the one who made Sensei uneasy. Who wouldn't be embarrassed at having to continue his voice lessons in front of a sudden intruder?

"This is my brother Kikuhito."

I returned her introduction with an inept something about how nice it was of him to put up with such noise pollution. If she were rehearsing at home, customers would check the window above the rental video shop and the 7-Eleven before entering. I said the same thing to Sensei I said to customers. Without acknowledging me, Sensei said, "How nice of you to come."

With that, the day's lesson finished and we had a cup of tea. I had intended to leave without interrupting the lesson, but my timing had been off. My sister kept the conversation going.

"Which food is best for the voice?"

"Beef," was my sister's immediate reply.

"I don't know why, but beef with red wine seems best. Melon, on the other hand, is not good. But, you know Sensei, it's all a matter of taste."

This was the first time I had heard my sister call him Sensei. Following her lead, I began to do the same. I knew if this were a mistake, they would let it pass; after all, his wife referred unnecessarily to him as Sensei. I remember vividly how his wife responded.

"The one of whom you speak never talks to anyone at home; he is sullen by nature. It's no wonder his voice is so rough. I believe that is why he has taken up singing; to be able to speak more happily. Isn't that so, Sensei?"

Sensei remained silent for the rest of the meeting. Gloom set in. Nodding or punctuating with an occasional "Oh," the conversation continued between the wife and my sister. I noticed that Sensei's attention had continued its flight to an unknown source. I knew from the complete ennui that engulfed his expression and from the way in which he hid this in a faint smile that this man was complex.

Husbands and wives often resemble one another, but Sensei's case was the exception to the rule. I felt sure that Sensei's wife regarded him more as a perverse outsider than as her husband.

My sister and the wife were getting on so well I imagined they must be nearly the same age. My sister looks older than her age, and the wife, much younger, so my visual mistake wasn't at all inappropriate. My sister was twenty-three; the wife was twenty-nine. That day, their conversation left Sensei behind as it turned to the vulgar subjects of foreign travel, the theater, and cosmetics. I was preparing to make my escape, looking for a lull in the conversation when suddenly my eyes met Sensei's. He telegraphed his entrapment.

As I left, Sensei whispered, not directing it to me.

"I wonder what goes on every day in the mind of a nineteen-year-old boy?"

My sister answered for me.

"Girls."

"I see. The same as me then. I have an emotional age of about nineteen."

For the first time, I heard Sensei laugh. Unfortunately, his joke was lost on the two women.

On the way home, I asked my sister.

"Is that woman Sensei's mistress?"

"Don't be silly. Couldn't you see she's his wife? She is pretty, isn't she."

"Yes, but she doesn't seem like his wife. Doesn't even act like it."

"We caused it. I'm sure they're a couple when they're alone."

"I like Sensei's taste in clothes."

"Do you? Are you sure it's not just to make himself appear younger? A middle-aged man still has just one thing on his mind: his next conquest."

"Isn't that what women do too; sit around all day thinking about men?"

Laughing it off, my sister rapped me on the head. Who, I wondered, was on Sensei's mind? His wife? His lover? My sister maybe?

Sensei was about to have his thirty-seventh birthday next month.

I don't remember when Sensei, my alternate man from across the river, came walking in the vicinity of my house. He couldn't have had any reason to cross to this side, but there he was, muttering something to himself and heading in the direction of the station. I had just come home from the university, so it must have been about 5:30 in the afternoon. The minute I saw him from the balcony, I set off after him like a blundering idiot. I had a special sideline now. Town crier. "There goes an author" was my refrain.

Sensei was not just strolling through the shopping arcade; he walked slowly, glancing around like a lost child.

Dressed in a turtleneck shirt and black corduroy pants, Sensei paused in front of a fish shop to ogle at a flayed sea bream on ice.

"Sensei, nice to meet you the other day."

Sensei started, then stared squarely at me.

"Oh yes, you're her brother." Sensei was struggling to remember my name.

"What are you doing?"

"I'm staring at a fish."

"Something for dinner?"

"No. I feel sorry for a flayed bream on ice."

"I hope your wife's well."

"She is. Working now. You live near here?"

"Yes. I'd invite you in if my sister were here, but she'll be late tonight."

"I see your sister every week. Any place around here to get a good cup of coffee?"

I took Sensei to a place about ten minutes away that specialized in classical music. The owner, a passionate fan of Richard Strauss, called the place Der Rosenkavalier. I usually had coffee there in the evening with Satoko. If I asked, the owner lent me his rare collectors-item recordings. When the store closed at midnight, he offered me beer. I brought him, in return, gifts from my travels. I wasn't sure how to introduce my friend the owner to Sensei. What if he didn't want his identity as a novelist known? I hardly knew him. I ended up avoiding the counter in favor of a table from where I made only eye contact with the owner.

Sensei sipped a cup of black Mandheling, preferring to puff on a cigarette rather than exchange words.

"Do you write all the time when you're home?"

I had no confidence in being able to have a conversation, so I pursued the ordinary idea of how he lived his life.

"Writing isn't all there is to the job. Killing time, like this, is also extremely important."

"Is singing part of your work too?"

"Sure. So is slurping my noodles, making telephone calls, and walking in the shopping district."

"What do you do for amusement?"

"That's the most important aspect of my work. I'm always on the lookout. Keeping yourself constantly amused is very tiring, you know. Truth is, I'm the sort of person who hates to have a good time. Yet I can't stop."

What a strange thing to say, I thought. Just idle talk, but he had been too emphatic. There would be time after I had become his disciple to ponder the meaning of these words.

"You mean, Sensei, that amusement is not fun for you?"

"The more I amuse myself, the more vulnerable, the less lovable, the less able to bear it I become."

"I've never had that pleasure. It would be nice, having so much fun I ended up hating it."

"You'd have no problem with it physically, but what's at stake is prayer. Debauchery requires a vow."

"A vow? Vow what before you go wild?"

"Oh, this and that."

Sensei wouldn't speak in specifics. His word *vow* was weird. Lighting a new cigarette, he changed the topic.

"Your sister says you're studying Russian at the university. Is that true?"

"Right. The daily drills are horrendous."

"Russian grammar must be difficult. You know, though, I think everyone ought to study a foreign language. So you can let loose anywhere in the world. Japanese restricts you to having a good time only in Japan."

I laughed and agreed. My sister told me that Sensei was fluent in English and Spanish. It seemed he could also get by in Italian when his travels called for it. From the moment I took the entrance exams to the foreign languages department, I held fast to one single maxim: a minimum of three languages would be required to get on with women. Sensei seemed about to confirm my golden rule.

Sensei waited for the entire performance of Berlioz's *Harold in Italy* to end before getting up from the table. He thanked me for introducing him to the shop and paid the bill.

Walking back to the station, Sensei suddenly stopped in the middle of the street as though he had recalled something. He blurted, "I smell teriyaki chicken. Let's have some."

His invitation seemed so natural I forgot my reticence and let my appetite be swayed by the smells enticing us both.

"Have as much as you want," Sensei said, filling his own glass with beer. I followed suit. After a moment, Sensei, asked, somewhat hesitantly: "Do you have a lover?"

"There's a girl at the university."

"Do you think one's enough?"

I smiled, thinking it was a joke, and said I wouldn't mind having more. Sensei continued in earnest.

"Do you really like this girl?"

I also thought this question was meant to be funny. Obviously so, if she was my lover, I thought. I grinned.

"She's the only one."

"I'm jealous. What's her name?"

"Satoko. Studies Italian."

"I see. I once wrote a novel about naive love among students. That's nice. You're living out the novel of your youth."

"No. I'm just seeing a girl, that's all."

"Yes? I was once like that. I'm jealous."

What, I wondered, did Sensei have to be so jealous about? Youth? Purity?

"What about your beautiful wife?"

"Ah, yes. You must think me insatiable," Sensei replied, biting into his teriyaki as though trying to conceal his interest.

I wondered if, in fifteen years, I wouldn't feel the same way as Sensei. My curiosity was piqued. I wanted to delve further into Sensei's inner consciousness.

Sensei went out to make a phone call after our second round of beer. He announced on returning that he had to leave. He said in parting: "How about inviting your sister next time?"

"Why don't you ask her yourself?"

Sensei laughed approvingly. The alcohol had taken effect and made me somewhat curt. I continued with a more polite wish to go out with him again, and he responded in kind that I should telephone him.

After coffee at Der Rosenkavalier, I saw Satoko as far as the station on the other side of the river on her way for tutoring. I had been called Sensei until quite recently by a ninth-grade schoolgirl. A more skillful tutor had been found, and so I was let go. My pupil Yumi had this to say on our last day, "I like you, but Papa's warning me."

Me leading Yumi on? Ridiculous. If that's the way her worrying father sees me, I'll quit. What if I had gone ahead and given Yumi that single little kiss?

That day, my sister came home by taxi after midnight. Quite drunk, she bumped into things getting to the kitchen, where she drank two glasses of water in an attempt to sober up. It had been her lesson day, and I knew she had gone that evening to Sensei's.

"What did you and Sensei have for dinner?"

"Italian."

"Nice. All I got was *teriyaki*."

"Well you're not in the same category. I am, after all, an opera singer. Get it?"

So Sensei was also good at flattery. Sister was in an unusually buoyant mood. I wanted to know what his wife was doing while Sensei and my sister were out having that dinner. I wondered whether Sensei had asked his wife if he could take his singing teacher out.

For about a month after, I was busy preparing for exams and writing papers. My simple life consisted of a solitary bead drawn directly between the university and home. Any date with Satoko was made in the library. We sat across the table for about an hour, me pouring over Russian documents, she doing the same with Italian, until we reached a convenient break point in the study to signal to each other that it was time to go back down to the stacks where old magazines and valuable rare volumes lie moldering eternally on the darkened shelves. We had been told that there were books dating to pre-Revolutionary time, lost in Russia that would fetch no less than 5,000,000 yen, yet nobody ever looked at them.

We spoke in whispers under the window admitting light to the deserted stacks. The light struck her face, outlining it so that she seemed like a talking sculpture. I could see deeply into the pale brown pupils of her eyes, hot stuff when it came to appreciating a lover. All that was necessary now was for her to have skin like marble. Cheeks brightened by the light, Satoko glowed faintly as though emitting a pale glow of fireflies.

"Let's go somewhere when we finish our exams," I said.

"I need to cut loose too. How about going skiing?"

"Too strenuous for me. Cold too."

"What are you talking about? You want to be Russian, don't you? You may find your future working in Siberia."

"I work better in a warm place, let loose easier. Let's go to a hot spring."

"How about a combination ski resort and hot spring?"

Satoko always made the decision, and I always followed. She always went the short way, and I always took the long way around. I got better at reading my own character going out with her.

People often ask me why I decided to study Russian. I was used to giving a variety of answers: I wanted to read Dostoyevsky in the original (despite the utter difficulty of even reading him in Japanese translation?!) or something romantic as if I wanted to set foot in that cinematic world Tarkovsky had created or that I just liked a country that had been left behind by capitalism. Things like that. It turned out that when I began to study Russian and delve into the forest of materials on Russian literature and history, I realized just how close I actually was to having a Russian disposition. I felt empathy with the poor oaf Oblomov. How moved I was by the stalwart actors in Dostoyevsky's novels and in Tarkovsky's films. More than a few of my classmates had plans to be hired by the Russian department of the university in four years or were aiming to be experts in international politics, but none of this seemed worthy of debate to me.

While arguments over the pros and cons of scholarly analyses versus television and print-media event coverage flew left and right in the graduate student offices, I offered nothing by way of opinion or addition; I muttered to myself something about what to do with people like the Doukhobors who lived a life in Siberia free of Western rationalist ideas? What was happening was I was choosing a world that already conformed to my character. This would be the most honest answer I could give to the question of why I studied Russian.

Tarkovsky made a film called *Nostalgia*. I knew the characters were a Russian man with an Italian woman. I took Satoko to see it. She looked puzzled when she found me shedding tears. In Italy the main character has a glimpse of his soul through the window of his inner recesses, not through his intellect. For some reason the story pointed at my own sense of guilt and complicity. What guilt, you ask? Something like guilt by association. It made me unbearably sad to think that I would not share his will to commune heart to heart with such religious zealots. I knew what he was capable of was forbidden to me: hearts in communion, peering into the recesses of the inner consciousness, praying for something, thinking of death. I felt in my own way dysfunctional.

Satoko brought it up later.

"You know, sometimes you just bury yourself in your own little world. But you come right back to this side again."

"Is that weird?"

"Weird, but fascinating."

I knew she must have been accusing me.

Why had Satoko taken up Italian? The reason was clear; she had lived as a child in Rome.

In the stacks we talked about clairvoyance: how everyone has it, how the way you make love would change if you had telepathy, how interesting it would be to be able to play an instrument without using your hands or mouth. It took thirty-five minutes that day before I first kissed her. I couldn't seem to get the timing right. In thirty-five minutes any real Russian or Italian would have done it close to a hundred times. What were we to do? We were impostors.

Deciding to make one last ditch effort at study, we went toward the stairs and up to the desk.

"Let's talk more about extrasensory powers."

I laughed and obliged her. Sensei crossed my mind.

"One of my sister's friends asked me recently whether I had a lover, and I said yes."

"Really? Who?"

Thinking for a second about what I would do if she didn't take it as a joke, I looked Satoko right in the face.

"As if you didn't know."

Our relationship had stalled at a kiss.

Translated by Kenneth L. Richard

This Conflict between Illusion and Brutal Reality: An Interview with Yoriko Shono

Larry McCaffery, Sinda Gregory, Mari Kotani, and Takayuki Tatsumi

Yoriko Shono was born in 1956 in Yokkaichi, Mie Prefecture. She lived with her parents in Ise until she finished high school; then she went to Nagoya where she spent two years at a university preparatory school. She was finally admitted to the Faculty of Law at Ritsumeikan University in Kyoto, from which she graduated in 1980. In 1981 she received the Twenty-Fourth Gunzo Prize for New Writers for her novel *Gokuraku* (Heaven). For the first four years of this period, she lived in a small apartment in Kyoto, and then she moved to Hachioji, where she continued to lead a reclusive life in a one-room flat. This lonely experience gave her a good opportunity to write a new existentialist novel *Nanimo Shitenai* (Doing Nothing) in 1991, for which she received the Thirteenth Noma Literary Prize. In the wake of the Japanese bubble-economy age from the late 1980s through the early nineties, which she found completely futile, Yoriko Shono became more and more creative in her writing. The year of 1994 was her annus mirabilis. She received two major literary awards: the Seventh Mishima Yukio Prize for the novella *Nihyakkaiki* (The 200th Anniversary of the Dead) and the 111th Akutagawa Prize for her haunting novella *Taimu Surippu Kombinato* (Time Warp Complex—an excerpt of which follows). Her late 1990s major works include: *Haha no Hattatsu* (The Development of My Mother), *Paradaisu Furattsu* (Paradise Flats, 1997), and *Tokyo Yokai Fuyu* (The Floating Ghosts of Tokyo, 1998). (TT)

Sinda Gregory: Since *Time Warp Complex* is your only book so far that's been translated into English, we're going to have to focus most of our questions on that work. Do you feel it's typical of your work so far?

Yoriko Shono: In retrospect, *Time Warp Complex* is not what I would consider my major work. But for translation purposes, since there are all kinds of proper nouns of the factories, I think this will help convey the atmosphere of the town even for English-speaking readers. What I consider as my major work is *Restless Dream*, but this would be very difficult to translate. *Restless Dream* was an effort to ascertain the construction of the Japanese language; all kinds of puns and anagrams appear, and it relies deeply on the fact that it was written in Japanese. Moreover, there appear many types of patriarchal discriminations by Japanese men toward women, and as an infrastructure, I used the Japanese genesis myth of Izanagi and Izanami. In this sense, I think that *Nihyakkaiki* or *The 200th Anniversary of the Dead,* which brought me the Mishima Literary Award, might be more appealing to the American or English speaking audience, if ever translated into English.

Larry McCaffery: Since *Time Warp Complex* is not representative in some ways of your work generally, maybe you can tell us about what made you shift into this other nonrepresentative way of writing?

YS: I started on *Restless Dream* when I was in my twenties, and I spent most of my thirties completing it. Through this work, I was able to capture the basic structure of Japan and the Japanese sensibility, in my own way. In other words, the story is about what Japan looks like when seen from my own perception, my own recognition of the Japanese world. *Restless Dream* was a starting point as well as a sort of main frame or foundation for my writing. Afterward, I came up with the motifs for *Time Warp Complex* by going to Umi-Shibaura, or for *The 200th Anniversary of the Dead,* for I had missed my dead grandmother so much that I wanted to meet her again. These experiences were no more than cues of not so much importance for what I wanted to write about in *Time Warp Complex* — but the basic framework for what I was doing had already been provided from *Restless Dream.*

LM: Do you recall what the initial impulse was that got you started? For instance, did *Time Warp Complex* start with the dream of a tuna that opens the book?

YS: As a matter of fact, yes, I *did* see a dream of a tuna, but it wasn't like I wanted to actually meet him. This tuna of my dream was somewhat cyborglike and quite handsome as well, but that doesn't mean I would really fall in love with him. What I had in mind from the beginning, as a theme of this story, was "does love really require an other?" For example, in the eleventh-century novel *The Tale of Genji,* Lady Murasaki wrote a story in which her simplest descriptions of the garden and the wind convey the atmosphere of love.

Mari Kotani: You can find many of these princesses in that novel. They write songs and they find themselves in the atmosphere of love.

Takayuki Tatsumi: They achieve this sense of love by looking at things, rather than human beings. This reminds me of what I have been thinking in terms of the "celibate machine," because you can fall in love even with yourself. You don't need any existence of the other.

YS: In my own case, at the outset of *Time Warp Complex* I thought, "Is this love without the other something that is universal?" So by immersing myself into the longing to meet the tuna, I wanted to pursue what it would be like to be in love without an other. But while I was writing this story, I was asked to do a report for a magazine and I visited Umi-Shibaura—the actual setting of *Time Warp Complex*. That is where this "feeling of love," which was a mere illusion, got knocked away by the powerfulness of reality. This conflict between illusion and the brutal reality functioned as a springboard that allowed me to finish up my story.

LM: The train station you describe in the story has one end that opens up onto the sea while the other end is at the factory. Was that based on a real train station? It seemed very symbolic.

YS: Yes, it's a real train station. I've described it the way it is.

SG: You said that *Restless Dream* has a discursive framework. Would you tell us what that means a little bit more specifically?

YS: Let's take sexual discrimination. Until recently, we used to employ the word *uwaki,* which means "having an affair" or "committing adultery," but then it changed to *furin,* which is frequently used these days. Since this term represents the relationship between men and women (although it connotes sexual descrimination depending on its usage), it is used for both sexes. On the other hand, *uwaki,* which is obsolete lately, is a concept applicable to men who take mistresses just for pleasure. However, if a married woman had a love affair outside her marriage, it meant adultery or infidelity. It was almost a crime.

Uwaki was negative while *furin* had a rather equal connotation between man and woman, but in the course of time, this word was consumed and again it was generalized. Although we coin new words to express something, the newness gradually wears the negative connotation again. This can be said about any word that has a discriminating implication. Within this contamination process, you can see that there is the fundamental construct. Within this construct, all the filth, the vice, and the responsibility, gathers to the weaker ones. *Furin* started out as an equal term, but gradually women ended up with disrespect. For me, "the weaker ones" means all those being discriminated against, including women. Also, what we call *Kegare* (the filthy, the unclean) is associated with various kinds of discrimination.

Another point is the fact that we Japanese use words that are easy to control and we try to be understandable, but this particular way of expressing ourselves is only tracing the way the dominator sees the world. In order to get out of this kind of invisible restriction, it was necessary in *Restless Dream* for me to do a linguistic experiment or decontextualization. But there is a limit to this, because if you go too far, it will make no sense to the general public.

MK: One way to express this "invisible restriction" is to say that women have to evaluate ourselves by using the words of the dominator.

YS: There is a distortion and I wanted to see this distortion, which is brought by the phoniness of the dominator. I just want to get back the word from the dominator. There is a prince who appears in *Restless Dream* who is not at all attractive, but he keeps the most beautiful woman in the world. This beautiful woman was greatly abused. The prince would have dozens of love affairs but this woman would always forgive him with a smile (although, ironically, she poses to be a woman of the seventies, being liberated and all, like Jane Fonda). Therefore, the prince would say "You are a good woman."

On the other hand, the main character (her name is Peach-Tree-Flying-Snake) is abused as well, but in a different way. For example, the prince would always say, "You are a *baka-onna* (stupid woman), a *histeri-onna* (a hysteric woman)!" Unlike an anima which is praised but ruled by the prince, this Peach-Tree-Flying-Snake is abused and despised. This is the reason why she can plan to defeat the prince someday.

What I tried to do was to analyze these repulsive words and find out what kind of fraud or hidden implications they are made of, why these words have so much power. The story ends with the main character destroying not only the stage on which the prince stands, but also the world.

SG: I understand you studied law. This seems perhaps relevant to *Time Warp Complex* because so much of the story seems to be about playing with language in a way that I associate with what lawyers do. Can you talk a little bit about your background generally, and how law might have prepared you to become a writer in particular?

YS: It was a matter of chance, of course, but I was influenced by the content of what I studied at law school. I specialized in civil-suit law, especially in the process of lawsuits involving civil and commercial matters. Civil lawsuits deal with nothing but the private rights, such as the rights of property; therefore they don't really have much to do with crime and punishment. The language in that field becomes very abstract, sometimes bringing about the arguments or the theories completely based on logic. The maniacs involved in these types of lawsuits for the money or the right of property are greedy but calm. Sometimes they will come up with all kinds of excuses, claims, and sophistry. Our duty is to hold them back to common sense. For example, a lawsuit over the boundary line—a person claims that the boundary line is here. He loses the case. But according to logic, he can have a whole case if he tries it again, changing his claim by one millimeter—which is rather ridiculous. Through this, I was able to see the gap between logic and common sense, and I also myself enjoy these sorts of logic games. Moreover, I was taught to doubt the most logical, to defamiliarize what we have long taken for granted. For example, women are taught to be "feminine" or "womanly." But from the perspective of civil law, we have to begin with the definition of the word *womanly,* almost to the last centimeter or last millimeter.

SG: One of the things that comes through in *Time Warp Complex* is that there is the power of logic and there is language that is logical, but these sorts of logical structures may not have anything to do with what is true.

YS: In the case of *Time Warp Complex,* by illustrating a certain person's point of view, I was hoping that I would be able to imply something to the readers. It was like a fight against the language and the world, or in other words, the world made up by words. What I tried to present in *Time Warp Complex* were people's activities in the age of Showa, and the city of Tokyo reflected on the narrator's view and her memories. I wanted to offer the very Zeitgeist, not in the mass-media way of representation, but from a very personal standpoint. Also in my other novel, *Doing Nothing,* I described through the narrator's viewpoint the scene of the ceremony of the emperor's accession on TV, and the bodyguards who protect the royal family who happen to get on the train with the narrator (these episodes are based on my own experience). In these cases, I avoided writing political discourse and criticizing it consciously at all. Instead, I tried to describe what I really felt and the details correctly rather than using some stereotype. I wanted to create a fictional space which contains a critique of Japanese language already deformed and of the thoughtlessness of mass media through the force of my extremely private compositions.

LM: You mentioned that you began *Time Warp Complex* with that dream of meeting a tuna, but how did this story evolve?

YS: I usually set the theme beforehand. The first one-third of all my books—twenty to fifty pages according to whether it is a novel or short story—is usually improvised or written quite offhand. The rest, I rather consciously try to follow the theme. I speculate, meditate, study a lot before starting to write. Not really planning, but more of a free-association, waiting for the muse to inspire me to write.

As for *Time Warp Complex,* I wanted to combine the fantastic scene of the sea and a tuna fish I dreamed of with a love without the substantial lover. I had already written a novel called *Sea Animal* dealing with the sea—not the real sea but the one in our dream or our TV screen. The protagonist keeps the love for that illusionary sea, such as the love without the substantial lover. However, when I actually went to Umi-Shibaura for conducting research, I came across a series of compelling realities that were to lead us to this fantastic sea. In other words, I had seen too many signboards on the way to Umi-Shibaura, which is located right in the middle of the industrial sea. In such a place, "the scene of the ruin" that I described at the very beginning of the novella is only a fantasy, since the area has historical necessity, and moreover, there are people living there. Therefore, I tried to walk around the area as indifferently as possible, just depending on my senses and cutting off my preoccupations. I went there twice, and one time I kept walking and taking notes for almost six hours with a short break for eating Soki noodle, as I depicted in the story.

SG: In the beginning of *Time Warp Complex,* the woman seems crazy, but by the end of the story, she seems to be more sane.

YS: Before capturing the "alternate reality," things often seem rather absurd in my writing. But while I hit the keys of my word processor, I find the point where I can come to terms with the meanings of the words and use expressions that are understandable to the common reader without killing or sacrificing this "alternate reality." I reflectively find the limit at which I can destroy the familiar and yet still create something my readers can relate to. As for *Time Warp Complex,* the main character just happened to turn out as seeming sane and balanced, but some of my other works end in a complete chaos for the main characters.

LM: I noticed that in *Time Warp Complex* there are references to *The Wizard of Oz* and several other children's stories. Were there any children's writers—or any other authors, for that matter—that you have been particularly influenced by? And when you were starting out as a writer, were there any woman writers that you could look to as a kind of model?

YS: I have always admired the works of Mari Mori, the daughter of Oogai Mori, a famous writer of the early 1900s, who introduced many things from German culture into Japan. She is one of the first writers who picked up *"yaoi,"* the Japanese equivalent of the K/S fiction as a literary theme. But I don't think I was "influenced" by her, although I liked her works, and while reading them, I did learn how to write sentences which go back and forth between illusion and reality. Maybe the way I punctuate sentences or my style and rhythm has a little something to do with my reading her. I also like Mishima's early works, especially *Confession of the Mask*. As for children's stories, I was very attracted by the retold stories for children such as *Kojiki* and *Ugetsu-Monogatari,* a Gothic story published in 1776.

Transcribed by Reiko Tochigi; translated by Hisayo Ogushi

The complete interview with Yoriko Shono can be accessed at www.centerforbookculture.org.

Time Warp Complex

Yoriko Shono

All of this happened last summer. I was upset about a dream of being in love with a tuna when I got a call from either the tuna himself or Super Jetter, boy wonder of the comic books I read as a girl. I wasn't sure which, but the caller kept saying, "There's somewhere you have to go," and I ended up having to go to a station called Umishibaura.

Umishibaura is the last station on the Japan Railways Tsurumi Line. It has one long platform that runs right out over the sea at one end. At the other end there's an exit of sorts, a staff-only entrance to a Toshiba factory, but it's strictly "no entry allowed" to anyone but Toshiba employees. At one end the sea, at the other the Toshiba factory, so to leave the platform you have two options: jump into the sea, or show your Toshiba staff ID. If you happen to get off at that station, and you're neither fish, sea snake, nor Toshiba employee, but rather just a person, you have no choice but to stay put on the platform until the next train comes along.

This was where I had to go.

I still wasn't sure who my caller was. I'd been fast asleep when the phone rang, and at first I thought the call itself might be a dream. After I said hello, there were a few seconds of silence. I decided it had to be X. I thought, I'm having a dream about a phone call from X.

"Well, it's me. Yes?" I said. This "yes" was my signal to hurry things along. It meant "I know exactly where we stand here, and I'm not planning to offer any small talk, so get to the point." Such unadorned greetings are the best I can manage when I'm half-asleep. But my caller was unfazed, and his response was all business.

"Have you given that . . . matter . . . some thought?"

"Well, let me see . . ." I replied provisionally. I hadn't, of course. I don't mean that I hadn't thought about the matter. I mean that there was no matter in the first place. In any case, even if it was just a dream, I was still in love with the tuna.

"Anyhow, you'll need to go somewhere for me. Anywhere you like is fine."

" I see. Yes. Yes, well . . ." was all I could say. Telling me I had to go somewhere didn't explain what this was about. And even if I was being told I could go anywhere I liked, there was nowhere I felt like going. What's more, being in love with the tuna made me feel like not wanting to go anywhere.

But if I did have to go somewhere, I wanted it to be where the tuna was. The Kasai Seaside Aquarium might seem like a good choice, but what they have there are actual, live tunas, and that's not exactly what I had in mind. With or without real tunas, the place I wanted to go had to be really *tuna-ish,* though if someone were to ask me what I meant by tuna-ish, it would be tough to answer. I was just obsessed with the idea of being in love with the tuna.

No, *obsessed* is the wrong way to put it. But it's true that I wanted to hang on to that intoxicated, addicted, floating-on-air feeling. And waking up was taking the edge off it, leaving me in a muddle. I couldn't get beyond saying that I was obsessed with the idea of being in love.

The dream sea where my dream tuna lived wasn't the blue color of love. Instead it had the dull gray sheen of greased metal; only the little waves seemed happy. The view beyond the concrete-reinforced hill of withered grass afforded only a glimpse of this sea. I was walking there when I came upon a fishmonger's shop, with a wooden box out front full of fish. I often dream of a fish circus, so I was vaguely thinking, oh, this again—but the circus didn't appear. There was just me, peering into the wooden box.

Along with the fish, there was a row of bottles in the box, each a unique shape. None of the bottles was in the least bit beautiful, but they were intensely transparent. I had a strange desire to have them for myself, so I went into the shop.

The salesman was the tuna. He was different from your average tuna, but nonetheless a living being with a distinctly *tuna* aura. His body as a whole was the body of a fish, but narrow at the neck. His eyes were like an excited cat's eyes, with wide-open pupils—not at all like the eyes of an actual tuna, of course. And his skin, rather than suggesting tuna, had more the silver and hardness of a fresh-caught bonito. The tuna was a little shorter than me, say five feet, with long thin fins sticking out like penguin wings, tips curled slightly like the leaves of an office plant. An inverted triangle of face was stuck on his front, like the face of a person.

This face was inclined to the left, looking my way. I felt a bit uncomfortable. My cat eats tins of tuna every day. I was starting to think that maybe this wasn't a tuna but a merman. Or perhaps I should say that I took refuge in that idea.

Maybe this creature had evolved from some natural species of tuna.

Just as this thought occurred to me, the two of us hit the same wavelength. The tuna looked at me and nodded. Tuna as lover. Although it could never go any further than that exchange of looks, we reached that peak together then. A touch-me-and-I'll-explode love-tuna; that's what he was. Nothing else happened after that. Love was simply there.

"You've got to go there for me. It *is* the twenty-first century, after all."

Well, so what if it was? . . . wait a minute. Are we already into the twenty-first century?

"Uh, I see. Yes, I'm listening." I always try to keep my mouth well clear of my mind, the better to lie at a moment's notice. One sounds much smarter that way.

"Well, I've thought about this . . . matter from various points of view," I continue. "A very wide variety indeed. It's just that . . ."

"Yes?"

This guy too could manage a pretty well loaded "yes." This "yes" meant, "Don't even start with 'I've thought about this . . .' If you'd thought about it, you'd come out and say what you thought."

But if you keep your mouth free from your mind, you can handle this sort of situation well enough. As long as you maintain some semblance of logic, you can come up with a flow of words that is completely equivocal.

"It's just that, well, there's the question of how I get to wherever it is I'm going, and what I do there. And how much do I pay to get there? Who will I go with? And what for?"

I was impressed at how reasonable I was being. But my caller was apparently no fan of reason.

"Oh, come now. Instead of saying all this, you could already be on your way. Won't you just go?"

Maybe it was because I'd woken all the way up now, but this business of just answering ad hoc, with no idea of the subject under discussion, was getting to be a strain. On the other hand, it occurred to me that it wasn't *that* much of a strain. And who was this guy? From the phone, the gray sea where my tuna might live began to hiss gently, like a breeze.

What if my caller is the tuna? I thought suddenly. But instead of letting my heart go thumping away wildly, I thought instead, you're obsessed. While I was distracted with the gray of the dream sea, the caller turned the conversation in a new direction.

"What I think, Ms. Sawano, is that rather than somewhere run-of-the-mill, what we need in your case is somewhere, oh, utterly bizarre. And I'd like you to take some snapshots there."

"Ms. Sawano," he'd said. So this call was indeed intended specifically for me. Here I'd begun thinking it must be a wrong number, not taking it seriously at all. Plus the guy throws in this business about photographs. Since when do I handle photography jobs? Probably best, though, just to keep the conversation going for now.

" 'In my case,' you say?"

This sort of conversational prompt is usually fine as long as it seems sort of meaningful. The caller, at any rate, sounded happy.

"Yes, that's right. Yes, indeed."

But then things went wrong.

"Yes," he said, "in as much as you never do anything normal, you're not remotely fashionable, and you're always getting involved in strange situations. You get into the silliest trouble with some honest soul, for example, then make yourself a victim and cause a fuss. You know nothing of the world, and you're particularly weak on politics and economics. So I want you to exploit these rather complete deficiencies of yours and get out there for me. Absolutely anywhere is fine. All I'm trying to say is, well, it is the Heisei era after all."

What does the current emperor's reign have to do with anything? I thought. And my caller hasn't left much out here, has he? Yet I'd let him go on as if it didn't matter one way or the other. If I didn't want to go, I could always just turn him down. I wasn't too stung by any of this anyway, though a lot of it was on the mark: an oddity, an amateur, removed from the culture—that's me. But then I thought, a camera *produces* culture. Even snapshots require at the very least good sense and good luck.

Still in the dark, I tried out an insecure-sounding voice in the hope of drawing the guy out. Or perhaps my taking an odd, sulky tone, rather than lashing out at him, was due to lingering drowsiness.

"Oh, photographs. Well, as long as you don't mind a disposable camera, then I suppose I have one of those, but . . ."

The moment I'd spoken, my mind—agile for still being half-asleep—cut to a memory of a camera.

I'd taken a picture of a weasel, nine years earlier. I took the picture through a glass door, and this caused something called halation. The image of the weasel and the Japanese-style garden in the background came out cracked and cloudy, while in the center of the photo there was a corona of light radiating from the weasel's back. Sort of a Weasel of God effect. Actually, I would have opened the door to take the picture, but that would have scared the weasel away. This was the extent of my photography career. I went ahead and told the caller about this to put him off, but he wasn't disappointed in the least. If anything he seemed impressed.

"I see. So you don't have a camera. Very, very interesting indeed."

I began to think this might be a crank call.

"You find that interesting, do you?"

I was hoping to put him off balance, to find some hint of unease behind this guy's "interest," but then things took another unexpected turn.

"I'll tell you what," he said. "If you go to Shinjuku or somewhere, they'll sell you a camera for around 50,000 yen."

That was definitely *not* interesting. I was flustered, but tried to sound indifferent.

"I do *not* need a camera at present, thank you."

So that was what this was about. He was a camera salesman. Though I wasn't sure that particular job still existed.

"Won't you buy a camera?"

Not a camera salesman, then, but a camera subscription salesman. They would come around with some free film or eggs and do their pitch for the camera. Turn them down and they'd throw in a serving mold for chicken pilaf. But then you'd get the morning and evening cameras piling up on your doorstep.

Come to think of it, didn't I hear an interview the other day where someone was saying, why not buy a fax machine, they're selling them for 50,000 yen or so in Shinjuku? Were these electrical appliances all one price, 50,000 yen?

But 50,000 yen is enough to affect my financial peace of mind for six whole months. And while I definitely could see a use for a fax machine, I couldn't imagine needing a camera more than nine times in my entire life. Aside from that, why were people so cavalier about electrical appliances? I remembered how the color TV that my parents bought around the time they started broadcasting the Hyokkori Hyotan-jima puppet show seemed so important, and how cameras and suits were major assets parceled out to relatives after people died.

I found myself wallowing in memories of the distant past. This was getting dangerous.

"Well then," he was saying. "Let's be on our way, shall we? In any event, think of some strange, strange place . . ."

"Ah yes. Somewhere incredibly strange. Let me see . . ."

I thought of places I could get to for less than 200 yen one way. I wasn't inclined to spend a lot; the caller had made me feel stingy. In recent months the amount of money in my apartment had been minuscule, and my bankbook made it clear that my savings were also minuscule. My daily life was such that I'd smile at the sudden recollection of a 500-yen coin that I knew was tucked away in an old bag. OK, then, the fare had to be no more than 200 yen.

I'd go somewhere where no tickets were needed.

A place that costs nothing, a place that costs nothing . . . my mind conducted a search on its own, and up floated an interesting idea that wouldn't require any train fare at all. My voice took on an exceptionally clear tone—a smoothness that suggested I'd had this in mind all along.

"Perhaps I'll go see an election. A photo of a polling station, maybe, or I can snap a shot of that Diet member who walks by on the street under my window."

When had that been? As I recalled, a Diet member did walk by under my window regularly at one point. Navy-blue suit, bent forward, trudging wearily. One time, he stopped in front of a boutique and turned to the window, still bent at the waist. He raised his arm demurely, like a woman putting on a coat over a kimono. Then, facing the shop window, he waved his hand and bowed. I wished I'd taken a photo of that. But why should I have to go outside?

I live in a one-room apartment on the third floor. My window looks out over a shopping district, with a view of everything from parades of Awa-odori dancers to election speeches, to patrol-car arrests, drunken brawls, and lovers' tiffs between heavy-metal types in the early hours. When I don't feel like going out, I just pretend that I'm looking out at the whole world from up there.

Now some kind person might say, "but you can't actually see other countries from up there now, can you?" just by way of giving me a chance to explain that in fact foreigners constantly pass under this window after dark, even though you hear that their numbers have dwindled since the recession set in. Dhaka and Dub and Hong Kong—just like the words in the song . . . *workers of every nation.* Now that I think of it, didn't I hear something recently about chocolate from Zimbabwe being sold for Valentine's Day? Or was it from Kenya?

That reminds me of the time a Kenyan named Ali came over from the hospital in Urawa where he worked to visit a friend who was a janitor in the hospital across the street from my place. Ali's friend wasn't there, so he wasn't able to ask the friend to lend him the train fare to get home. If he'd gone to the local police station for help, they would have arrested him as an illegal alien since he hadn't brought his passport. So instead, he made his way up to my place and asked to borrow 700 yen.

At that time I'd just moved to Toritsu Kasei, and simply hearing that Ali was from Kenya . . . it wasn't so much pity because it was cold outside; it was more that I couldn't conjure up the remotest physical sense of the distances involved when I heard the word *Kenya,* and this made me feel sad. Anyway, I ended up lending him the 700 yen. It's been more than a year, and he still hasn't paid me back. I wonder what happened.

"An election, huh? No, even better than that—because we're in a recession after all, and 'recession' puts one in mind of the former Showa imperial reign, wouldn't you say?—there's this station called Umishibaura. Why don't you go there?"

"What was that name again?"

"Umishibaura. U-mi-shi-ba-u-ra."

I must not quite have made it from the Showa era to the Heisei. That was one tough name to catch . . .

"Um, I'm sorry, but . . . what was that again? Umishinagawa? Umashiroura? What was it? Something '-shimaura?' "

"What I said was, U-MI-SHI-BA-U-RA."

"Ohhh . . . Ki-mi-shi-ma-na-ra. Kimishima-Nara, is it? In the mountains, right?"

I was sure I'd heard of a place called Kimishima near Nara, so I put the two together immediately. That's because I'm from Ise, and most of the places around there seem to have that sort of double-barreled name, like Ise-Matsuzaka or Ise-Kawasaki—except for Ise itself, of course. So I just assumed that some person born in Nara and living in Kimishima had fond childhood memories and started calling the place . . .

"What? In the mountains? No! Listen, what I'm saying is *umi,* as in 'sea.' U, MI, SHI, BA, U, RA."

"Oh! Umi as in 'sea,' shiba as in 'grass,' ura as in 'shore.' "

"Well, of course. You've heard of it?"

"No. Never."

This was how I came to know the station's name. Umi and shiba and ura. U-*way*-mi-*way*-shi-*way*-ba-*way*-u-*way*-ra-*way*, as kids playing with the sound of the word would say nowadays. We'd have said u-*yay*-mi-*yay*-shi-*yay*-ba-*yay*-u-*yay*-ra-*yay* . . . but things have gotten stranger.

My sleepy-agile mind leapt into overdrive, bringing forth a completely unsolicited image to match this name, a sea as artificial as a backdrop, like a piece of glittery cloth. You couldn't see any islands, but there were several large patches of grass on the shore. A ghostly hand popped up from within my mind to pluck a single blade of this grass. But the blade seemed to be connected to the rest of the grass by a thread which the hand was rapidly winding in, like the stitching of a piece of fabric, and the sea unraveled together with the grass and everything got tugged up. Then from out of nowhere, riding on a stuffed, decorative, endangered sea turtle, came a crumbling mummy dressed in bright, kabuki-colors. It was Urashima Taro in a grass skirt, the boy from the folk tale who returned from beneath the sea to find everything changed. He swished on his turtle through the white space which the tugged-up sea had exposed, and when he disappeared, there finally emerged a realistic seacoast worthy of the word *shore.*

It was pretty similar to the sea where I'd met the tuna.

This wasn't obsession, just obstinacy. But . . . I loved him. My love-tuna.

"So as I was saying, let's get going to that station. At one end of the platform is the sea, after all."

Aha! So that's where Urashima Taro was swishing off to. The gray sea where the tuna lived grew vivid again. But it soon faded away, and though it was summer a shiver ran down one side of my body, leaving me with goose bumps.

"The Urashima Taro legend . . . and the platform . . . ?" I asked.

"What? What kind of stupid nonsense are you getting at? The other end of the platform is a Toshiba factory!"

Then, all of a sudden, I heard a voice that unleashed a wave of nostalgia.

". . . Do come . . ."

Were the phone lines crossed? That wasn't just nostalgia; it was a voice I'd never heard before. The tuna. He was calling me. But those words, ". . . do come . . . ," did he mean come to Umishibaura? I had no idea. Flustered, I addressed the tuna directly:

"What did you just say? Where are you?"

I spoke in a serious, in-love sort of voice, but I could tell that my delivery stank. And my caller hadn't heard the tuna on the crossed line.

"As I was saying, the sea breeze blows along the platform, like in a dream."

The Umishibaura in my head now took on the appearance of a seaside resort. There was a glass-encased showroom and a perfect Japanese garden on the grounds of the Toshiba factory. A sign on the platform said "Welcome to Umishibaura," and out at sea, tour boats plied their trade. On the first floor of the factory there was a restaurant looking out over the water, with nothing to interfere with the view but the train platform. In the foreground, of course, there was an old man in a cheap jacket passing out leaflets about gathering natural gems, and a loud young man in a livery jacket held up a banner for a local inn. Just like the Nagasaki I'd visited on a school trip.

I reminded myself that even if the station was only there because of the factory, we were talking about a station by the sea, and there must at least be a café. Even so, I didn't want to go to Umishibaura.

"Do you think they sell postcards on the platform?"

"No, that's not what it's like," he said. "It's more like *Blade Runner.*"

"Are they making replicants at the Toshiba factory?"

"No! No, no, no, no, no!"

A very firm denial. I began to think my caller might be a replicant himself.

"What I mean," he said, "is that that railway line is a vestige of economic expansion."

My head reeled. Here was an idea that I found even less comprehensible than foreign languages. I know *nothing* about economic expansion. Between the struggle to write fantasy dream fiction and to bring in enough for the household necessities, I could trace economic history back no farther than the strong yen and the consumption tax.

In other words, I remembered only the part of it that had affected me personally. When the yen strengthened, imported meat and American cherries became cheaper, then Japanese beef and cherries followed along. Up to then I'd been eating ham and cabbage curry toward the end of each month, but with the strong yen I was able to manage broccoli and beef-shank curry. Then they introduced the consumption tax and, in a virtuoso performance, sucked up what slight leeway the exchange gains had allowed me.

It wasn't just that the price of beef returned to its original level, but that *all* of the curry options became exorbitant, and I had to search for other areas to make up for the monthly shortfall. It wasn't a matter of giving up any one thing in particular, but one way or another things got tighter. I went to concerts less often. I gave up buying even a single high-quality notebook. Come to think of it, I stopped buying flowers for the apartment around then.

All of this was during the days of the so-called economic bubble, but I'd just made the transition from living off an allowance to living by the pen, so the craze for trips abroad, designer goods, and city-hotel-getaways more or less passed me by. The strong yen did bring a stream of my favorite jazz musicians to Japan, and by stretching things I was able to hear Steve Gadd and Jacques Dijonnet at small clubs. The ticket prices had skyrocketed though, and even with all of the advertisements, the programs still cost 2,000 yen each.

Then the bubble economy pushed up rents, and I was thrown out of my apartment. The only affordable places were exclusively for students or for companies providing housing for their single employees. While I was looking for a place, those "Corporate Contracts Only" signs were my enemy. I searched on and on for a new place to live, growing ever more exhausted.

Which reminds me that the good times are over now. Now we're in a recession.

I moved into this apartment just before the bubble burst; by summer, the rent had dropped a full 6,000 yen. The very day the rent went down, a muddy and emaciated silver tomcat took to hanging around outside the door of my apartment. He stayed for the next three months. Boy was that cat big! He ate a ten-ounce tin of the cheapest beef cat food in one sitting, and the cost of feeding him came to exactly 6,000 yen per month. One day he simply vanished—I suppose he decided to go home when the mating season ended. But for that three-month period, every time I saw the cat I felt there was some strange law in effect which held that the amount of money available to me must remain constant, no matter what.

But what has economics got to do with it? Is my caller an economic authority, or is he someone who's read a book that some authority wrote and sold for 680 yen?

"In the seventies there was the oil crisis, you see, and after that the area gradually went into decline. It remained depressed throughout the bubble economy years, and what with the outlying dormitory towns all being in recession, there you have it: a vestige of the earlier economic expansion. The scenery's rather interesting—near-futuristic . . . a real *Blade Runner* type of place. And you're to go and see this aftermath of the industrial dream, this scene of what's left after everything is over."

"Scene of what's left . . ."

"As I've been saying, Umishibaura."

For some reason, this pushed me right past the end of my rope. Words started to well up.

"Oh really? As you've been saying? As you've been saying!? Now look, I don't mind a visit to the sea, but one end of the platform *being* the sea—that's outright scary. Half of your body might as well be sucked *into* the sea. A place like that . . . how can you keep your balance?"

I imagined the train to Umishibaura disintegrating, held together by threads. Half of the passengers were oozing out through the windows like fermented breakfast soybeans on sticky strands, crying *aaaaaaaaagh,* eyeballs glued to the sea they were returning to. Their heads changed into creatures from an ancient ocean . . . nautilus shells . . . trilobites . . .

In the middle of all this fear and anxiety, my caller burst out laughing, *woah-ho-ho-ho-ho-hohhhh!* He sounded like a nautilus himself.

"Hooh! Anyone would feel the same, I'm sure. Hee-hee-hee. Half your body carried away by the sea . . . If you find the sea frightening, the Hanayashiki amusement park in Asakusa should be fun for you. After Hanayashiki, why not go to the races and have a bite of horse meat?"

He certainly seemed to be enjoying my comments. Well, then why not give him something even stupider?

"No, horse meat is definitely out. Basically, I see horses and ducks as my friends. I know it's kind of a contradiction, but I don't eat those guys."

"Pardon me?"

"I do not eat horses and ducks. Or sparrows. It's not that I think of sparrows as my friends. I just don't eat sparrows. If it's something to eat that I'm looking for, then I prefer an all-you-can-eat cake buffet, I suppose."

That didn't get through at all.

"What's this you're saying?" he said. "You keep horses and ducks? And sparrows? Hmm, yes. I see. Well, this station really *is* interesting. By the way, where is this all-you-can-eat cake buffet you mentioned? It sounds disgusting."

I no longer had the slightest idea of how to communicate with this caller. Despairing, I floundered about with the only word left in my head, *photograph*.

"Hmm, yes. Now that I think of it, there's a supermarket right near my place. I'll take a photograph of that. I saw an American couple taking photos there, so it must be okay."

"That sort of thing is not in the least bit bizarre."

"Yes it is!"

I'd shouted reflexively, getting all worked up about this for some reason. It occurred to me that this was just the way I lose my temper in dreams. Nonetheless, I couldn't stop myself. I became oddly childish.

"If it was a supermarket in Hawaii, you'd certainly think *that* was unusual! Great big cartons of Gatorade. Ice cream in buckets. Chocolate . . . I once had some American chocolate . . . my father . . . I thought it was American, at least . . . I always thought it was American . . ."

Now I was crying. What was this all about? I thought, and suddenly I understood: chocolate! My mind grew instantly clear. What I still didn't understand, though, was why chocolate? And what had cleared my mind? Somehow—through dream or the unconscious or hallucination, I don't know which—a body-warm association, like a weaving of nerves, had formed between Umishibaura, the tuna, and the chocolate. It was making me laugh and cry at once. The caller, of course, didn't pick up on any of this. Only the first words I'd said even registered with him.

"You've been to Hawaii, have you?" he said.

Why was it that only a sea-related topic would have gotten

through to him? I decided to play along with the caller for now, but that took us even further off-track.

"No, I haven't. I've never been anywhere but school trips. Kyoto, Nara. Then there was the trip to Tokyo for my university entrance exams. I'd love to go to Hawaii, though."

For some reason, the caller didn't take any of this in.

"Oh yes, how very nice," he replied with great happiness. "Yes, do go to Iran. At your own expense. Or perhaps some place in the mountains where you can find a suspension bridge. In that case, somewhere in Japan would be fine. Yes, I can just see you doing that, Ms. Sawano."

I should never have bothered to play along with this stupid guy. My voice dropped to a whisper, but finally I managed to assert myself.

"No. No, what you're suggesting is definitely out. What I'm looking for is somewhere that's less trouble and more fun. Some place where you can enjoy a meal, then come home. Besides, if you go to a hotel in Iran, they're sure to ask about your political identity."

"What's that supposed to mean?" My caller sounded angry.

Reflexively, I hurried to appease him.

"Anyhow, I'll go. I'll go. Somewhere. Okay?"

I remembered reading in a psychology text that appeasement always brings dire consequences, but I was too sleepy to suppress the instinct. Anyway, the caller seemed to appreciate that I was trying. He backed down too, offering a relatively hassle-free option.

"By all means, go somewhere. Go and see *Jurassic Park* or something."

"I'd love to know if those dinosaurs are real."

The conversation was heading toward a conclusion. In my mind's eye I saw a mathematical formula about limiting values which I'd studied at school. I could see every symbol clearly, right down to the tiniest character. The caller's voice was growing kinder and kinder.

"Ah, yes. But now that it has come down to really going . . . I'm sure you'd like to see the sea, wouldn't you? The sea is real."

Then that voice again.

". . . Do come . . ."

A great sadness washed through me. I responded without thinking.

"In that case, I'll go to the sea."

"And that station?"

"Yes, I'll go to that station," I said, and hung up.

This had gone beyond the limiting value equation to the limit itself. I'd just been trying to placate this guy, then before I knew it I was going to Umishibaura. Or perhaps that way of looking at it was itself part of some solo performance I was putting on.

Three minutes later the phone rang again. That same initial

silence, even though he was calling right back.

"Hawaii is one thing, but would you go to Okinawa Hall?"

"You want me to go to the shore in Okinawa? But it's the hot season down there now."

"I said Okinawa Hall. The temperature is constant. You've heard of Tsurumi Station?"

"No, I haven't."

"It's on the way to . . . your destination. So once you find it, get busy. In the underground mall at Nakano Broadway, they're selling tuna eyes for 600 yen a pair. Be sure to look for the most near-futuristic-looking station. Get off there and cut across Irifune Park. Walk under the overpass, and you'll find Okinawa Hall."

"Is the airport in Okinawa near the shore?"

"What? Look, we're not talking about Narita. This is over by the harbor."

It seemed I'd been told to get on a train and go to Okinawa. Some seabed-bound train leaving from the platform for Okinawa. Just great. Okinawa! Hawaii or Okinawa. As words do in childhood, Okinawa suddenly reverted for me to its constituent sounds, o-ki-na-wa. O-ki-na-wa-re-ver-sion. My mind swam with underlined text and photographs from school textbooks on Japanese history. The reverted Okinawa led to the Reversion of Okinawa, and the common theme linking Hawaii to Okinawa shifted from pleasure travel to politics.

"Um, about the relationship between Umishibaura and Okinawa and Hawaii, well . . . uh . . ."

As I was formulating my question, the line went dead.

I was in a real fix. I didn't want to go anywhere. I had no use for the real sea; the dream sea was the only one that I wanted to see.

But then there was that mention of tuna eyes, and that ". . . do come . . ." I wanted to meet that tuna again and find out exactly what was going on in my heart.

Well, if that's what I wanted, then—horrid thought—I'd have to go.

In the end I didn't know if the telephone call was a dream or if it was real. But I had to get to that strange station. Crossed phone lines or whatever, I had heard the voice of the tuna. The next day I set off for Umishibaura.

Translated by Adam Fulford, with assistance from Takahashi Yuriko and Ito Nobuji; stylized by Michael Keezing

Why Not Have Fun? — An Interview with Gen'ichiro Takahashi

Larry McCaffery, Sinda Gregory, and Yoshiaki Koshikawa

Gen'ichiro Takahashi was born in 1951. A radical student activist, he dropped out of Yokohama National University in 1969 and worked as a manual laborer throughout the 1970s. In 1982 he won the Gunzo Literary Award for First Novels for his *Sayonara Gyangu Tachi* (Good-bye Gangsters). His strong interest in American postmodern fiction was apparent in his novel, *Niji No Kanata Ni* (Over the Rainbow, 1984), which was acclaimed as one of the first Japanese metafictional works and was also notable for its typographical innovations. His *Jon Renon Tai Kasai Jin* (John Lennon vs. the Martians) was a metafictional manual on pornographic writings, and his *Yuga de Kansho-teki na Nippon-Yakyuu* (Japanese Baseball: Elegant and Sentimental), which bears comparison with Robert Coover's *The Universal Baseball Association,* won the Yukio Mishima Award in 1988. Takahashi's other works include *Penguin Mura Ni Hi Wa Ochite* (Sunset in Penguin Village, 1989), *Wakusei P-13 no Himitsu* (The Secret of Planet 13, 1990), and *Goosutobasutaazu* (Ghostbusters, 1997). Takahashi has also published numerous essays on literary themes, as well as on horse racing. (Hisayo Ogushi)

Sinda Gregory: What is the role of a writer like you in Japan?

Gen'ichiro Takahashi: First of all, in Japan nearly all critics tend to be severely critical about modern writers and postmodern writers as well. It has been so for more than a hundred years, since modernism was first attacked as an imported trend and not having any roots in Japan. So how can you avoid their harsh attacks? The best way is to become a critic yourself! At least that is what I do. In fact, I've somehow managed to create this sort of camouflage for myself too effectively! As a result, nowadays I am usually considered more of a critic than a fiction writer. However, in my case, I don't limit myself only to literature. I also write about mangas, cinema, fashion, etc., and in this way, I am attempting to expand the definitions of "literature," just as Roland Barthes has done.

SG: Do critics have power over writers in Japan?

GT: Until about twenty years ago, there was collaboration between good writers and good critics. After that, there was a lack of good critics—that is, critics who read new works and who were aware of what was happening in other countries as well as Japan. Nowadays, the fiction writers are apt to know more than the critics. This imbalance has made it so difficult to build a positive writer-critic relationship which our predecessors used to enjoy.

SG: Do you have a particular theoretical position that you are coming from as a critic? Or do you write criticism that mostly reflects your own individual interests as a fiction writer?

GT: Probably both. But I try not to mix them up. As I have already mentioned, when I am writing as a critic, I try to expand the definition of "literature," and the style becomes that of a critic. On the other hand, when I write from the interest of a writer, my criticism comes quite near to fiction. I take one stance or the other according to the context that I am put in.

Larry McCaffery: Then, what about your theoretical position? Is it singular? Do you consider yourself as a Marxist critic or a deconstructionist critic or whatever?

GT: No. It's far from singular. Marxist theory, deconstruction, poststructuralism—of course, I am interested in them and have read them. Their weapons are useful, but they lack the sensibility which, I think, is quite necessary to a good critic. For my defining "literature," these kinds of theory are not valid. To me, this sensibility is my greatest weapon, and I try to refine it as precisely as I can. Remember, Paul Valéry had no theory, but had other strong weapons—his intelligence and knowledge of literature.

LM: I understand that, rightly or wrongly, your writing has mostly been called metafictional. Do you agree with that—and if so, where did you get your interest in metafiction? Was there a tradition of that in Japan or was that something coming from outside?

GT: Metafiction is something that mostly comes from outside Japanese literary traditions. And it's true that my novels are rather cut off from the traditional Japanese novel lineage. (By the way, right now I am talking as a critic.) Of course, writers are influenced by many things, but objectively speaking, I consider my creative roots as being modern Japanese poetry rather than novels. In Japan the world of poetry is composed of a system totally different from, or independent of, that of the novel. There's simply almost no interrelationship between Japanese poetry and novels, which is quite different from the literary scene of America or Europe, where many fiction writers have been influenced by poetry and even written poetry (I'm thinking of everyone from Poe up through James Joyce, Faulkner, and Raymond Carver). This might be oversimplifying, but in Japan, the mainstream novel is dominated by realism, being premodern, whereas the world of poetry is high modern. And as I have just said, poetry and fiction are cut off and are not interested in each other. But in my own case, I have been a reader of this high-modern Japanese poetry for many years. For example, I have read the works of poets such as Ryuichi Tamura, Gan Tanigawa, Shuntaro Tanigawa, Gozo Yoshimatsu. They are all pursuing the style of language and are really self-conscious about what they are trying to do. This trend cannot be seen in the mainstream novels of Japan, and that is why I must say that I am very dissatisfied with them. So, to answer your question, I guess my model has been Japanese high-modern poetry and also the metafictional novels from overseas.

SG: What type of writers are you talking about?

GT: There are many of them. For example, Faulkner, Pynchon, and Calvino. My favorite is Calvino. I bought Calvino's last essays in criticism, *Six Memos for the Next Millennium,* in New York, read it in my hotel, and wept. That was in Algonquin Hotel, and there was a small lithograph that happened to be the same one used for the cover of Calvino's book.

LM: In the late seventies, when you were beginning to write, was there a movement of what you might call postmodernism, in the way there was in the United States in the sixties?

GT: No, there wasn't—at least not in the novels. But there was in the field of poetry, comics, music, television programs, and also copy writing. In other words, the novel was left behind.

LM: Why was that?

GT: Even among the critics, this is considered a big mystery. It might have something to do with the incestuous publishing system in Japan, where you have the "great masters" from the pre-WWII era and all of these old-fashioned critics who swarm around them. They have lived long, and they continue to have power. The characteristic of these people is that they ignore what is going on outside, and they think that attitude is aesthetic. For example, Hideo Kobayashi, who was one of the most famous critics, came to consider even war as destiny—in other words, a natural phenomenon. What he did was completely exclude the "meaning" of a social context. This attitude was considered as aesthetic and was fondly accepted by the Japanese. Now the procedure through which one goes in order to become a novelist in Japan is unique; I am sure there is nothing like this in America or in any other country. In Japan there are five or six high-literature magazines which give out awards for newcomers. These awards are the one and only gateway that leads to the writing profession.

LM: Sinda and I both noticed in going through the fiction selections included in *Monkey Brain Sushi* that at the end of every single story there always seemed to be a reference to awards. It seems that there are so many of them—many more in Japan than we have in America. We even speculated that these awards might actually have the effect of controlling things rather than merely of rewarding the good works that do appear.

GT: And that's exactly the case. The awards function as a kind of permission, just like a governmental permission given out from an office.

LM: Everything I've heard about your new book, *Ghostbusters,* makes it sound like it's a perfect example of avant-pop. I understand that the main characters in this book are the famous Japanese haiku master, Basho, Butch Cassidy, and the Sundance Kid. What gave you the idea to write a book with that combination?

GT: It was originally going to be a "road story" about a traveler trying to go across the continent of the United States from east to west. It didn't need to be the U.S.—actually it could have been set anywhere, but I knew I wanted to write an adventure novel in that form. There are many people who have gone on the sort of adventures I had in mind, but I chose Butch Cassidy and Sundance because I loved the movie, *Butch Cassidy and the Sundance Kid.* I had in mind making an adventure story which moves horizontally, from west to east (or east to west), but I also wanted another story that would cross or intersect this horizontal movement at right angles, from north to south. I decided to use Basho, the Japanese haiku writer who, as you know, wrote about his travels from south to north and north to south. Of course, historically speaking, the two adventures took place in two different countries, but since I was telling their stories in literature, I thought, why not have their stories intersect so I could put them together?

LM: This east-west trajectory has all sorts of historical and mythic resonances in America—you can see this in everything from the early Fenimore Cooper novels up through *Huck Finn, The Great Gatsby,* and *The Crying of Lot 49*—whereas in Japan these are associated with the north/south movement.

GT: A good point. For details, just read my book! But I should add that the origin of my own novel has more to do with *Don Quixote*—the very first novel—than with those American works.

LM: Not the *Tales of Genji*?

GT: No! Cervantes sent Don Quixote off on an expedition in the first novel. I've always wanted to write a road novel just like that of Don Quixote's.

SG: But how is this adventure related to the other two storylines?

GT: The version of *Ghostbusters* which has already been published in a Japanese magazine is incomplete. I'm a little reluctant to give away too much, but I will reveal that even though Shikibu Murasaki, the author of the *Tales of Genji,* does not appear in my novel, there will be a poet who was about 100 years older than her. And Don Quixote himself is also going to be making a guest appearance in the novel.

Yoshiaki Koshikawa: When I read that version of *Ghostbusters,* I realized that the movement was not only geographical but also temporal—they are time travelers as well.

LM: So it's four dimensional. But why isn't the author of the *Tales of Genji* going to appear? And why do you think that *Don Quixote* is the first novel rather than *Tales of Genji*—which appeared several hundred years earlier.

GT: Novels and stories are two different things. *Tales of Genji* is a story whereas *Don Quixote* is a novel. And quite frankly speaking, I like *Don Quixote* much better than *Tales of Genji* because it has a sense of humor. *Tales of Genji* is too precious—and pretentious.

LM: This introduction of Japanese characters and narrative archetypes into Western ones—or allowing different characters and stories to intermingle and collaborate with each other—seems to be part of the postmodernism of Japan. *Ghostbusters* obviously is doing this. This seems to me to be the obvious approach for Japanese postmodern artists—not imitating American materials but combining them with Japanese elements. Why isn't there more of that happening?

GT: I'll answer you as a critic. When Japan underwent the Meiji Restoration in 1868, the Japanese literary tradition, which started off with *Tales of Genji,* was completely diminished. As a result, the Japanese literary works produced after 1868 had no connections with the works of the pre-Meiji Restoration. For example, a whole new style started to emerge that was very different from the formal "literary style" you find in all the pre-Meiji Restoration works.

YK: What was happening is a little bit like what you find in America in the late nineteenth century with the colloquialisms of Mark Twain and even Whitman. That was, in terms of style, a cutoff from the former literary tradition strongly influenced by British literature.

GT: That's right. Anyhow, with the former tradition extinguished, the Japanese writers were essentially restarting from zero when they began basing their works on colloquialism, and it took them about twenty years to build up a new tradition of literature. This kind of basic overhaul was naturally a huge cultural trauma whose effects are still being felt on our writers even now.

LM: One of the things Mr. Shimada was saying when I interviewed him was that you're seeing more recent Japanese writers becoming more conscious of their lost tradition—and are beginning to intentionally express their need to recuperate it.

GT: Yes. You can see this, for example, in the ways that writers are bringing back or reviving the old usage of words and expressions into their books. On the other hand, there is a tendency to affirm the hundred years of postrestoration literary works as well. But then, writers like Mr. Shimada and I think that we can take both strands, using the traditional and also the modern. Combining is a big aspect of postmodernism, but we've learned that from the particularly Japanese situation rather than from the Western idea.

LM: Let me ask about the title of your new book. Clearly, *Ghostbusters* has to do with the American movie, but could you talk about how the idea of ghosts evolved as you were working on the book?

GT: The title did come from the movie *Ghostbusters,* but the original idea of using a ghost came from a different context. What I am going to tell you is a secret which my editor doesn't even know. Many novels have ghosts in them, but I wanted to create a ghost that was unique, nothing like the ones that had already appeared. It had to be a metaphor of literature itself. So in my story there are no ghosts that actually have forms. But at the end I will reveal what this ghost is. I'll give you a hint (everybody always asks me to give them hints!). As I've said, these ghosts have no particular form—they exist not as a substance but as a certain system of rules.

SG: Do you think literature has any power anymore to change people or to affect politics?

GT: Yes, I do think that literature still has some sort of power—perhaps a power even greater than politics. But there is a difference between the situation of writing in America or Europe and that of Japan. In America or Europe, there were many novels that have had strong political influence over the years, but in Japan, only poetry was able to attain that power. Maybe this is because Japanese readers do not like to read political messages in the form of novels. In our novels, emotion is dominant.

SG: But what if you are an idealistic writer and you want to change things? How do you do it?

GT: Basically speaking, it is not so much the political system as the way of thinking that really matters. I believe that a writer is still able to change the way of thinking. Therefore I think writing a work of fiction is in itself a very political thing to do.

LM: I know you were very active in the student movement in the sixties—perhaps even too active, in a sense, since after one student protest, you wound up having to go to jail. And apparently during that period you suffered autism or aphasia. I've interviewed other writers who had physical problems in speaking or writing—for instance, Samuel Delany, the science-fiction writer, is dyslexic. I'm wondering to what degree having these sorts of problems might wind up making someone particularly aware of language or heighten one's self-consciousness about its functioning. How would you say your own problems might or might not have had effects on your writing?

GT: I'll answer that question from a critic's point of view. It's hard to see myself as a writer objectively, but on the other hand, I suppose I should be the best critic to explain the writer "Gen'ichiro Takahashi." I think that there are three types in the usage of words. One is the very political usage—for example, the way language is used as a vehicle for propaganda. To me, that usage is incorrect. People using language like this are nearly always using words not so much to persuade but to confute, to attack, and, if possible, to beat the disputant. So the users of these words are most often trapped in their own contradictions. That is what I mean by "incorrect," but I have to admit that this type of language was a part of my mental background. The second usage is poetic usage. As I have mentioned before, I have always loved modern Japanese poetry even though it was the exact opposite of the political usage of words. That is, the poetic use of language aims at absolute correctness or precision. Both the political and poetic usage of words are very far from the everyday language, which is the third type—words as we use them ordinarily in our daily lives. Back during my student activist days, I was in jail for about ten months, and when I came back to everyday life, I had trouble using my words. I was sort of torn apart between the two extremes of the political and the poetic usage of language since those were the only words that I had been using before being imprisoned. Then when I suddenly slipped back to the real world, I was at a loss. And so I went through a period when I suffered from aphasia. Before long, I started writing novels in which the words seemed to be very moderate or close to the everyday usage and I began to feel more comfortable again using language. Actually, even though I just said "before long," it actually took me ten years before I was able to find the most comforting, adequate usage of words to express myself.

LM: What was there about the form of the novel that allowed you to feel like you could express yourself—that words in novels somehow seem to function in an ordinary way—the way they do in real life?

GT: Novels have more capacity to be flexible, to exist in some kind of "in-between" status that is neither political and deceptive or absolutely correct. Words used in novels can be correct and incorrect at the same time. I know this sounds pretty contradictory but that's what I think.

LM: I'm not sure if this is directly related to what you're talking about, but there always seems to be an element of playfulness and humor in your works. How do you see the role of playfulness or humor—and how does that relate to the seriousness of your purpose?

GT: The best way to answer that would be to cite Cervantes or Calvino! But in my own case I feel that the writer is at the same time the best reader of his work. So when I write, I write in order to satisfy myself as a reader. And I get that satisfaction by playing with words. Of course, true life as it really is involves suffering. Therefore, at least in novels, why not have fun?

Transcribed and translated by Reiko Tochigi

The complete interview with Gen'ichiro Takahashi can be accessed at www.centerforbookculture.org.

Ghostbusters—An Adventure Story

Gen'ichiro Takahashi

Butch Cassidy and the Sundance Kid set off for the east. The detective from Pinkerton, together with the sheriffs, followed close behind them. A step out of town, there lay the desert.

"So," the Sundance Kid asked Butch Cassidy, "Where are we heading?"

Butch Cassidy took out a folded piece of paper from the back of his pants and spread it out. It was a small crumpled map about 6 x 6 inches with the whole of the United States drawn on it. "This is where we are now," Butch said, pointing at the very left edge of the U.S. with the index finger of his right hand. "And, we are going this way." The finger started to move, heading very slowly toward the right edge. It was a long, long journey.

Sundance stared hard at Butch Cassidy's index finger. The merciless sun glittered on it. Then came the attacks from the rain, wind, and Indians, while the tenacious sheriffs and detective continuously pressed them close. The roads running through the glens would easily crumple and the river water would overflow with no indication at all. Right about the center of the map, the index finger stopped its proceeding. The Sundance Kid strained his eyes to see Butch Cassidy's motionless, uncouth finger. Eventually he realized that the finger had not really stopped but was in confusion, quivering delicately around a certain minute point. "He has fallen in love with a saloon-girl," thought Sundance. Her age was about twenty-four or twenty-five. She had become a bar girl after leaving one of the many prairie wagons that were carrying a full supply of brides-to-be for the men who had settled in the west.

"So, your name is Butch," she murmured.

"Yep, sure is. I'm a man of Belial wandering about the west."

"What's 'a man of Belial?' I can't read so I don't know much."

"Don't you worry 'cause there's no need to read. 'A man of Belial' is something like a vagabond."

"That means you don't have a wife?"

"Well, ma'am, as an answer, do you know this song?"

Footloose and fancy-free, I go wherever I want.
A gun in my right hand, monkey-rum in my left,
And a hurdygurdy-gal on my lap.
Blacks, Whites, Mexicans, you name it.

You wanna fight, then here I am.
But one thing I just can't stand,
That's a wife, to pin me down.

The bar gal was impressed. "You're a poet, Butch."
"Not really."
"Kiss me, Butch. Kiss me hard, so my head spins round and I go dizzy."
But then came the day when the finger and pretty girl had to say good-bye. They loathed to part and made love with burning passion till the crack of dawn in the second-floor room of the saloon. The Sundance Kid, who had nothing to do but drink while waiting for the finger, suffered from a heavy hangover. Hurry up, Butch. There is a limit to things, you know.

His wish was answered, and once again the finger started to move on the crumpled surface of America. More than ever, it was a difficult journey. There were storms and floods, and after much struggle, the finger toiled its way to a town, only to find all the people dead because of an epidemic. Fleeing away from town, they were attacked by a tornado. Then came a buffalo stampede followed by a starving wolf and a coyote which would appear most unexpectedly. The corn was brown and withered because of a long spell of dry weather. The finger gaspingly looked up at the sky. The Sundance Kid looked up, too. A whole cloud of flying locusts covered the blue sky. Sundance screamed to himself. The finger stumbled along the dry and arid wasteland. Not a leaf of grass grew. Drought and famine. They had not seen rain for a long time. Spring came, then summer, and of course autumn, but there was not even a trace of a cloud. It seemed like a long time had passed. The Sundance Kid felt as if he had become old and senile. He couldn't even ride a horse anymore. Going to the ice cream parlor in a wheelchair pushed by a black man was just about as far as he could get. His eyes were gummed up and tears would run down his cheeks without his noticing. He wanted to chew tobacco but there were no teeth to chew with. America was impossibly big, and the Sundance Kid had no idea when they would ever get to "the east."

"Here we are," said Butch Cassidy. The index finger of his right hand had reached the right edge of the U.S. on the map. "This is where we are heading." With that, he put the map back into his pocket.

"You know, Butch," the Sundance Kid said, his eyes becoming watery.
"What?"
"That's a long way to go."
"Yeah, I guess."

Translated by Reiko Tochigi

Keeping Not Writing:
An Interview with Yasutaka Tsutsui

Larry McCaffery, Sinda Gregory, and Takayuki Tatsumi

The Japanese guru of metafiction, Yasutaka Tsutsui is a novelist, playwright, literary critic, actor, and musician. The oldest of four brothers, Tsutsui was born in Osaka, 24 September 1934, and educated from 1953-57 at Doshisha University, Kyoto, where he majored in aesthetics and art. Giving up his boyhood dream of becoming an actor, he started with his brothers *NULL,* an SF fanzine, in 1960. Discovered by Edogawa Rampo, the creator of the modern Japanese detective genre, Tsutsui made his debut as a professional writer with the publication of a short story "O-Tasuke" (Help Me, which had originally appeared in the first issue of *NULL*), in the detective fiction magazine, *Hoseki*. But it was in the field of SF and fantasy that Tsutsui would achieve his earliest acclaim. In 1962 his story "Muki Sekai e" (Toward the Inorganic) obtained an honorable mention in the Hayakawa SF Contest and "Okon Shoten" (The Death of Okon) became his first publication in Hayakawa's prestigious *SF Magazine*.

In the second half of the 1960s and early 1970s, Tsutsui was nominated several times for the Naoki Prize without ever winning. In the 1970s and 1980s his stylistic abilities, ranging from slapstick to fabulism and metafiction, began to attract a wide readership. In the 1980s, Shinchosha published his complete works in twenty-four volumes. A member of the Science Fiction Writers Association of Japan and the Japan PEN Club, Tsutsui has received a number of literary prizes, including: the 1981 Izumi Kyoka award for *Kyojin-Tachi* (Imaginary People); the 1987 Tanizaki Jun'ichiro award for *Yumenokizaka-Bunkiten* (The Yumenokizaka Intersection); the 1989 Kawabata Yasunari award for "Yoppa-dani eno Koka" (A Descent into the Yoppa Valley); and the 1992 Japan SF award for *Asa no Gasuparu* (Gaspard of the Morning). In 1997 he was awarded the rank of *Chevalier des Arts et des Lettres* by the French government for his literary work. (TT)

Sinda Gregory: A lot of your sensibility was influenced by surrealism and yet you have used the structure or form of SF in your works. Why have you not written more traditional surrealism? What was your initial impulse toward SF? Was it just a form that would allow you to create surrealism?

Yasutaka Tsutsui: To me, SF is an approach to deconstruct reality, just as surrealism was. Of course I could have employed other approaches. For example, I would have wanted to become a painter if only I had the talent. So, anyway, writing or écriture was the only way left for me to deconstruct reality. Now when I was in university, I wanted to become an actor, a comic actor. That seemed to be another way to deconstruct reality. Comedy was a very important medium for me, but in my time, there weren't so many avant-garde theaters. My awareness of myself being a comic actor led me to write slapstick fiction.

Larry McCaffery: Do you plan your stories out beforehand as in an outline, or do you work, in a sense, improvisationally?

YT: As long as a writer is good and professional, he will have his own blueprint for what he would write. Before writing a piece of work, he should be able to envision almost every detail, the slightest detail of the text-to-be. However, from my experience, this kind of vision or blueprint testifies to the fact that the very writer is obsessed with what he has already done in his past successful works. He is apt to follow them in the blueprints. He is delimited, encircled by his past accomplishments. Therefore, he must transgress the boundary. This is why I employ the improvisational approach. By that way, I am able to write something different, something new.

For me, a true masterpiece must be new and more often than not, it should leave the critics at a loss. As long as the writer follows the line set by his past works, it would be easy for the critics to analyze his works. But I strongly believe that a good piece of art should be something that bewilders the critics. Of course, I have a blueprint but then I employ improvisation and try to destroy the whole. Now will this make the work a failure? No, because I can never destroy a text enough. It is strange, but the work ends up in a certain settling way.

LM: What was responsible, do you think, for the sort of independent rise of the metastances in art in the sixties, in genre writing? Was it a coincidence or was there something going on?

YT: When a writer is ambitious enough to write fiction that has never existed, there would be several ways, and one of them would be a metafictional approach. However, even before this method had been employed consciously by artists, whether he be a writer or a filmmaker, there were many works that had already suggested this way of creating. For example, there were those hilarious road movies of Bing Crosby and Bob Hope from the 1940s. One of them would say "Here are some flashbacks," and flashbacks would really appear on the screen. They were already self-referential.

And there were even mangas which had this metafictional tendency (without yet being aware of it). For example, often in Osamu Tezuka's works, the author would appear and have something to say. So there was a sort of accumulation of these metafictional tendencies, and we were very amused by all of this. We would think how this effect had come about, and start to employ them ourselves. That was how the "coincidences" worked, I would say.

LM: Ironically, in the U.S., some critics criticize metafictionists as being only engaged in playing games with words and fiction and not interested in reality. But it seems to me that metafiction is a way of returning people to reality by revealing the artifice. It's a gesture in getting at "the real."

YT: I think that metafiction is a game, only in the sense that games are a commitment to contingency. Some people would think that in order to make a story realistic, there would have to be a linear structure, which is in itself a dominant narrative. However, having a linear structure is not close to reality at all. As we all know, reality is full of coincidences and contingency. Now I am not sure how exactly metafiction and games are related to each other, but if you think of the main aspect of games as being dependent on contingency, then saying that metafiction is but a game would be the same as saying metafiction is reality itself.

SG: One of the things that is striking about the tales included in *What the Maid Saw* is that by the end of this work, there is a sense where Nanase is doing things that are not ethically correct but are necessary for her self-preservation. Is her decision to choose self-preservation at the expense of everything else more acceptable because she is a woman? If a man had chosen self-preservation over the ethical choice, would the response to the character be different?

YT: Yes, you are asking about the important relationship between social justice and femininity. In my opinion these two are completely different and it is misleading to discuss these two together. Now let's start with the former issue. There is what we call social justice as opposed to social evil. This includes very large-scale evil to a punkish kind of evil which a meager sneak crook might perform. But these are different from the evil which literature is trying to pursue. Of course, this has much to do with the effect of the representation of evil. But anyway, it is irrelevant to attack an evil depicted in literature in terms of social justice, because these two work on a completely different level.

In this context, we can go on to the problems of feminism. Assume that you are a talented woman and became popular, started to appear on TV, media covers you, etc., etc., but from a certain point people start to find faults and bash you, ridicule you, and thus you start to fall, ending up as a fallen idol. There is a close relationship with the problem of feminism and individual talent. If you are talented, the case would be that you might become a target of a social bashing. Nanase is a talented woman because she has supernatural powers. What I have just explained is an application of the problem of Nanase in a post-PC era. Nanase can be reinterpreted from this context.

LM: Do you remember how you got the idea for *What the Maid Saw*? I know that within *What the Maid Saw,* you make a number of references to actual studies of telepathy and parapsychology—were these studies part of what got you initially interested in developing the book or were you already familiar with them beforehand?

YT: When I started acting in an actor's group, I was still very young, so it was very difficult for me to fully grasp the characters of the roles that I was given. You have to be familiar with all kinds of human characters to be a good actor. So I started to read books about characterology written by Takehisa Takara. From there, I went to Freud. I thought it would be very helpful for my own understanding of acting out dramatic characters. But gradually, I became interested in them for their own sake, rather than for the application of these theories into my acting. It was not until I started to write fiction that the books of Jung's were translated into Japanese. I read many of his works as well, according to my own interest, but needless to say, I realized that my studying will also help me understand the psychological aspects of surrealism which I had always been fascinated with.

Takayuki Tatsumi: By the way, the topic of his B.A. thesis was the psychology of surrealistic creative writing with special emphasis on psychological automatism.

YT: I was not particularly interested in parapsychology, but I was aware that if I used this in fiction, it would be very experimental. It turned out that what I had studied according to my own interest happened to end up as very useful in my writings.

LM: Did your conception of your central character, Nanase, change at all while you were writing these stories?

YT: This change in Nanase comes from both Nanase's growth and my own growth, too. In such a story, a writer develops a deep sympathy with the protagonist. So the writer should know that the protagonist will not act as she or he would have because she or he has gone through several experiences. And again, this also shows the evolution of the writer himself. The series of Nanase's stories were first published in an entertainment magazine called *Shoosetsu*

Shinchoo. I kept writing these stories every two to four months for two years. It was natural that I went through evolution as much as I developed a sympathy with Nanase.

SG: I have a question about the manifesto. Toward the end, it says that every author basically wants to represent his own romantic love for literature. I was wondering about the relationship of this statement to the author who is doing something for his love of literature as opposed to the author who wants to translate his experiences in the world. Do you consider your fiction only an aesthetic form that is removed from the world, or is it something that conveys your own personal experience?

YT: Insofar as we are living in the real world, we have to be aware of the society or reality to a certain extent, no matter how committed we are to the aesthetic aspects of our works. In the sixties or maybe in the early seventies, when I was still at my early stage as a writer, I had very often been asked to write fiction that was closely related to current events. Sometimes I accepted their suggestion if the incident was appropriate enough to fit into my fiction, but needless to say, I don't do that anymore.

However, I do think that a writer should have the ability to predict. Now this is not in the sense of a supernatural power. The context is completely different. For example, almost one or two years before the Kobe earthquake, I had already written several stories that were, in a way, predicting it. This is very important for a writer. Fiction predicts future reality.

LM: How is it possible to create avant-garde art today when even the gesture of the avant-garde is so quickly assimilated by the mass media?

YT: If you want to do something new and avant-garde, you need to know what you are trying to reconstruct or deconstruct, appropriate or reappropriate, what there was in the past, the heritage of avant-garde, the history of philosophy, literature. For example, take philosophy. You might start off with Aristotle, go to Hegel, Heidegger, Derrida. You might want to build up something new, but the fact is, you might not even have reached Aristotle.

In today's *Nihon Keizai Newspaper,* a Japanese equivalent to the *Wall Street Journal,* there was an article saying that Japanese literature has been emptied, because Oe and I have ceased to write. This is not so. But I do regret that younger generation writers have never read the classics. Of course they can try things new but at the same time it is possible to read or reread the given heritage as well. What I truly recommend—particularly to the younger generation of writers in Japan—is deconstructing classics. That should be astonishing and radical to those who have never read those classics and it would be very useful for the writer, too.

LM: In the very beginning of "Standing Woman" the narrator says something like "these days, you can't write stories that might do either harm or good." These comments seem to take a pessimistic attitude about the ability of the contemporary Japanese writer to have any real impact on the culture.

YT: Even while I was writing this short story, I thought that in the near future, there would be many writers who would have to stop writing, just because of social justice. It could have been that I predicted this PC kind of age. What matters most is that it was not just I but also other writers behind me who may have to give up writing. My giving up writing represented other writers as well. It is not an exclusive case. It can happen to other writers any time.

The complete interview with Yasutaka Tsutsui can be accessed at www.centerforbookculture.org.

Just a Nobody
(from The Rumors about Me)

Yasutaka Tsutsui

That morning, while commuting to work in a packed train, I glanced up at one of the hanging posters for a women's weekly magazine. I then let out a sharp cry of alarm.

Reported: Mr. Tsutomu Morishita (28, Average Office Worker)
Dated Miss Akiko Mikawa (23, Typist) In A Coffee Shop!!

It was printed in the biggest Gothic type under a blow-up of my face. Next to it, in small letters:

That Night, Mr. Morishita Masturbated Twice!

I tore my hair, ground my teeth, and screamed. "It's a violation of my rights! I'll sue! What's it to you if a guy jerks off two times, or three!" The moment I arrived at work, I planted myself in front of my section chief's desk, and shoved a copy of the women's magazine at the station toward him.

"I request permission to leave the office on private business. You know of this, don't you? This article? I'm going to have it out with the publishing company that puts out this magazine!"

"I can appreciate how you feel," the chief said, trying to calm me in a tremulous voice. "But wouldn't it be better not to be so short-tempered? The mass media is a frightening opponent. Of course I'll give you permission to leave the office on personal business any time. You well know I'm a paternalistic fellow about things like that. You do know that, don't you? Yes. I think you do know. But I'm just thinking of your own good when I say this. Now, certainly this is a terrible thing. This article is horrendous, I agree. Yes, I can sympathize with you on this."

"Yeah, it's really bad."

"Oh, it really is. It's just too awful."

I hadn't noticed my colleagues gathering around us, and now they all began sympathizing with me. Some women workers even cried.

But I wasn't fooled. Behind my back they were all whispering ill about me, and they were helping the mass media. It was the inevitable two-faced nature of all those around the famous.

After the president himself came out to persuade me, I finally gave up on the idea of bursting into the publishing company. But the funny thing was that even though I had been so raving mad and had made such a commotion, none of it was reported on the television news or in the day's evening papers. That led me to think back over the way the mass media had selected news about me over the previous days.

They had left out of the news everything that I did in conscious awareness of the mass media. My attempts to shake my shadowers, for instance, or the way I would fly into a rage and shout at the television news or newspaper articles were either completely ignored or reported as if they had happened for different reasons. Far from reporting them as they had happened—even an incident like the helicopter that had crashed into a building while trying to tail me—they were reported as if they were totally unconnected events. In that respect, the coverage was very different from when the media investigates and reports other famous personalities. In short, they were treating me as if I was in a world devoid of mass media.

But thinking about it, I found it ironic that that was the very reason that the news about me gradually grew more prominent, that people began to take an interest in it, and that I became *the nobody that nobody didn't know*. For instance, one day the morning papers played up a story with a six-column headline topping the front page.

TSUTOMU MORISHITA EATS EELS!
THE FIRST EXTRAVAGANCE
IN 16 MONTHS!

There were times when I would unexpectedly encounter some of the crowd that were secretly reporting me. Once, when I came out of a stall in the company toilet, I tried opening the doors to the rest of the stalls in the line and found most packed solid with guys dangling cameras and tape recorders. If I suddenly used my umbrella tip to poke through the shrubbery in front of the empty lots on my way home, female announcers would spring out and dash away, microphones in hand.

Once I raised the tatami straw floormats, pried up the floorboards, opened the closet doors, and poked at the ceiling with a broomstick. The announcers and onlookers who were packed under the floor ran wildly about, shrieking; from the closet, four or five reporters, including several women, tumbled onto the tatami; and one cameraman behind the ceiling put his foot through a panel and came crashing down as he hurriedly tried to get away.

Of course, none of this kind of thing ever became news. Only the daily incidents of my life were taken up and grandly reported as the big news of the day, outstripping important stories about politics, diplomacy, and the economy.

For instance: "Mr. Morishita Orders New Suit on Installment Plan!"

For instance: "Mr. Tsutomu Morishita Dates Again!"

For instance: "Complete Investigation—Mr. Morishita's Weekly Dietary Life!"

For instance: "Who is the Woman in Mr. Morishita's Heart? Is it Really Miss Akiko Mikawa? Or . . ."

For instance: "Mr. Tsutomu Morishita Argues with Colleague, Mr. Fujita, 25, about Voucher Error."

For instance: "Shocking! Mr. Morishita's Sex Life!"

For instance: "Today, Payday for Mr. Morishita!"

For instance: "How Will Mr. Morishita Use His Pay Check?"

For instance: "Mr. Morishita Again Buys 350 yen Socks (Blue-Gray)!"

After a while, even commentators specializing in my affairs appeared. This surprised even me.

Finally my picture embellished the cover of one of the big newspaper's weekly magazines. It was a color picture. Of course, I had no idea when it was taken. It showed me mingled among commuting office workers on my way to work in the business district. I was slightly pleased that it was so well taken.

Even if I couldn't expect anything for the articles about me, it seemed natural that there should be some kind of acknowledgment from the newspaper company now that they'd used me as their cover model. But three days passed from publication date, then four, and there was still no word from the paper. One day, unable to contain myself any longer, I detoured by the newspaper office on my way to work.

Although everyone I passed when walking around town would turn to look back at me, when I entered the newspaper office both the receptionists and on-duty editors were unpleasantly cold. Their attitude seemed almost to say that they'd never even heard of me. While I sat in the reception room I'd been guided to, wondering if it would have been better not to have come after all, a sober-faced man appeared and identified himself as the assistant editor of the magazine.

"Mr. Morishita. You do know you're causing us a lot of trouble by coming here."

"So that's it. It's because I'm just a nobody who has nothing to do with the mass media, right?"

"You're neither a celebrity nor a man of the hour. You're not even a famous person. That's why you shouldn't come to places like this."

"But I *am* famous, in fact, aren't I?"

"All that is just gossip in the press about someone who isn't famous. Even after your face had become known, we still wanted you to remain nameless forever. We thought you fully understood that yourself."

"In that case, why did you need to make news out of a nobody like me?"

The assistant editor sighed.

"How should I know? I imagine it was because someone judged that you could become news."

"You mean the mass media? Who was the ringleader who came up with such nonsense?"

"The ringleader? If there were a ringleader, the newspapers would never have all gone chasing after you like this. The mass media pursues things with news value, even if there is no one there to give the order."

"What news value is there in my daily routine?"

"Very well, just what kind of articles would you say were big news?"

"Let's see now. For instance, whether or not the weather forecast was correct or that there was a war some place or that there was a ten-minute power failure in such-and-such a block or that an airplane crashed and a thousand people died or that the price of apples is going up or that a dog bit a man or a dog was caught shoplifting at a supermarket or the president of the United States was shoplifting or Man landed on Mars or an actress got divorced or World War Three is likely to break out or polluting industries are making money or another newspaper's making money."

The assistant editor had been watching my face absently. But at last he sadly shook his head.

"So in other words, you think that kind of material is big news."

I was stunned.

"It's not?"

He waved his hand irritably.

"No, no. Of course those things could be big news, too. Isn't that why we always report them? Yet at the same time, we're also writing stories about an ordinary office worker. Therefore, as long as the mass media reports on it, anything can be big news." He nodded. "Once the reporting has been done, any amount of news value will emerge. But the point is, by coming here today, you've destroyed that news value yourself."

"But it doesn't bother me."

"I see!" The assistant editor slapped his knees. "Now that you say it, it doesn't bother us, either!"

I quickly returned to the company. The moment I arrived, I called the typists' room from my desk and asked for my girlfriend, Akiko.

"Akiko," I said loudly. "Will you go to a hotel with me tonight?"

At the other end of the line Akiko gasped.

For a moment, the whole room fell perfectly silent. My co-workers and section chief stared at me round-eyed.

Finally Akiko answered, on the verge of tears.

"Yes, I'll go with you."

And so that night I stayed at a hotel with Akiko. It was of the lowest class in a hotel district awash with garish neon lights.

As I had expected, nothing about it appeared in the newspapers. It was not broadcast on TV. From that day on, news about me vanished from the mass media. From that day on, a middle-aged office worker of a type you might see anywhere appeared. He was thin, short, had two children, and lived in a suburban high-rise. He was chief clerk for general affairs at a shipbuilding company.

I became, once again, truly nameless.

I tried asking Akiko out just once after that to see what would happen. I asked if she would meet me after work at a coffee shop. But Akiko refused. Since I knew what kind of woman she was, I felt quite satisfied.

After a month, there was no one left who remembered my face apart from my own acquaintances. Yet even so, there were sometimes people who would look startled on seeing my face.

One day, in the train on my way back to my apartment, one of two girls sitting on the seat in front of me had that kind of expression on her face.

"Gosh. I've seen that man before somewhere," she whispered, nudging the girl beside her with her elbow. "Look. That guy. What does he do, I wonder?"

The other girl gave me an annoyed glance. Finally she replied uninterruptedly, "That guy? Oh, he's just a nobody."

Translated by David Lewis

A (Very) Selective Bibliography of Modern and Postmodern Japanese Fiction and Culture (English Translation Only)

Larry McCaffery and Sinda Gregory

Postmodern and Contemporary Japanese Fiction: Novels and Anthologies

Abe, Kobo. *The Ark Sakura*. New York: Vintage, 1989.

—. *The Box Man*. Tokyo: Tuttle, 1974.

—. "The Crime of S. Karuma." *Beyond the Curve*. Trans. Julie Winters Carpenter. Tokyo: Kodansha, 1991.

—. "Dendracacalia." *Beyond the Curve*. Trans. Julie Winters Carpenter. Tokyo: Kodansha, 1991.

—. *The Face of Another*. Trans. E. Dale Saunders. Tokyo: Tuttle, 1966.

—. "Friends." *Contemporary Japanese Literature: An Anthology of Fiction, Film, and Other Writing Since 1945*. Ed. Howard Hibbett. New York: Knopf, 1977.

—. *Inter Ice Age 4*. Trans. E. Dale Saunders. New York: Knopf, 1970.

—. *The Ruined Map*. 1969. Trans. E. Dale Saunders. New York: Vintage, 2001.

—. *Secret Rendezvous*. Trans. Julie Winters Carpenter. New York: Perigee, 1980.

—. "Song of a Dead Girl." *The Mother of Dreams and Other Short Stories: Portrayals of Women in Modern Japanese Fiction*. Ed. Makoto Ueda. New York: Tokyo, 1986.

—. *Woman in the Dunes*. Trans. E. Dale Saunders. New York: Knopf, 1964.

Apostolou, John, and Martin H. Greenberg, eds. *The Best Japanese Science Fiction Stories*. New York: Dembner, 1989.

Birnbaum, Alfred, ed. *Monkey Brain Sushi: New Tastes in Japanese Fiction*. Tokyo: Kodansha, 1991.

Kaiko, Takeshi. *Darkness in Summer*. Trans. Cecilia Segawa Seigle. New York: Knopf, 1973.

—. *Into a Black Sun*. Trans. Cecilia Segawa Seigle. New York: Tokyo, 1980.

Komatsu, Sakyo. *Japan Sinks*. 1973. Trans. Michael Gallagher. New York: Kodansha, 1995.

Lippit, Noriko Mizuta, and Kyoko Iriye Selden, eds. and trans. *Japanese Women Writers: Twentieth Century Short Fiction.* Armonk, NY: Sharpe, 1991.

Mitsios, Helen. *New Japanese Voices: The Best Contemporary Fiction from Japan.* New York: Atlantic Monthly, 1991.

Murakami, Haruki. *Dance, Dance, Dance.* Trans. Alfred Birnbaum. New York: Vintage, 1995.

—. *The Elephant Vanishes: Stories.* New York: Vintage, 1994.

—. *Hard-Boiled Wonderland and the End of the World.* Trans. Alfred Birnbaum. New York: Vintage, 1993.

—. *Norwegian Wood.* Trans. Jay Rubin. New York: Vintage, 2000.

—. *South of the Border, West of the Sun.* New York: Vintage, 2000.

—. *Sputnik Sweetheart.* Trans. Philip Gabriel. New York: Vintage, 2002.

—. *A Wild Sheep Chase.* New York: Vintage, 2002.

—. *The Wind-Up Bird Chronicle.* Trans. Jay Rubin. New York: Vintage, 1998.

Murakami, Ryu. *Almost Transparent Blue.* 1976. Trans. Nancy Andrew. Tokyo: Kodansha, 1977.

—. *69.* 1987. Trans. Ralph McCarthy. Tokyo: Kodansha, 1991.

—, dir. *Tokyo Decadence.* Based on his novel, *Topaz.* Image Entertainment, 1992.

—. *Coin Locker Babies.* New York: Kodansha, 1980.

Newman, Charles, et al., eds. Special issue of *TriQuarterly: Contemporary Asian Literature* 31 (1974).

Nosaka, Akiyuki. "American Hijiki (Amerika hijiki)." Trans. Jay Rubin. *Contemporary Japanese Literature.* Ed. Howard Hibbett. New York: Knopf, 1977.

Shimada, Masahiko. *Dream Messenger.* Trans. J. Philip Gabriel. New York: Warner, 1994.

Tanaka, Yukiko, ed. and trans. *Unmapped Territories: New Women's Fiction from Japan.* New York: Women in Translation, 1991.

Tsushima, Yuko. *Child of Fortune.* 1978. Trans. Geraldine Harcourt. Tokyo: Kodansha, 1991.

—. *The Shooting Gallery.* Trans. Geraldine Harcourt. New York: Pantheon, 1988.

Tsutsui, Yasutaka. *What the Maid Saw: Eight Psychic Tales.* Tokyo: Kodansha, 1990.

Yamada, Amy. *Trash.* New York: Kodansha, 1994.

Yoshimoto, Banana. *Kitchen.* 1988. Trans. Megan Backus. New York: Washington Square, 1993.

—. *N.P.* 1991. Trans. Ann Sherif. New York: Washington Square, 1994.

—. *Lizard*. Trans. Ann Sherif. New York: Washington Square, 1996.

Selected Modernist (i.e., pre-1970) Japanese Fiction: Novels, Story Collections, and Anthologies

Akutagawa, Ryunosuke. "The Autumn Mountain." *Modern Japanese Stories: An Anthology*. Trans. Edward G. Seidensticker. Ed. Ivan Morris. Tokyo: Tuttle, 1965.

—. "The Hell Screen." *Short Stories by Ryunosuke Akutagawa*. New York: Liveright, 1961.

—. *Kappa*. Tokyo: Tuttle, 1974.

—. *Rashomon and Other Stories*. Trans. Takashi Kojima. New York: Liveright, 1970.

Dazai, Osamu. *Blue Bamboo*. Trans. Ralph F. McCarthy. Tokyo: Kodansha, 1993.

—. *No Longer Human*. Trans. Donald Keene. Norfolk, CT: New Directions, 1958.

—. *A Return to Tsugaru: Travels of a Purple Tramp*. 1944. Tokyo: Kodansha, 1985.

—. *Self-Portraits*. Tokyo: Kodansha, 1991.

—. *The Setting Sun*. Trans. Donald Keene. New York: New Directions, 1956.

Dunlop, Lane, trans. *A Late Chrysanthemum: Twenty One Stories from the Japanese*. Tokyo: Tuttle, 1988.

Enchi, Fumiko. *Masks*. New York: Vintage, 1983.

Endo, Shusaku. *Scandal*. Tokyo: Tuttle, 1988.

—. *Deep River*. Trans. Van C. Gessel. New York: New Directions, 1994.

—. *Silence*. 1966. Tokyo: Kodansha, 1989.

—. *Stained Glass Elegies*. Trans. Van C. Gessel. London: Owen, 1984.

—. *The Girl I Left Behind*. Trans. Mark Williams. London: Owen, 1994.

—. *The Sea and Poison*. 1958. Trans. Michael Gallagher. New York: New Directions, 1992.

Gessel, Van C., ed. *The Showa Anthology: Modern Japanese Short Stories: 1929-1984*. Tokyo: Kodansha, 1985.

Hibbett, Howard, ed. *Contemporary Japanese Literature: An Anthology of Fiction, Film, and Other Writing since 1945*. New York: Knopf, 1977.

Ibuse, Masuji. *Black Rain*. Trans. John Bester. Tokyo: Kodansha, 1969.

Ishikawa, Jun. *The Bodhisattva*. Trans. William Jefferson Tyler. New York: Columbia UP, 1990.

Kaiko, Takeshi. *Darkness in Summer*. Trans. Cecilia Segawa Seigle. Tokyo: Tuttle, 1973.

Kawabata, Yasunari. *House of the Sleeping Beauties: and Other Stories*. Trans. Edward G. Seidensticker. New York: Ballantine, 1969.

—. *The Izu Dancer and Other Stories*. Rutland, VT: Tuttle, 1974.

—. *Palm of the Hand Stories*. 1929. Trans. Lane Dunlop and J. Martin Holman. San Francisco: North Point, 1988.

—. *Snow Country*. Trans. Edward G. Seidensticker. New York: Knopf, 1956.

—. *Sound of the Mountains*. Trans. Edward G. Seidensticker. New York: Knopf, 1970.

—. *Thousand Cranes*. Trans. Edward G. Seidensticker. New York: Knopf, 1969.

Keene, Donald. *Anthology of Japanese Literature: From the Earliest Era to the Mid-19th Century*. New York: Grove, 1955.

—. *Dawn to the West: Japanese Literature in the Modern Era*. 2 vols. New York: Holt, 1984.

—. *Japanese Literature: An Introduction for Western Readers*. 1955. Tokyo: Tuttle, 1987.

—. *Modern Japanese Literature: From 1868 to Present Day*. New York: Grove, 1956.

—. *The Pleasures of Japanese Literature*. New York: Columbia UP, 1988.

—. *Seeds in the Heart: Japanese Literature from Earliest Times to the Late Sixteenth Century*. New York: Columbia UP, 1993.

—. *Some Japanese Portraits*. Tokyo: Kodansha, 1978.

Lippit, Noriko Mizuta, and Kyoko Iriye Selden, eds. and trans. *Japanese Women Writers: 20th Century Short Fiction*. Armonk, NY: Sharpe, 1991.

Masuji, Ihbuse. *Black Rain*. Trans. John Bester. Tokyo: Kodansha, 1969.

Miyazawa, Kenji. *Night of the Milky Way Railway*. Trans. Sarah Strong. Armonk, NY: Sharpe, 1991.

Mishima, Yukio. *After the Banquet*. Trans. Donald Keene. New York: Knopf, 1963.

—. *Confessions of a Mask*. Trans. Meredith Weatherby. Norfolk, CT: New Directions, 1958.

—. *The Sailor Who Fell from Grace with the Sea*. Trans. John Nathan. New York: Knopf, 1965.

—. *The Sea of Fertility*. 4 Vols.: *Spring Snow*. Trans. Michael Gallagher. *The Temple of Dawn*. Trans. E. Dale Saunders and Cecilia Segawa Seigle. *Decay of the Angel*. Trans. Edward G.

Seidensticker. New York: Pocket, 1978.

—. *The Sound of Waves*. Trans. Meredith Weatherby. New York: Knopf, 1956.

—. *The Temple of the Golden Pavilion*. Trans. Ivan Morris. Intro. Nancy Wilson Ross. New York: Knopf, 1959.

—. *Thirst for Love*. Trans. Alfred H. Marks. Intro. Donald Keene. New York: Knopf, 1969.

Morris, Ivan, ed. *Modern Japanese Stories: An Anthology*. Trans. Edward G. Seidensticker, et al. Tokyo: Tuttle, 1962.

Natsume, Soseki. *Botchan*. 1904. Trans. Umeji Sasaki. Rutland, VT: Tuttle, 1968.

—. *I Am a Cat*. Trans. Akiko Ito and Graeme Wilson. Rutland, VT: Tuttle, 1986.

—. *Kokoro*. Trans. Edwin McClellan. Chicago: Regnery, 1957.

—. *Light and Darkness: An Unfinished Novel*. Trans. V. H. Viglielmo. Honolulu: U of Hawaii P, 1971.

—. *The Miner*. Tokyo: Tuttle, 1988.

—. *Ten Nights of Dream*. Rutland, VT: Tuttle, 1974.

—. *And Then*. Trans. Norma Moore Field. Baton Rouge: Louisiana State UP, 1978.

—. *The Wayfarer*. Trans. and Intro. by Beongcheon Yu. Tokyo: Tuttle, 1969.

Oe, Kenzaburo. "Agwhee the Sky Monster." *Contemporary Japanese Literature: An Anthology of Fiction, Film, and Other Writing since 1945*. Ed. Howard Hibbett. New York: Knopf, 1977.

—. *Death in Midsummer and Other Stories*. New York: New Directions, 1966.

—. "Japan's Dual Identity: A Writer's Dilemma." *World Literature Today* 62.3 (1988): 359-69.

—. *A Personal Matter*. Trans. John Nathan. New York: Grove, 1969.

—. *The Pinchrunner Memorandum*. Armonk, NY: Sharpe, 1974.

—. *The Silent Cry*. 1967. Trans. John Bester. Tokyo: Kodansha, 1974.

—. *Teach Us to Outgrow Our Madness: Four Short Novels by Kenzaburo Oe*. Trans. John Nathan. New York: Grove, 1977.

Ooka, Shohei. *Fires on the Plain*. Trans. Ivan Morris. New York: Knopf, 1957.

Osaragi, Jiro. *The Journey*. 1960. Tokyo: Tuttle, 1987.

Saikaku, Ihara. *The Life of an Amorous Man*. Trans. Kengi Hamda. Tokyo: Tuttle, 1963.

Sato, Haruo. "The House of a Spanish Dog." *Modern Japanese Stories: An Anthology*. Ed. Ivan Morris. Trans. Edward G. Seidensticker, et al. Tokyo: Tuttle, 1962.

Tanizaki, Jun'ichiro. "The Bridge of Dreams." *Contemporary Japanese Literature: An Anthology of Fiction, Film, and Other Writing since 1945*. Ed. Howard Hibbet. New York: Knopf, 1977.

—. *Diary of a Mad Old Man*. Trans. Howard Hibbett. New York: Knopf, 1965.

—. "Longing for Mother." Trans. Edward Fowler. *Monumenta Nipponica* 35.4 (1980): 467-84.

—. *The Makioka Sisters*. Trans. Edward G. Seidensticker. New York: Knopf, 1957.

—. *Naomi*. Trans. Anthony H. Chambers. New York: Knopf, 1985.

—. "Portrait of Shunkin." *Seven Japanese Tales*. New York: Knopf, 1963.

—. *In Praise of Shadows (In'ei raisin)*. Trans. Thomas J. Harper and Edward G. Seidensticker. New Haven: Leete's Island, 1977.

—. *Quicksand*. 1947. Trans. Howard Hibbert. New York: Vintage, 1994.

—. *Some Prefer Nettles*. Trans. Edward G. Seidensticker. New York: Knopf, 1955.

—. *The Reed Cutter*. Tokyo: Tuttle, 1984.

Book Reviews

Gilbert Sorrentino. *Little Casino.* Coffee House, 2002. 220 pp. Paper: $14.95.

A little over halfway through the series of vignettes that compose *Little Casino,* an interlocutor steps in to remark, about the preceding passage: " 'Dolores asserts herself again in this memoir, although I use the word "memoir" as a figure of speech, of course.' " To which another interlocutor, ostensibly standing in for the author, responds: " 'Memoir' or not, Dolores and her lady friends are heartbreakers all." The passage is ironic and playful (as is much of the book), but beyond this it may strike the reader as *odd,* since there's not much about *Little Casino* that suggests a "memoir" in the first place. The vignettes do follow a roughly chronological progression, starting in the 1940s or fifties and moving toward the present day, but there's no "Gilbert Sorrentino" character to follow through a series of formative adventures. Rather, the book is an ingenious assemblage of stories, jokes, remarks—anything and everything—the "logic" of which is articulated in an epigraph from Joseph Cornell: "Although we may catalogue a kind of chain mysterious is the force that holds the chain together." Stories are told and then commented upon, speculations concerning recalled events in one section are verified in a companion section, only to be called into question again later on. Characters reappear, as do items, for example, a pale blue dress, which may or may not be the same dress that appeared elsewhere, on a character who may or may not have figured into a previous scene. There are also lists of received ideas, narrated photographs, metafictional wisecracks . . . in short, most of the stylistic and formal techniques that Sorrentino has developed throughout his career appear, one way or another, in this book. He includes characters and quotes from his other books, along with quotes and intentional misquotes from Joyce, Céline, Beckett, Stein. He includes his most excruciatingly dismal single line of poetry (from *White Sail*) as well as the ridiculous stewardess voice from *Misterioso*—"Hi!"—quite possibly the pinnacle of ironized banality in Western literature. What all this amounts to is a meticulously constructed catalog or "chain," but it is also, in fact, a kind of memoir.

Throughout Sorrentino's career, life has served as the material for his art—"material" in the sense of *what an artist uses to build something*—and the same material has often reappeared in new forms, not just scenes and items, but entire books being recast in new language. The result has been a body of work unmatched (since Flaubert, I'd say) for its prolific formal and stylistic variety, each book a unique rethinking of language and its uses. It is in the context of such a lifework that *Little Casino* becomes most fascinating—a surprisingly personal book. As Sorrentino has written elsewhere: "A writer knows that he is a writer when he has lived long enough to see that his writing defines, as clearly as a graph, his life. The shock of this is not caused by anything so homely and acceptable as 'the record of the passing years' . . . but by the fact that this 'graph' is not a metaphor for his life, but a merciless representation of it." Life is the material of art, but eventually that notion flips, and the artist recognizes artistic forms as the material of life itself (his own). That this same material should then cycle back and be once more claimed for artistic ends seems a logical extension of one of the most profoundly artistic careers (not over, of course) in contemporary American literature. [Martin Riker]

William H. Gass. *Tests of Time*. Knopf, 2002. 319 pp. $25.00.

This fifth collection of Gass's essays covers several timely issues at the intersection of writing and politics. Among them are canon formation, moral influence, the impulses behind censorship, and the possibilities of protest. Also in this volume are a number of topical sermons that condemn the persecutions of Salman Rushdie, Assia Djebar, Ken Saro-Wiwa, and Tahar Djaout. Despite the politically charged subject matter of these essays, Gass repeatedly challenges efforts to pin down a definite relation between literature and politics: "it may be useful to remember that coins and paper have sides but value and language haven't." Typical of his essayistic style, all of these pieces reveal his dedication to particulars and his distrust of theories and systems. He has little interest, for example, in literary critics' attempts to define the laws of canon formation. At the same time, essays like "The Test of Time" and "The Shears of the Censor" make daring efforts to go beyond the truism that aesthetic judgments are always contingent. In the collection's central piece—a very long "litany" on writers and politics—Gass provides an exhaustively detailed, rhapsodically organized, yet continuously fascinating catalog of the uneasy, indeterminate, contradictory relations between writing and power. Ultimately, the point of this catalog is that "there isn't a single important point of view which has not been beautifully praised. There is scarcely an important truth which hasn't been brilliantly traduced." Out of context, this might sound like uncommitted political relativism or cultural conservatism hiding behind aesthetic disinterestedness. But Gass's meditations on the nature of literary creation reveal a highly complex—and subtly instructive— awareness of writing's capacity for social use and abuse, and his topical sermons put the lie to the fear that such a complex awareness cripples political and ethical judgment. [Thomas Hove]

Claude Simon. *The Jardin des Plantes*. Trans. and intro. Jordan Stump. Hydra/Northwestern Univ. Press, 2001. 288 pp. $29.95.

In the style of the French nouveau roman, Claude Simon's 1997 book *The Jardin des Plantes* makes its debut in English. Told as a fragmented retrospective, the novel melds both past and present, autobiography and fiction, in a haunting narrative centered around the atrocities of the Spanish Civil

War and the catastrophic engagement of the French and German armies in the early days of World War II (confrontations in which the author was personally engaged). At the age of eighty-seven, winner of the 1985 Nobel Prize for Literature, Claude Simon has reached the summit of his productive career. His novel is a testament to a life's work and a memoir of a century of upheaval, turmoil, and despair, and leaves us torn between hating and loving the words on the page. As if to willfully reconstruct the deconstructed, abject world of war in the twentieth century, Simon's stor(ies) not only are told through fragmented memories, they are placed as pieces of a puzzle on the page. The text is physically disjointed, often written on the page as two separate columns, each containing a separate story, or as multiple bits of paragraphs with no beginning or end. Although difficult to read at times, the reader remains engaged as the narrative oscillates between the glory of cavalry infantrymen and the heinous, bloody destruction of tanks, bombs, guns, and ammunition. "Will man ever learn to avoid self-destruction?" seems to be Simon's question. Made uncomfortable by the fragmented style, searching to find closure to horrendous stories of torture, war, and despair, we are left fatigued at the end of the novel. In *The Jardin des Plantes* Claude Simon takes us to another realm of reality by showing us the complexity and the chaos that make up the human condition. [Valerie Orlando]

George Garrett. *Going to See the Elephant: Pieces of a Writing Life*. Ed. Jeb Livingood. Texas Review Press, 2002. 195 pp. Paper: $18.95.

George Garrett has made important contributions to American literature, both prominent (his memorable three novels on the Elizabethan period) and inconspicuous (his jaunty and fearless overviews of American fiction over the years for the annual *Dictionary of Literary Biography*). In this essay collection, Garrett is merciless about that world's pretensions, yet idealistic about the writer's vocation. Punches are not pulled. New York is censured for literary parochialism, and also, more subtly, for its editors promoting second-rate books as "palliatives" for their own metropolitan isolation. The grim self-interest that characterizes far too much of a writer's "mission" is fully revealed. An acute introduction by Jeb Livingood foreshadows Garrett's own point that his was the second generation of American modernists, which sought to emulate the work of Eliot, Hemingway, and Faulkner while living an academic life completely different from theirs. Garrett takes a bus from Vermont to Rhode Island to attend what he thinks is an elephant festival, desperately works up elephant jokes in preparation, only to find a beaming Ralph Ellison greeting him upon disembarkation—it was an *Ellison* festival! In "The Good Ghost of F. Scott Fitzgerald" Garrett comes to grips with the mystery still surrounding Fitzgerald's "impeccable and inimitable craft," and remembers how parlously his canonicity was achieved. And for other deserving writers canonicity may still be in the balance, as in the position of Fred Chappell, Madison Jones, and James Dickey, writers about whom Garrett writes affectionately and hilariously. These pieces, though, are not ceremonial *éloges*; they are honest, candid, and comprehending of the whimsicality of literary endeavor. Humor is also the manifest chord of two mock-essays by alter-ego "John Towne," whose undersong is a profound commitment to high standards. [Nicholas Birns]

Vladimír Páral. *Lovers & Murderers.* Trans. Craig Cravens. Catbird, 2002. 409 pp. $27.00.

Vladimír Páral's lurid, graphic, wildly satiric 1969 novel mingles the conflicts of two breeds of comrade, Blue (having a private apartment) and Red (without one), jostling uncomfortably in the same wretched building near the dusty industrial heart of a Czechoslovakian border town in the grip of late Socialist rot. While awaiting translation to—or scheming to snatch—a precious flat of their own, Páral's dispirited pilgrims seethe with jealousy, ambition, and sexual appetite, their follies at once pathetic and unruly. The author complicates their situation by distributing his account of it among several voices, alternately ascendant ("Conquerors") or descendant ("Besieged"), in pursuit of questionable advantage. Páral's contrapuntal mixing-and-matching captures the dissatisfaction and discontinuity of grimly absurd lives, while his furious pace and bleakly outrageous sense of humor leave few conventions standing, nothing sacred. Borek Trojan, down but not out, sick of the rampant squalor of the ground floor, wants an upstairs apartment, love, and freedom from the grasping, crushing oppression of his life. But everyone else wants this, too. "Besieged," he marks time, making love to the boss's eager wife from the second floor as all manner of mayhem explodes about him. When the scene abruptly shifts years ahead, Borek, having murdered his lover, Zita, finds little pleasure in succeeding to her home. As a new cadre of apartment dwellers undertakes his overthrow, Trojan the "Conqueror" succumbs to a "sexretary" half his age. Being Red or Blue matters not at all; both "Besieged" and "Conquerors" are complements, predictable and deadening. In vivisecting the pervasive dreariness of the Communist provinces, Páral mocks and exalts his frenzied rabble's appetite for life-without-restraint. His frenetic harlequinade expanding and contracting to uproarious effect, Páral projects no end to the clamor—just stress, briefer respite, more of life's yearning self-deception. [Michael Pinker]

Brion Gysin. *Back in No Time: The Brion Gysin Reader.* Ed. Jason Weiss. Wesleyan Univ. Press, 2001. 368 pp. Paper: $24.95.

This splendid array of out of print, difficult to find, and previously unpublished work, spanning more than four decades, provides readers with a basis to gain greater appreciation for Brion Gysin's unique vision and amazing achievement. Included here are substantial portions of three full-length works: *To Master—A Long Goodbye* (1946), a biographical treatment of Josiah Henson, the real-life model for Harriet Beecher Stowe's Uncle

Tom; *The Process* (1969), a novel written in Tangier, set primarily in North Africa, and narrated by an African American dubbed Hassan Merikani (a Gysin persona); and *The Last Museum* (1986), a surrealistic romp (with illustrations by Keith Haring) that draws on Gysin's experiences at the Beat Hotel in Paris, outlandish fictions, and the *Tibetan Book of the Dead*. Similarly, Gysin inextricably intertwines autobiography and fantasy in his fine piece, "Fire: Words by Day—Images by Night," which moves back and forth between the hospital room where the narrator (a Gysin persona) is recovering from a colostomy and memories/hallucinations of the Sahara, childhood initiations into sexuality, etc. Also included are descriptions of the cut-up technique, developed by Gysin and used by Burroughs in *The Soft Machine, Nova Express,* and *The Ticket that Exploded;* descriptions of the Dream Machine he invented and hoped to market; excerpts from a *Naked Lunch* screenplay (not the one used by Cronenberg); a marvelous travel piece, "A Quick Trip to Alamut"; "Potiphar's Wife," a Bowlesian story featuring only Moroccan characters; and a preface to a cookbook containing the recipes of Hamri, Gysin's partner in the famed 1001 Nights Restaurant in Tangier that featured the master Jajouka musicians. The few examples of Gysin's paintings and lyric calligraphic art only begin to hint at his contributions to the visual arts. In sum, Brion Gysin: collaborative, exuberant, experimental, honest, nomadic, uncompromising, versatile, visionary. [Allen Hibbard]

Cees Nooteboom. *All Souls Day.* Trans. Susan Massotty. Harcourt, 2001. 338 pp. $25.00.

The German word for history is *Geschichte,* and the Dutch one, *geschiedenis*. The suffix for the Dutch term, *-nis,* also means *niche,* notes Arthur Daane, the documentary filmmaker who is the protagonist of Nooteboom's novel, and if the novel is about what of the past remains in our lives, it is also about our place in that past—our niche. At the same time, as our place in the scheme of things explains our lives, it also protects them. "After all," Daane thinks, "a niche was a place to hide in, a place to find hidden things." Daane is between assignments in Berlin, where the presence of the past is everywhere and becomes the subject of his daily reflections. His friends worry that he has not recovered from the deaths of his wife and son in a plane crash ten years before. He meets a woman whose citizenship is Dutch, her blood Spanish, her name that of a Scandinavian male (Elik). "Too much past will kill you," Daane tells her. "The past has to 'wear out' before we can go on." Between Daane and Elik the past never does, and in their lives All Souls' Day, the day the dead come back and dance, is day after day after day. *All Souls Day* is more than twice as long as any of Nooteboom's books, which are less novels than fables. Size matters, but if *All Souls Day* is less a novel than a series of meditations (the meditation is often the basis of the fable), it also needs the weight novels provide for us to comprehend the pain of Daane and Elik's lives; in this sense, it is a more powerful work than his fables. All of his work possesses an erudition, a command of language, and skill that we find in America in Nabokov and

Guy Davenport. Consider it a niche, if you will, but one we must keep. [Robert Buckeye]

David Mamet. *Wilson: A Consideration of the Sources*. Overlook, 2001. 336 pp. $26.95.

Born-again Christians, earnest lawyers (and the subphylum politicians), diligent academics: late-century postmodern sensibility finds irresistibly comic the antics of each, not merely their audacious search for order (that is the sorry century's most profound dilemma) but rather their smug certainty that they can conjure it. Prayers, affidavits, and footnotes create an order reliable to them but inevitably ironic (and chillingly comic) to the rest of us. Skewing a familiar speculative fiction premise (a distant future assembling history through the fragmentary records of a lost era), Mamet targets with luscious savvy and deadpan irony the limitless pretense of academics, hungry for tenure, to suture history from such bits, to talk their way into reasonable order. Centuries down the road, the Internet has apparently crashed (sparked, apparently, by massive riots after the truth that Coke and Pepsi are the same formula is revealed), and what is left is the hard drive of a Mrs. Wilson, most likely a future president or perhaps the wife of Woodrow. Mamet understands that the laughable premise of the Internet—that the world is now within range of cataloging—has led us to the earnest silliness of brain-heavy humanity: the illusion that order is finally possible. We get chapters of academic investigations into comic books, tattoos, jokes, commercial jingles; we get footnotes within footnotes; we get allusions elegantly interwoven within text, signals of an overarching designer (Mamet himself) having the time of his life. All of this is set in the pitch-perfect turgidity (under Mamet's sensibility it is hilarious) that apes academic discourse. Without the distraction of plot, we get enticing fragments that pretend to mimic narrative, and we see beneath the infinite jesting of such high-tech lexical gamesplaying the disturbing notion that sense and nonsense, certainty and uncertainty, are (and always have been) synonyms, not antonyms. [Joseph Dewey]

Carla Harryman. *Gardener of Stars*. Atelos, 2001. 179 pp. Paper: $12.95.

Not knowing what a city should be anymore, Carla Harryman invents one. In *Gardener of Stars* we are in a city as dreamworld. In this imaginary landscape, fragmentation, ruin, and loss are three—we cannot call them characters—three aspects of the psyche, emblems, states of being, or "borders of words." These—we cannot call them women, exactly—dual-gendered psyches or signifiers—wander through and tend to a city that overflows with images of the unconscious. We can enter anywhere. Deriving its ethos from the surrealist poetics of ruins, Harryman's sensibility emerges from the modern metropolis that contains fragments of lives, ruined buildings, inchoate languages, multiple peoples, collisions of values, obscure stories, and varied encounters in erotic space. The amorphous "gardeners" play gender games, and in the end, "all they could say about it is everything is sex." Everything in this novel is moving. The question is how do we read it with its kaleidoscope of diffuse images and unsettling language. Does the writer care? It is a novel that takes on the attributes of the city, and the city has been torn open. As readers, we wander in this city, this linguistic wilderness, this dream book that incorporates words as well as blank pages, visual images, gaps, epigrams, memoir, prophecy, and various forms of poetry and prose. It's no wonder then that we, as readers, have difficulty orienting ourselves to the "outside" of words or surface events as we flow through this stream of surrealist images (feathered women, headless torsos, dolls), ruins, and states of mind and body. This work is like a raft of words, writer and readers alike having survived a catastrophe; the heroic quest "replaced by a collective trauma." We float on the words and images, not really understanding them, but pulled along by the current of writing. Though we may remain puzzled readers of this dream city, it is Carla Harryman's gift to shore up words against its psychological, cultural, and architectural ruins. [Patricia Laurence]

Leonid Tsypkin. *Summer in Baden-Baden*. Trans. Roger and Angela Keys. Intro. Susan Sontag. New Directions, 2001. 146 pp. $23.95.

Just when Susan Sontag thought she knew all the masterpieces of the late twentieth century, along came Leonid Tsypkin's *Summer in Baden-Baden*. As she rightly explains, her failure was understandable: Tsypkin was not a professional writer (he was an esteemed pathologist before his request for an exit visa placed him on the medical blacklist) and chose not to submit his work for publication. *Summer in Baden-Baden* was smuggled out of the Soviet Union and published in a small émigré journal. The book begins with Tsypkin on a train headed for Leningrad to visit the Dostoyevsky Museum. On his way, he is reading the episode in Mme. Dostoyevsky's memoir of her husband where she recounts the summer they spent in Baden-Baden, a period when Dostoyevsky's gambling reduced them to more and more abject states of poverty, when each desperate attempt to regain his dignity turned into a further exercise in degradation. Tsypkin's account is unsparingly frank. As a specialist in cancer's response to lethal viruses, Tsypkin approaches Dostoyevsky's self-destruction with the same unflinching, clinical fascination. Yet Tsypkin understands that he is not a neutral observer. His own obsession with Dostoyevsky, a virulent anti-Semite, is part of Tsypkin's self-abjection, made all the more vital because it takes place at a time when his career, his wife, and his art are all at risk from the Soviet anti-Jewish policies that Dostoyevsky would have applauded. Is there no difference between Tsypkin and Dostoyevsky? Can Dostoyevsky teach Tsypkin anything? Does their art grow out of the abjection they so single-mindedly pursued? *Summer in Baden-Baden* refuses to answer these questions; it merely places the work on a slide where the tissue, stained and illuminated by the imagination, can have its anatomy precisely studied. [David Bergman]

António Lobo Antunes. *The Return of the Caravels*. Trans. Gregory Rabassa. Grove, 2002. 210 pp. $24.00.

One of Antunes's slimmest books, *The Return of the Caravels* is also one of his most ambitious and most distinctly Portuguese. Constructed from Portugal's history, the plot centers around several famous explorers and colonists who are returning to a Lixbon that is both stuck in the seventeenth century and strangely modern. Caterpillar tractors block traffic while workmen illuminate their stores with cane-wick candles. Iraqi tankers are anchored next to caravels. Despite this apparent fluidity, the events in the novel also take place at a very specific time, 1974, following Portugal's socialist revolution and the granting of independence to Angola. The return of the colonists from Africa is the occasion for the novel, an exploration of the decrepit state of a fatherland without order, without glory, without money, and most importantly, without heroes. For instance, Vasco da Gama and King Dom Manoel are arrested and sent to an insane asylum despite the King's continual protests that "all this crap belongs to me," Diogo Cão is hired as a water inspector and ends up a drunken lout searching for nymphs in the Tagus, and Pedro Álvares Cabral's wife deserts him after becoming a prostitute to work off his debts. Throughout it all Luis Camões pens his epic poem *The Lusiads,* to which *The Return of the Caravels* owes its unique style. The novel can be a difficult read if one doesn't recognize (or research) the importance of the figures from Portugal's past, but these characters exist outside of their historical significances and thus are accessible to all readers. One can, and should, read *The Return of the Caravels* for its depiction of a crumbling empire— where the heroic actions of the colonists have been replaced by the monopolistic tendencies of the businessman—its sarcastic bursts of humor and its depressing yet touching scenes that combine in such a deft fashion as to reaffirm Antunes's reputation as one of the great contemporary writers. [Chad W. Post]

David Mitchell. *Number9Dream*. Random House, 2002. 400 pp. $24.95.

Mitchell's first novel, *Ghostwritten,* was a deeply humanist and intellectual novel that told a complex story in a readable and immediate manner. His second novel is even more accomplished, managing to depict the thoughts of a young man in a masterful style. Eiji Miyake, a twenty-year-old from rural Japan, heads to Tokyo to find his anonymous father. Over the next several weeks, his search leads him through a series of misadventures both comic and absurd. Eiji's dealings with cinematically violent yakuza gangsters, Japan's best hacker, and the girl with the world's prettiest neck force the country boy to adjust quickly to the pace of the city's chaotic beat. *Number9Dream*'s Tokyo is a vibrant, light-speed city running on the power of Mitchell's megawatt prose. Mitchell gives the reader the sense that anything can happen, that Eiji can sashay down any alleyway and find fascinating and dangerous characters to interact with. But instead of just anything happening, everything does. Eiji's daydreams compose a good deal of *Number9Dream,* and his fantasies spin constantly, supplying variant realities to the novel's main thread. As Eiji procrastinates about trying to find his father, his mind is hard at work concocting elaborate detective yarns, as a wiser Eiji of the imagination tracks down his father by noon, with plenty of time to drop hardboiled catchphrases and strike cool poses. *Numer9Dream* is so versatile it even manages to be an homage to a host of first-rate twentieth-century Japanese novels, though its chief achievement lies elsewhere. The novel's portrayal of the workings of the human mind— the way it associates, sorts information, constructs meaning, makes sense of reality, and, when necessary, proposes its own reality—is nothing short of astonishing. Simply put, *Number9Dream* succeeds on so many levels that most novels seem impoverished by comparison. [Jason Picone]

William Kennedy. *Roscoe.* Viking, 2002. 291 pp. $24.95.

Throughout his career, William Kennedy has anatomized life in Albany, New York, city of his birth and muse to his imagination. Set in 1945, *Roscoe* centers on Roscoe Conway, sometime lawyer and astute politico, who has shunned the limelight to run the local wing of the Democratic party and control the city for his boyhood friends. Just as Roscoe plans an overdue exit from public life, his world spins off its axis when his best friend commits suicide and his ex-wife, the sister of his friend's widow, reemerges to wreak havoc on all around her. At the same time, Roscoe must oversee the reelection of the city's boy-mayor and resolve a gambling feud that could destroy the political machine. *Roscoe* is a sprawling book, chronicling the machinations of the famous as well as the obscure. Kennedy has created a rich tapestry of mid-twentieth-century America, but this is the "other" America, home to schemers and swindlers, crooked politicians and charming rogues, the America often unacknowledged in the euphoria of the postwar years. No one knows the Irish-American experience the way Kennedy does, and each of his books is an examination of a unique ethnic group that is anything but a pale imitation of Anglo culture. Instead, his Irish are irascibly distinct, perversely idiosyncratic, and wholly their own. Self-destructive and melancholic, they are also wildly comic and vibrantly alive. These are the insiders who never quite got inside, and for all their influence and power they never attain a place in the mainstream. *Roscoe* is further proof of Kennedy's fecund imagination and immense skill. His characters are sharply drawn, his plot intricately designed, and his vision of American society unsparing. He is one of American literature's great regionalists, a writer who can conjure the nation from the convolutions of a single city. [David W. Madden]

Percival Everett. *Erasure.* Univ. Press of New England, 2001. 265 pp. $24.95.

Percival Everett's new novel offers a compelling exploration of "the notion of a public and its relationship to the health of art." The protagonist, Thelonius "Monk" Ellison, an avant-garde writer, woodworker, and fly fisherman, becomes offended by critics' charges that his dense novelistic parodies of poststructuralism are "not black enough." Unable to find a publisher or an audience for his most recent book, Monk becomes infuriated by the national success of Juanita Mae Jenkins's *We's Lives in Da Ghetto,* as the "ghetto wanna-be" novel is celebrated as one of "the true, gritty real stories of black life." Hiding his identity behind a pseudonym, Monk composes a bitter parody of Jenkins's blaxploitation novel, but the literary community hails Stagg R. Leigh's *My Pafology* as the new voice of black America, a genuine representation of the animality of ghetto life, and an authentic "glimpse of hood existence." *Erasure*'s acerbic satire on race and publishing is balanced by Monk's heartfelt attempt to reconcile himself to tumultuous changes in his family life: his sister's murder, his mother's Alzheimer's disease, his brother's coming out, and his father's suicide. At the same time, Monk faces a defining crisis in his artistic and racial identity when he serves as a judge for a book prize and Leigh's misunderstood novel is named as a finalist. While Everett imports various texts into the novel's frame, including an excerpt from Ellison's Barthesian novel and ten chapters of *My Pafology,* he further expands the boundaries of his art and his critique with extended intertextual references to *Native Son* and *Invisible Man.* In some ways *Erasure* echoes Ishmael Reed's *Reckless Eyeballing* and Trey Ellis's *Platitudes,* but Everett's brilliant and incisive anger, as well as his sincere understanding, makes me hope this provocative novel will find the audience it deserves. [Trey Strecker]

Michael Martone. *The Blue Guide to Indiana.* FC2, 2001. 120 pp. Paper: $12.95.

The disclaimer pasted to the front of Michael Martone's latest exposé of Indiana notifies readers that the book neither "factually depicts nor accurately represents the State of Indiana"; only a reader entirely isolated from modern America could possibly mistake this hilarious collection of wry observations as "real." Martone toys with our usual expectations for a travel guide by providing glimpses into the inner workings of this state, while simultaneously questioning how *useful* information is. We learn about the "Trans-Indiana Mayonnaise Pipeline," which supplies Chicago's condiment giants, and how to prepare marshmallows, "the coup de grace on many a Hoosier dessert." Martone also notes that a Hoosier's true sign of rebellion is his disavowal of Daylight Savings Time. The most rebellious spirits here are Eli Lilly and Michael Graves, two Indiana natives who have achieved notoriety both in and outside these fictional pages. Architect/designer Graves has recently turned his talents to objects marketed in Target stores, and Martone echoes the mass appeal in Graves's work by assigning to him fictional buildings, including the John Chancellor Memorial Pavilion, Orville Redenbacher's tomb, and a Knights of Columbus Hall. Graves is even credited with designing the Visitors Center at Eli Lilly Land, a postmodern theme park celebrating the American Dream's nexus of money and happiness. Martone meticulously describes the park's many attractions, and manages to leave even the most jaded Prozac patient/consumer giggling nervously over his renderings of "It's a Prozac World" and "The Possible Side Effects Funhouse," attractions that highlight the edgy power of today's pharmaceuticals. Martone certainly has a penetrating eye for all that is Indiana, but what seems to be his greatest contribution is his razor-sharp observations of American culture writ large—a decidedly unnerving portrait of contemporary life. [Anne Foltz]

Dee Goda. *Orchid Jetsam*. Tuumba, 2001. 172 pp. Paper: $15.00.

Experimental in every sense of the word, *Orchid Jetsam* defies the very convention of the novel. Perhaps more important, however, is the fact that this is a detective novel (or a "detective series," as Goda, who is really the accomplished poet, Leslie Scalapino, refers to it). As Paul Auster demonstrated in his now classic novel *City of Glass,* the detective novel is not only an established convention, it virtually defines the conventional reading experience. In the detective novel, the reader lives vicariously through a detective who ultimately solves a mystery, but also creates a unified meaning from the disparate and incoherent elements of the story. Unlike *City of Glass,* which essentially embodies the hardboiled detective novel only to turn it on its head, *Orchid Jetsam* seeks to disrupt the reader's experience on a more primary level. Instead of skewing stock characters and hardened themes, Scalapino skews the very lens by which the reader perceives such themes. Her use of disjointed syntax and unconventional punctuation forces the reader to think about the text as much as what the text might represent. Where Auster played within the rules of language to alter the common reading experience, Scalapino changes the rules, smashes them, in an effort to create something entirely new and original. That's not to say Scalapino's work is in any way better than Auster's. Moreover, the two take different roads to reach a similar destination. Both authors call upon the convention of the detective novel, and both display expert skill in showing the multiplicity of language. The difference with *Orchid Jetsam* lies within the language itself. There are no handrails here, there is no Sherpa. The reader is at the whim of the text, at once floating through ephemeral transitions, then wading through chunks of dense signification. [Christopher Paddock]

Magnus Mills. *Three to See the King.* Picador USA, 2001. 167 pp. $19.00.

Mills's third novel, *Three to See the King,* has many of the qualities that made his first novel, *The Restraint of Beasts,* a finalist for the Booker Prize. The narrator and the prose are stripped and laconic, the situations absurd and comic, and the human relations at once vital and parodic. Like a happier and less existential Kobo Abe, Mills has an ability to render the absurd with a light touch that nevertheless preserves its profundity. *Three to See the King* is the story of a man living alone on a flat plain in a house made of tin, spending his days listening to the sound of the wind. Out of nowhere a woman he hardly knows shows up and moves in, gradually structuring his life. As the book progresses, distant neighbors who also live in tin houses show up, eventually bringing with them word of one Michael Hawkins, a sort of guru intent on building a society in the bottom of a man-made canyon. The narrator, trying at first to maintain his solitary life, is slowly incorporated into Michael's world, finding himself occupying a role in regard to the developing cultish society that he can't quite understand. Functioning at once symbolically and literally, the novel has a great deal to say about the dynamics of power, the role of religion, and people's ability to become fixated on an idea. Yet it is finally Mills's ability to render these larger themes through daily concerns (whether or not to have a weather vane, what sort of plank to use to make a sidewalk for a wheelbarrow) that makes the novel effective and unique. *Three to See the King* lives up to the promise of *The Restraint of Beasts.* [Brian Evenson]

Alfred Jarry. *Collected Works of Alfred Jarry, Volume 1: Adventures in 'Pataphysics.* Trans. Paul Edwards and Antony Melville. Ed. Alastair Brotchie and Paul Edwards. Atlas, 2001. 334 pp. Paper: $14.95.

While widely known for his seminal work *Ubu Roi,* Alfred Jarry wrote other significant works that have not until now been available in English. Atlas's proposed three-volume set promises to bring Jarry's major works to the English audience. This first volume, which includes Jarry's first two books, *Black Minutes of Memorial Sand* and *Caesar-Antichrist,* in addition to a series of essays and a selection of Jarry's speculative journalism, more fully illuminates what was later to be coined pataphysics: "the science of imaginary solutions." Jarry remains a major literary figure, as his work is an important precursor to the surrealist movement as well as to the Theater of the Absurd. Even though Jarry originally composed symbolist poetry, he quickly migrated through new territories as he toyed with the various new schools of writing. In fact, the one constant throughout his brief career seems to have been experimentation. His experimentation, though, would open new terrain—a terrain that would later host Raymond Queneau and Eugene Ionesco, among others. The strength of the Atlas project is twofold. First and foremost, it brings to light some of Jarry's important works. The second strength is the admirable apparatus of commentary. Nearly 20 percent of the first volume, about sixty pages, is dedicated to finely tuned

commentary. And, as the Atlas project unfolds, there will be even more commentary. In fact, the entire third volume, titled *The Commentary*, will be
dedicated to "notes, iconography, supplementary translations, essays and
bibliographies relating to the works translated in volumes I and II." The
second volume will contain four novels: *Days and Nights, Visits of Love,
Absolute Love,* and *Messalina.* We are fortunate that after almost one hundred years, Jarry's oeuvre is now available in English. [Alan Tinkler]

Frederick Crews. *Postmodern Pooh.* North Point, 2001. 175 pp. $22.00.

At the beginning of his career Frederick Crews published *The Pooh Perplex*
(1963), a lighthearted parody of literary criticism found in freshman
casebooks. Thirty-eight years later, as Professor Emeritus at Berkley,
Crews presents *Postmodern Pooh,* a vicious attack on contemporary literary
theory, where some critics are so bound to their own theoretical hobby-
horses that their work becomes absurd. By designing the book as eleven
papers from a mock panel on A. A. Milne at the 2000 MLA convention,
Crews parodies not only the theories themselves, but the convention's aggressive nature. The papers represent such diverse fields as Derridean
deconstruction, new historicism, gynocentrism, neoplatonism, culture studies, and queer theory. Topics include such things as the absence of genitalia
in Ernest H. Shepard's original illustrations, Pooh's desire to sodomize
Eeyore, parallels to Shakespeare, and a suggestion that Virginia Woolf
might be the real author of the Pooh stories. The individual contributors'
notes are themselves wonderful satire, with position titles such as "Exxon
Valdez Chair in the Humanities" at Rice University and "Joe Camel Professor of Child Development" at Duke. The Oxford-educated Das Nuffa Dat
rants at the imperialist Pooh's stealing honey from downtrodden bees, yet
the speaker reveals his own privileged origins: his grandfather was a ma-
harajah and his father drives a Bentley. A few chapters include illustrations, the best of which is a chart in the biopoetics essay showing the
"Stochastic teddy bear descent rate" as Pooh falls from a tree into a gorse
bush. Documentation is another tool for satire. The Marxist essay, for example, is so full of citations from Frederic Jameson that it becomes a fawn-
ing celebration of Jameson rather than a discussion of Pooh. We laugh at
Crews's satire, but somewhat uncomfortably as we recognize that his message—literary criticism often pushes itself too far—is regrettably correct.
[Geralyn Strecker]

A. J. Perry. *Twelve Stories of Russia: A Novel, I Guess.* Glas/Ivan R. Dee,
2001. 448 pp. Paper: $14.95.

Twelve Stories of Russia: A Novel, I Guess documents one character's six-
and-a-half years living in Russia during its troubled transition from the
Cold War to upheaval and reform. A. J. Perry's protagonist—an English

teacher identified only as James—pieces his story together using a variety of forms—lists, alphabets, grammar lessons, card-game scores, even the seating chart for a wedding banquet. The effect is at first disorienting, but so is the experience that the narrator struggles to articulate. He is soon introduced to the grim realities of Russian life. Eventually, he learns Russian and makes friends in his adopted country. But the complexities of relationships are beyond the narrator's capacity for quantification and analysis, whether they come in the form of romantic trysts or everyday encounters with Russians who are dubious of the democratic ideals represented by their American guest. Despite his deadpan humor, it becomes apparent over the course of the book that the narrator's play with tone and form masks an urgent need to connect, both with the culture he is visiting and with the estranged family he has left behind in the United States. Episodes from the past punctuate the narrator's affectionate skewering of Russian life, adding a resonance that goes beyond easy satirical cleverness. At one point, a Russian friend advises James to write the usual book about a foreigner arriving in Moscow with high hopes but encountering instead "bread lines . . . toilet paper shortages . . . people yelling and shouting . . . . " The narrator's response is emblematic of this inventive fictional memoir: "I came expecting toilet paper shortages . . . and instead discovered poetry." [Pedro Ponce]

David Gilbert and Karl Roeseler, eds. *Here Lies*. Trip Street, 2001. 248 pp. Paper: $13.00.

The best anthologies these days center around a theme, whether it be private eyes, erotica, or war. True to its title, *Here Lies* presents stories that contain a lie or a character who is a liar. It "raises the question," the editors tell us, "of what is and what is not a lie." What follows is an eclectic—for want of a better word—compilation from familiar names such as Gilbert Sorrentino and Lydia Davis to notable newcomers like Deborah Levy and ZZ Packer. I'd never heard of Packer before picking up this anthology, but I'll be sure to seek out the author's debut collection from Riverhead. Packer's "Drinking Coffee Elsewhere" deals with young lesbians in college and the denial of sexuality, and reads so smooth and sharp the perfection hurts. The same can be said of Lewis Warsh's "The Russians," a story that draws you so deeply into its world of Russian immigrants, love, incest, and desperation, that you'll have a difficult time leaving it. To say that "The Russians" is haunting doesn't do this gem of fiction justice. There's plenty of humor in *Here Lies*. George Saunders's "I Can Speak!™" is a letter written by a sales rep to a dissatisfied customer who has returned a talking baby mask. Despite all the technical research the rep uses as justification for the product, in the end all he wants is not to lose his commission. One of the best surprises in this collection, and hilarious on its own weird level, is Mac Wellman's "Muazzez." Those familiar with Wellman's plays and the "alien" elements in them will appreciate this iconoclast's view of the world. There are many anthologies out there, and most of them fade away as quickly as they appear. *Here Lies* rises above the foam and should last. [Michael Hemmingson]

Lucius Shepard. *Valentine*. Four Walls Eight Windows, 2002. 181 pp. $18.00.

This valentine is a "complicated construction that has at its paper heart new memories, a painful history." It is sent by the narrator (a journalist) to "you," a woman whom he meets (by chance or by design) after a long absence of six years. The valentine is a description of their encounter in Piersall, a town in Florida, which waits for a hurricane. This "funny" (pun intended) valentine explores their erotic adventures, their secrets (from themselves and each other), their theatricals. The text begins with a temporal and spatial metaphor: "There are countries that exist only for a matter of days, sometimes for hours, not lasting long enough to be named or even recognized for what they are by their temporary citizenry." Consider the oddity of the metaphorical country that seems to be a *state* of consciousness, "a world elsewhere." The name "Piersall" can be read as "pierce-all" or "peers-all." We look for clues in the couple's conversation, but their dialogue is cloudy, occluded. They go to the Beach Theater, where they watch a movie called *Class* (a "remake") and read the movie as a representation of their situation. Theatricals within theatricals. As if these elusive, playful touches were not enough, the narrator imagines "the two of us tucked into a corner of this canvas, savage figures by Rousseau, shadows with burning eyes." Although the narrator maintains that "we had no reason for speech, both knowing all the other knew," we are unsure of his statement because at times they really don't know their fate, their "exits and entrances." And this valentine, uncanny as it is, is unforgettable because it poses such simple questions as: "Where are we going? What can we hope for? What should we want? Will you be mine?" [Irving Malin]

Robert Coover. *The Grand Hotels (of Joseph Cornell)*. Burning Deck, 2002. 64 pp. Paper: $10.00.

The fantastic hotels described in this slim and beautiful volume—the first half of which was first published in the collection *A Convergence of Birds* last year—are inspired by the boxes/sculptures of Joseph Cornell. Coover imagines a chain of metaphysical hotels and offers a chapter describing each one. The hotels are fairy-tale, childhood, fun-house, spage-age, nature, and even avian themed. More important, however, than their impossibly imagined physical features are the psychological and emotional comforts the hotels offer their guests: there is a hotel for "repressed desires and eventless lives"; one for "eternal verities" and "tragic estrangement"; one for the "literal reexperience of one's own lost childhood"; one for the "frame and image of [guests'] fleeting love"; one "to experience the deep structures of nature itself"; one for the "reassuring continuity between [guests'] present and their pasts." Each hotel also symbolically offers commentary on the creation and reception of art. Coover's book is a funny and moving mediation on the nature of desire and comfort. [Robert L. McLaughlin]

Cesare Pavese. *The Selected Works of Cesare Pavese*. Trans. and intro. R. W. Flint. New York Review Books, 2001. 397 pp. Paper: $16.95.

In four first-person novels Pavese renders with formidable talent extreme isolation, where people group only out of obscure necessity. As one character observes, "Having money means you can isolate yourself." Everyone is removed from the world, whether or not it be wartime or post-WWII Italy. Refuge is sought in cellars, tombs, cloisters, sheltered bathing spots. Jobs and studies mean little, women somewhat more. The primary haven for the three male narrators is the natural world, the repository of beauty, fecundity, and responsibility—husbandry carries a dual meaning in "The Devil in the Hills"—which unites with a nostalgia for boyhood to create a modern form of pantheism. Operating from that complex base Pavese attacks the industrial world's cities, bombs, and killings, scorns the idea of God—surviving the war, says the narrator of "The House on the Hill" after an epiphany that is only like grace, is "all chance, a game"—and, slyly, Italian fascism's destructive love for earlier, more glorious times. Significantly, the female narrator of "Among Women Only" has less time for nature and is nervous about her past. Nevertheless, her constant fearfulness is present, in subdued form, on the sands of "The Beach," as men jostle for position with other men and with women. Pavese's sentences look languid but the prose hides and reveals motivations and connections. "There's nothing to take away from life, it's already zero," remarks a female character in a typically aphoristic fashion. Clearly Pavese's intelligent, probing narratives, which possess their own brand of wit, brought forward in a clear, smooth translation, add more to an understanding of life and of peculiar kinds of solitude and ennui. [Jeff Bursey]

Chris Bachelder. *Bear v. Shark*. Scribner, 2001. 251 pp. $23.00.

Constantine, the typical tyro playwright in Chekhov's *The Seagull*, famously rejects convention, cries out for new forms, and produces a tedious flop. Thankfully, Chris Bachelder, a first-time novelist, realizes the value of having something relatively old to say. *Bear v. Shark* tells the satirical tale of an ordinary American family traveling to Las Vegas to witness the greatest—that is, most-hyped—spectacle of this or any age, a staged battle between two of nature's most perfect killing machines. The deadliest thing in the novel, unsurprisingly, is the inescapable, soul-deadening mass media machinery that promotes the event and turns domestic life into a cartoon. TV a vast wasteland? Imagine that. Bachelder freely acknowledges that this point has been dulled by repeated use, however, and he resharpens it by doing so. Part of his fun is referencing nearly all of the literary lions who've said something about consumer culture, borrowing styles and dropping names along the way. Rather than seeming derivative, the book is a veritable primer on postmodernism, a metafictional homage to everyone who's written countercultural essays in the form of metafictional novels, an entertaining set of Cliffs Notes for every undergraduate who hasn't read the overstuffed masterworks of the last forty years. In one chapter of *Bear v. Shark,* the *American Vacation* reality program chronicles the family's trip, with commentary provided by a young unknown — Chris Blackletter? Backacher? Badchildren? Something like that. A viewer e-mails: "Where's Pynchon. My Internet cable listing said it was going to be Pynchon doing color. That guy with the cummerbund ain't Pynchon." No, he isn't, and neither is he Barth, or DeLillo, or David Foster Wallace, but he's a pretty good simulation and he's funny as hell. [James Crossley]

Hanif Kureishi. *Gabriel's Gift.* Scribner, 2001. 223 pp. $23.00.

Kureishi's latest book continues with the theme of existence in a postcolonial society, ground which he's already covered nicely in *The Buddha of Suburbia* and *The Black Album.* His books are peopled with lost souls, men and women legendary in their own minds, but seemingly (and often humorously) insignificant in modern culture. Thankfully, however, in this book social issues are secondary; the intimacy of familial relationships is at the front. Gabriel, just coming into his teenage years, pulls himself through life in London as his aging rocker father is expelled from the family home by a neurotic, alcoholic mother. When Gabriel's father desperately attempts to grasp at the disintegrating straws of his past, hijinks ensue. At least on the surface. This novel is by far the most stripped down of Kureishi's. His choices in this book are crystal clear; in fact, my initial impression was that the novel felt incomplete, that the absence of the gritty detail that made his previous works so unique displayed a distinct lack of attention toward the material. However, as he did in his previous novel, *Intimacy,* and as he's always done in his short fiction, by tossing away all that is *not* to do with the characters, Kureishi's prose becomes far more deft at representing the nuances of human folly and casualty than most writers can accomplish with exhaustively specific detail. Kureishi isn't really breaking any new ground for himself here, but what may have been lost by excising the grander social themes is more than recovered with the genuine and perfectly tender rendering of an ordinary family breaking to bits and calling on its youngest member to grow up too quickly in order to fix it. [Brian Budzynski]

Richard Burgin. *The Spirit Returns*. Johns Hopkins Univ. Press, 2001. 191 pp. Paper: $13.95.

Burgin's landscape is a wasteland, its inhabitants suffering some form of ennui yet incapable of creating relationships that would sustain them. The opening story, "Miles," acts as the imprimatur on Burgin's canvass. In it a lonely young man feels that what he wants from women is to "have his way" and proceeds to allow an angry black man to draw him into a clandestine meeting with a woman for a purely sexual tryst. Yet this meeting simply brings his loneliness to the surface, for Miles realizes that having his way cannot bring him what he truly longs for—sex *and* a soul mate. As each story unravels, it becomes clear that in this world where alienation reigns it is difficult to obtain either of those needs and impossible to gain both. In "The Spirit Returns," a fight in a subway and a horrendous storm drive Eugene from New York, where his "passion" for frightening people threatens to overwhelm him. When he returns for a visit, his addiction leads to an encounter with a beautiful woman whom he fails to frighten and also fails to win, leaving him busted and more alone than he ever was. The final story, "The Usher Twins," concerns a stillborn relationship between kindred souls; it is a grand fugue on unending longing. These tales, taken together, point to a disturbing conclusion: In the U.S., the social contract has become null and void. But for all this dry analysis, Burgin's prose is invigorating. Bravely and imaginatively, he characterizes that feeling of being adrift in a consumer-driven society and is particularly astute and funny dealing with the male viewpoint. Yet he also reveals much about the total disconnect between the genders. In another solid story collection, Burgin continues his haunting exploration of the condition of contemporary America's psyche. [Jean Timmons]

Steve Aylett. *The Crime Studio*. Four Walls Eight Windows, 2001. 156 pp. Paper: $14.95.

Steve Aylett's first book, originally published in Britain in 1994, embodies the point that laughter is many things, not the least of which is a shock-reaction to righteously deft wit: we laugh partly out of admiration for the degree of skill with which the humor is conveyed. *The Crime Studio* is a comic-noir tour-de-force in which otherwise trite hardboiler elements are the raw materials for Aylett's cockeyed take on genre fiction. In Beerlight, U.S.A., everyone is either crook or cop, and the entire population is spastically nihilistic. "How crisply I recall the summer when . . . the denizens of Beerlight burst hollering onto the streets and began arbitrarily shooting the life out of each other. For the first time there was a real sense of community." Aylett's language is deadpan British, using light and matter-of-fact diciton to describe acts of thuggish depravity. From a lesser writer this m.o. would produce a wake-me-when-it's-over "gritty" street drama, but Aylett's action is cartoonish, never explicit, which keeps the book from sinking into a grim post-Tarantino gratuitous-mayhem quagmire. The characters' demented reasonableness (one delinquent thoughtfully informs his victims "that the report they had heard was just a cough from my handgun") contributes to the book's cheerfulness; the book's goons are endearingly earnest in their rationale for their outrageously illegal pursuits. Literate, too: one hack alters Don DeLillo's work in progress "so that one of the characters smiled." Aylett pulls off the neat trick of creating stories (twenty-seven of them—it's like the Ramones wrote a book) whose over-the-top abandon belies a firm hold over the material, demonstrating that it takes a very careful hand to write such chaotic stuff. *The Crime Studio* manages to subvert genre fiction without descending into sniggling postmodern ridicule, which may be the last brave thing left in contemporary literature. [Tim Feeney]

Steve Weiner. *The Yellow Sailor*. Overlook, 2001. 220 pp. $26.95.

Steve Weiner's first novel, *The Museum of Love* (1994), drew comparisons to Burroughs, Céline, and Genet, as well as filmmakers Cronenberg, Lynch, and Todd Haynes, for its blend of surrealism and sadism. *The Yellow Sailor* extends his strangely traumatic aesthetics, evoking an unpleasant world of lost hopes. The novel opens in Hamburg in 1914 and continues to explore the grotesque and tense environment of northern Europe at the dawn of World War I. It extrapolates from this particular moment a mood or sensibility of desperation and desolation, where love, religion, and nationalism are emptied of their value. The novel begins on the titular merchant ship, but the ship is wrecked in the first chapter, leaving most of the work to follow the separate journeys of the five main characters. A dream or nightmare quality surrounds their episodic adventures, as if Hasek's good soldier Schweik had been dropped into a war landscape crafted by Genet, Dennis Cooper, or de Sade. Most of the novel takes place in bordellos, bars, labor colonies, and the streets, where encounters with nomadic workers, soldiers, corrupt police, and prostitutes—straight, gay, and child—are often marked by violence. The most pronounced feature of the novel, though, is the elliptical, telegraphic prose that is delivered in a consistently sharp, staccato fashion. Everything is described and spoken in a dead, affectless tone, which heightens the cold, empty feeling of the world described. The rhythmic minimalism also affects the content in that central scenes and actions are often hinted at or summarized curtly rather than delineated in detail. While Weiner uses flat language effectively to create an environment of devastation, *The Yellow Sailor* runs the risk of numbing the reader to the pleasure of reading the book itself, though its sick humor and beauty save it at critical points. [David Ian Paddy]

Ray Vukcevich. *Meet Me in the Moon Room*. Small Beer, 2001. 253 pp. Paper: $16.00.

Ray Vukcevich is a master of the last line. Almost every one of his stories has a zinger at the end, but not the kind of zinger that shocks the reader or causes annoyance. Often it's a perfect line of dialogue that opens up the whole story and, at the same time, avoids a heavy-handed conclusion. Example: " 'Me,' he shouted, 'pick me!' " from "Pink Smoke," a story involving a beloved pickpocket turned magician. Or, from "Doing Time," a poetic statement of disappointment: "I get real discouraged, and I wonder if maybe I'm just pissing into the wind." My favorite—"Nothing happens"—comes from the story "Season Finale," in which sitcom television mixes with supposed real life. Of course, the stories that go along with these last lines are pretty good too. One of Vukcevich's favorite themes seems to be reincarnation or, at the very least, spiritual ventriloquism. His characters seek each other out as beings that have been transformed into fish, ghosts, and small children. The connections between them, though questionable, show desperation and sadness, and, in a way, dire hope. A few of the stories lack the originality that the others possess ("We Kill a Bicycle" and "Home Remedy" manipulate the reader a little too much), but the majority of them prove that Vukcevich is ingenious with the short-story form. Although the stories read as playful vignettes, Vukcevich covertly works in ideas of self, identity, destiny, and obsession. And occasionally, the dangers of outer space. [Amy Havel]

Peter Rock. *The Ambidextrist*. Context, 2002. 214 pp. $21.95.

The Ambidextrist focuses on Scott, a vagabond who comes to Philadelphia to outpace his past and who hooks on at a hospital, making money as a subject for medical experiments. Scott quickly becomes entwined with the lives of three others living in the city's margins. One is an eccentric homeless man named Ray, with whom Scott develops a softly stated trust. Another is Terrell, a young teen entering the minefields between puberty and manhood and to whom Scott aspires to be a mentor of sorts. Scott also tries to make a connection with Terrell's sister and guardian, Ruth, but his advances (while not without a certain charm) tend to border on low-level stalking. This sort of tension, between potential and despair, between beauty and a darkness lurking just behind it, permeates the novel. The teenage Terrell is certainly a sympathetic character, but he becomes involved in increasingly violent and destructive behavior as the novel progresses. Ray is a homeless man romantic enough to have fashioned a hidden "garden" out of bits of glass and other junk, replete with even a reflecting pond. Still, there are strong hints that Ray has exiled himself into homelessness as a way of escaping what may be pedophilic tendencies. It is Ray's garden that in some ways emerges as the central trope of the novel, more so even than Scott's ambidexterity which gives it its title. While the novel raises issues of homelessness, mental illness, and inner-city gangs, it doesn't do so with an aim at something like social realism per se. Instead, like Ray's garden, *The Ambidextrist* seems more interested in mining for the aesthetic possibilities lurking in its downtrodden terrain. [T. J. Gerlach]

Reinaldo Arenas. *Mona and Other Tales.* Selected and trans. Dolores M. Koch. Vintage, 2001. 190 pp. Paper: $12.00.

Regardless of what some may say in this age of content over form, there is a melody to some prose that announces to the reader that the melody-maker is a lyricist of significant measure. Such are the songs sung by Reinaldo Arenas in *Mona and Other Tales.* There's a line in the story "The Glass Tower" in which the narrator says of the protagonist (Alfredo Fuentes, a Cuban novelist in exile) that there were those who were "critical of his facile eloquence." In that phrase, "facile eloquence" (whether meant ironically or not), lies much of the poetic strength in Arenas's prose, and what distinguishes that prose is its versatility. That is, he can write a short story in the traditional mode (à la Chekhov and Poe), keenly focusing on the linear fundamentals of singleness of effect, active detail, and epiphany (as in "With My Eyes Closed"); or he can write a story that is as layered and multifaceted as a story from Cortázar (as in "Mona"). For some reason (known only to the publicist for Vintage Books) the *New York Times* blurb that graces the cover, "His stories are fresh, slightly lyrical, surprisingly subtle," was presumably meant to be something laudable; however, it is the kind of "encomium" no writer of Arenas's stature would have been happy with. Adjectives like "fresh" and adverbial phrases like "slightly lyrical" and "surprisingly subtle" are either hackneyed or condescending or both and in no way relate to the real writing. Apparently the stories are not "lyrical," merely "slightly lyrical." Even a cursory reading of Arenas would indicate that one is reading the work of someone totally in control of his material, whose prose, even in English, is as lyrical as he had planned and as subtle as he had envisioned. [Mark Axelrod]

Mary Robison. *Why Did I Ever.* Counterpoint, 2001. 200 pp. $23.00.

Mary Robison's first novel in ten years is less a novel than a collection of 536 fragments chronicling the life of Money Breton, a failing Hollywood script doctor, three-time divorcée, and mother of two grown children. The book's structure nicely reflects and reinforces the disorganization in Money's life and mental state. She's afflicted, as she lets on before page ten, with Attention Deficit Disorder. She explains, "Without Ritalin I can sustain an evil thought or two, such as: 'That there feels like cancer of the esophagus.' However, I'm liable to skip over more routine kinds of thinking, such as, 'Move up in line here,' or 'Steer.'" Without the Ritalin, she stays "in bed," a line nicely reminiscent of Joan Didion. It's likely this obsession with psychosomatic health that led one reviewer to compare Robison to Didion, though the novel's voice more readily brings to mind Lorrie Moore. For all the unreliable narrator flaws ADD might imply, Money's voice is sincere, and full of a dark, wise humor. She isn't losing her mind; rather, she's laughing out loud at just how unbelievably, absurdly awful life can get sometimes. This is the main charm of the novel: her blunt take on the ridiculous state of her life, and, too, the people in her life. Indeed, Money's alternately confident and self-loathing perspective is what makes the book as painful as it is hilarious. (It might seem an odd comparison, but Money's voice and predicament—particularly the non sequitur series of letters to Sean Penn—bring to mind Bellow's *Herzog*.) The only complaint I might make is with the novel's length. In 200 pages and fourteen chapters, its fragments breeze by fast, making it a very quick read. Money's voice is so kooky, smart, brave, and wicked, you'd be happy to read 536 more. [Suzanne Scanlon]

Arthur Bradford. *Dogwalker*. Knopf, 2001. 144 pp. $20.00.

The epilogue to this collection of stories describes a dream about a book that is not restricted to reality but that follows the course of its own invented reality. It is worth reconsidering this epilogue after you've finished *Dogwalker* because the realities invented here, with dogs as their common motif, are disorienting, though delightful in their way. Bradford has succeeded in transforming our notion of storytelling by reacquainting us with the central reality of dream narratives: they are strange, but recognizable, and they follow a certain alternative logic. Like a contemporary Sherwood Anderson, Bradford is fascinated by and sympathetic to grotesque characters. Many of these spare, crisp stories center around an unusual experience precipitated by the narrator's encounters with odd people, like a roommate named Catface who eats the food the narrator had intended to feed his three-legged dog, or another roommate who kidnaps his landlady, then slices himself in two under a freight train. The first-person narrator of all twelve stories draws us into his reality and lets its bizarre circumstances dictate the action. His clarity is almost arresting, given the surreal quality of the subject matter, and he manages humor even when his raw material is disturbing. The strangeness of the stories is relative, but it reaches a marked crescendo in "Dogs," the longest story in the collection. Here the narrator sires a muskratlike offspring with his girlfriend's dog, finds out that the muskrat has in turn impregnated a woman who lives in an iron lung, and . . . you get the idea. The author's imagination may prove too rich for some readers, or maybe there's a limit to how far a story can follow its own invented reality. If so, Arthur Bradford is intent on pushing at that limit. [D. Quentin Miller]

Jean-Patrick Manchette. *3 to Kill*. Trans. Donald Nicholson-Smith. City Lights, 2002. 134 pp. Paper: $11.95.

What's essential is not so much a reinvention of the novel as an ongoing redefinition of it. Beginning in the early seventies, Jean-Patrick Manchette achieved for the French crime novel just such a redefinition, rescuing the genre from the sludge of police procedurals and stylized exoticism it had become and setting it like a cur at the heel of contemporary literature. "The crime novel," he said, "is the great moral literature of our time." A massive presence in France and throughout Europe, Manchette to this point has remained untranslated and wholly unknown in the States. Now City Lights, in its new series of European crime novels, offers *3 to Kill*, the first of Manchette's stream of ten great novels, with the last, *The Prone Gunman*, promised soon. For Manchette, and largely for the generation of writers who followed him, the crime novel is far more than entertainment: it's a means to combat and decry the failings of society, burning its way through pages and the blitz of the everyday to rivers of power and influence beneath. *3 to Kill* tells the story of an ordinary man who, arbitrarily set upon by killers, steps out of his life to turn their killing back upon them. As ever, the novel is brilliantly written, replete with allusions to art, literature, and music, papered with the very texture and furniture of our lives. Manchette is Camus on overdrive, at one and the same time white-hot, ice-cold. He deserves much the same attention. [James Sallis]

Paul Wilson. *Someone to Watch Over Me*. Granta, 2001. 244 pp. £12.99.

This novel, both a theological and secular mystery, takes its title from the Gershwin song, in which a young woman sings longingly for a lover. The implications here are more sinister, because we live in a paranoid world where a watcher could invade our individual rights or protect us from pickpockets or terrorists. There is also less belief in a spiritual force that can keep us and our loved ones from harm. Brendan Moon is a watcher. He investigates religious fraud for the Maslow Company, a firm that does not want to pay out £7 million for a prize established by their founder for anyone who can prove that a miracle has taken place. Moon is sent to a small town in Lancashire, where a sexually abused young man has shot over a dozen schoolchildren. This is not a remarkable or miraculous occurrence in a violent age, but the appearance of parchments in ancient Hebrew raining on the village is. Moon, a lapsed Catholic who is mourning the untimely death of his son, a wife who has left him, and the loss of his faith, must try to make sense of these events as well as these mysterious "letters from God." He realizes that, especially in the face of truly awful occurrences, people want some explanation, "the soothing comfort that *someone somewhere* was in control of events." His investigation causes him to revisit a priestly mentor from his childhood, a simple-minded groundskeeper, and the writings of a twentieth-century Jewish poet. At the end, although the secular mystery is solved, the theological one is still in the hand of this "professional doubter." Moon realizes that for him, as well as the other confused and hurting souls he encounters, the human connection is the most important, that "this fragile mystery of life itself . . . is the wonder to rejoice in." [Sally E. Parry]

———————

Paul LaFarge. *Haussmann, or the Distinction*. Farrar, Straus & Giroux, 2001. 382 pp. $24.00.

The central figure of Paul LaFarge's second novel is Baron Georges-Eugéne Haussmann, the architect of modern Paris, who introduced the civic order of the modern metropolis into the chaos of the medieval city. LaFarge's captivating prose navigates the intricacies of city life as the ambitious Baron conspires with a duplicitous demolition man and secretly conducts an affair with his adopted daughter. The story, which masquerades as a translation of Paul Poissel's *Haussmann*, chronicles the Baron's tumultuous struggle for imperial favor and immortality, a struggle that breeds motives and countermotives as complex as the city map: "here is only one design superimposed upon another, replacing the parts it covers, lines obscuring and obscured by other lines." Haussmann and LaFarge represent Paris's architectural, political, and spiritual transformation to modernity in the Baron's elaborate plans for an underground network of sewers and his blueprint for a grand cemetery, "a Necropolis as large as all Versailles"—"the ideal city, perhaps: clean, bright, and regular, above all, regular." As the novel balances modern tensions between life and death, the natural and the man-made, the past and the future, LaFarge's Baron inhabits "a city which never existed: the new Paris as imagined hopefully by the old, or the old Paris as remembered with regret by the new." Yet while this is a promising novel, the author—either LaFarge or Poissel—maintains too much ironic distance from his characters, including Haussmann, who remains a mystery. A greater disappointment, I believe, is that LaFarge does not exploit the metafictive frame of the translation within the body of his narrative and misses the opportunity to superimpose design upon design and to truly translate this historical fiction into the present. [Trey Strecker]

———————

Frederick Busch. *War Babies*. New Directions, 2001. 114 pp. Paper: $12.95.

During Frederick Busch's prolific career there have been some notable gems, including *War Babies*, first published in 1989. *War Babies*, like his superb early novel *Manual Labor*, is about the tenuousness of identity. An American, Peter Santore, travels to Salisbury to confront his father's past by finding Hilary Pennels, the daughter of an English war hero who died in a Korean POW camp. Peter's father, who survived the conflict by turning traitor, may have been responsible in some measure for Pennels's death. Peter, the narrator, explains his mission: "It had always been simply to be in the same town as the child of the hero of a moment during which my father had distinguished himself by turning coat." The simplicity of this symmetry underscores the difficulty of resolving the past, as the past refuses to be so readily contained. While Santore joined the Peace Fighters on his own volition, Pennels ordered his men to join so they would gain access to food and medical supplies. After ordering his men to join, however, Pennels remained behind, and during the interrogation that followed, at which Santore may have been present, Pennels died. While Peter attempts to cope with his traitorous father, Hilary is burdened with her father's heroism. His heroism, she claims, was more important to him than his family, and now she is marked by a father she knows only through the narratives provided by her father's sergeant-major, whom Hilary admits "lives more in 1951 in Korea than he does here or the present." Even as the novel attempts to resolve itself around Hilary's claim that "We have a right, both of us, to live our own lives," the novel commendably avoids closure as the past inextricably remains an active component of the present. *War Babies* is Frederick Busch at his best. [Alan Tinkler]

Barry Hannah. *Yonder Stands Your Orphan*. Atlantic, 2001. 336 pp. $24.00.

Hannah's latest novel is his first in ten years—since 1991's *Never Die* he's published only two collections of (quite strong) stories. Taking its title from a Bob Dylan song, *Yonder Stands Your Orphan* has no real central character and only the loosest of plots. But plot and focus are hardly the chief reasons why Hannah should be read. It's all about the sentence, about style, and about the way in which style crafts character. Unique, Hannah's rippling prose creates sorry, down-and-out and (sometimes quite literally) mangled characters who still manage nonetheless to struggle through. These characters are manifold, with none really dominating. Indeed, the novel seems more to focus around a place, Eagle Lake, though finally the novel chooses to disperse rather than to gather into a coherent whole. The players include the nasty but Conway-Twitty-faced pimp and killer Man Mortimer, the dramatist-lawman Sheriff Facetto, Facetto's seventy-two-year-old girlfriend Melanie Wooten, ex-biker and pastor Egan, ex-doctor and saxophonist Max Raymond, and orphan-lovers Gene and Penny. As the characters collide and come into each other's orbits, they grind each other up a little further, but sometimes transform one another. There are echoes of Hannah's past books here. Sidney Farte reappears from Hannah's "Water Liars," from the masterful collection *Airships*. The method in which Man Mortimer kills Sidney's father recalls Hannah's second book, *Nightwatchmen,* and overall the novel recalls both *Nightwatchmen* and Faulkner's *Sanctuary*. It is a book to be read for its brilliant, crystalline moments, rather than the whole—with bereft parents nailing their feet to the floor, orphans running mad, and Man Mortimer engaging on a path of mayhem even as he physically wastes away. *Yonder Stands Your Orphan* shows that despite having found Jesus, Hannah can still write alarming, harrowing scenes and sentences, that he remains an American original. [Brian Evenson]

Dan Chaon. *Among the Missing*. Ballantine, 2001. 258 pp. $22.00.

Among the Missing, Dan Chaon's second collection of stories, is a fascinating blend of postmodern conditions many writers and readers tend to skip over in their attempts to find meaning in life as a whole. Chaon skillfully brings to life the high-wire acts in which many contemporary families are unwillingly engaged as he re-creates a variety of tensions: between parents and their children, among siblings, and especially the mental twists and turns within the human mind. Children are hurt by their parents' harsh words, sexually misused, and made to feel they have little significance in either their families or their communities. These painfully isolated individuals strive for validation by attempting to engage with anyone who may offer consolation and/or affirmation of their existence. Chaon's characters, however, are brought to life with a compassion and understanding that allows the reader to step confidently into their worlds without the usual and expected ennui of a fractured postmodern sensibility. In "Big Me" a young narrator secretly visits a neighbor he believes to be himself at an older age. Alienated by this discovery of another "Big Me," his adult personality is forever manipulated by his desire to keep the events of his childhood contained and inaccessible, even to himself. The slippery nature of reality and the function of memory is also a significant part of the title story, in which an entire family, buckled into their car, disappears into a lake. Almost no one in the town wants to believe the family is dead, and although the townspeople desire and need "that there would be some rational explanation," none is forthcoming. Chaon's work suggests that—like life itself—even the best stories have no neat and tidy connections, and this is what makes fact and fiction the painful, yet enchanting, journeys they are. [Anne Foltz]

Gerald Locklin. *A Simpler Time, A Simpler Place: Three Mid-Century Stories*. Event Horizon, 2000. 167 pp. Paper: $12.95.

The three stories comprising this collection perform a meticulous examination of repressed sexuality and the desires that motivate the often-absurd behavior of humans. Set in the 1950s and sixties, Locklin's stories present characters who fight against their cravings only to give in to them in the most destructive and unsatisfying of ways. The first tale, a 140-page novella, focuses its attention on a sexually tormented young priest as he moves toward an epiphanic renunciation of his vows. Singular in this portrayal is the attention Locklin pays to the most banal aspects of the priest's existence: a dinner with his aging parents, a picnic with his parishioners. With an economy of language and a precision rare in the current atmosphere of linguistic exorbitance, the author is able paint vividly the comic torment of this man of the cloth: "A few minutes later she directed him to a bare spot behind some oak trees, near a canal. The moon did not penetrate the canopy of leaves. They had come here to talk and neither of them said anything." As if to allow a view of opposing sides, a parallax of sorts, Locklin

follows his novella with two shorter stories—in one, the narrator specu-
lates about the possible perversities of the old priest he used to wrestle in
his childhood; in the other, we witness a conversation between men who
doubt the existence of the female orgasm. Rendering these portraits with
inference and irony, Locklin brilliantly exposes the myths that infect our
nostalgia of the mid-twentieth century. With a humor and a mastery of
craft that might, in some ways, remind readers of a more traditional George
Saunders, Locklin reveals the true obsessions of the 1950s, a time that was,
in the view of these stories, anything but simple. [Aaron Gwyn]

Edward Carey. *Observatory Mansions*. Crown, 2000. 356 pp. $23.00.

I am pleased that Vintage has just reprinted this novel in paperback. There
were few reviews of the cloth edition, despite the fact that it was hailed as
"brilliant" by John Fowles and as a "striking debut" by the *Times Literary
Supplement*. The novel has an epigraph by Marin Sorescu: "I gloved and
greased / my hands, my legs, my thoughts / leaving no part of my person /
exposed to touch / or other poisons." The lines suggest that the body is
threatened by "reality," that it needs protection from external poisons.
Carey implies that identity, perception, and consciousness are so tainted
that they are nightmarish, grotesque, and perverse. Almost every page suggests the fluidity of existence. People and objects are blurred. And as the
observatory—emphasize vision!—goes to pieces, it seems as if, like the
body, it is threatened by objects. The narrator, unsure that he exists, decides to collect objects, to *possess* them (as he is possessed by his infantile
possessions). Of course, he begins to believe that he doesn't exist except as
an object in *someone's* collection. He makes much of the fact (or delusion)
that he—and perhaps the six other occupants of the decayed mansion—
cannot move: "Under the terrible inertia of pyloric stenosis we tried to move
no more than was necessary, movement was painful to us now, painful to us
and to our home—too quick a movement might bring us down . . . if our
home was to die, and we realized it must, then definitely, we should die with
it." Perhaps he can save himself by recognizing that he is an object and that
he is really no more than one of a collection. Carey offers a final terrifying
(and unbalanced) idea—he seduces us into believing that his words are so
powerful we are marked by his black lines on the white page. [Irving Malin]

Lydia Davis. *Samuel Johnson Is Indignant: Stories*. McSweeney's, 2001.
201 pp. $17.00.

In her latest collection, the author of *Break It Down* (1986) and *Almost No
Memory* (1997) delivers fifty-six scintillating stories that showcase her almost tactile love of language in sentences reminiscent of Baudelaire's prose
poems or Kafka's fables. If these diverse tales share a subject, it is the difficulty of communication and the modern impulse to objectify other individuals.

Davis's stories—some as brief as a single elliptical sentence—do not depend upon verbal pyrotechnics; rather, her stories are quiet and introspective, nuanced meditations of minimalist precision that flower into complexity and urge the reader to see anew. Even in a short review, there can be no substitute for the texture of her beautiful sentences: "Because they were fantasies she had alone, at night, they continued to feel like some sort of betrayal, and perhaps, because approached in this spirit of betrayal, as perhaps they had to be, to be any comfort and strength, continued to be, in fact, a sort of betrayal"; "It is certainly true that the larger and older the living thing is, the harder it is to know how to care for it"; "The useful thing about being a selfish person is that when your children get hurt you don't mind so much because you yourself are all right." Whether writing about marital infidelity and memory or lawn mowers and jury duty, Davis's contemplative, poetic prose and her deft characterization brilliantly underscore the subtleties of modern life, subjectivity, and conscience. These are stories meant to be savored. [Trey Strecker]

Annie Ernaux. *Happening*. Trans. Tanya Leslie. Seven Stories, 2001. 95 pp. $18.95.

In *Happening* Ernaux returns to the experience of her illegal abortion that she plumbed in *Cleaned Out*. While that book used fiction to explain and expunge, this book self-consciously returns to convey and contemplate. I say self-consciously because Ernaux has written a detailed, explicit book not only about her pregnancy and abortion, but also about remembering and writing. The book was written over the course of nine months; by beginning many sections with "Yesterday" or "Last night" Ernaux makes explicit the construction of this narrative in time. As such emotions veer, statements are made and contradicted. "Reality" in one section connotes the everyday world from which Ernaux in her condition has been exiled, and is the stark physicality and emotional landscape of that same condition in another. After seeing a documentary on Nazi death camps, she thinks, "the pain I was about to inflict on myself would be nothing compared to the suffering experienced in death camps," yet goes on to describe delivery as "D-day." Such contradictions not only convey the emotional complexities of the ordeal, but also prove successful her desire to "revisit every single image until I feel that I have physically bonded with it." Written words are not revisited because it would obfuscate the truth of the experience—writing bred of memory and sensation. At times her approach proves frustrating. Some sections are written a bit clumsily for a writer of Ernaux's skill, some statements clichéd for someone of her intelligence. However, these problems are subordinated to the honesty and truth (is it not true that even great writers pen lousy sentences? And keen minds think in cliché?) Ernaux has set as her goal. Moreover, she succeeds in rendering the numbing grind of diurnal unhappiness, fearful accounts of her trips to the abortionist, and harrowing the miscarriage in her dorm room with beauty and riveting detail. [Gregory Howard]

Terry Southern. *Now Dig This: The Unspeakable Writings of Terry Southern 1950-1995*. Ed. Nile Southern and Josh Alan Friedman. Grove, 2001. 263 pp. $25.00.

Now Dig This collects thirty-five miscellaneous outrages perpetrated by the esteemed author of *The Magic Christian* and *Barbarella*. These "unspeakable" and often very amusing writings prove amenable to classification, and readers are administered roughly equal doses of tall tales, letters, glimpses "behind the silver screen," forays in the new journalism, send-ups of "the quality lit game," and "strolls down memory lane" in the form of interviews, articles, short stories, and sundry communiqués both previously published and unpublished. The reader will herein learn, for instance, Slim Pickens's criteria for a happy life ("jest a pair of loose-fittin' shoes, some tight pussy, an' a warm place to shit") and why, according to a letter to *Ms.* magazine, Southern believes women will never be taken seriously (they writhe and sob and "Oh, my god" too much when coming). A tribute to Edgar Allan Poe ("King Weirdo") rolls its eyes at some very astute comments on fiction in the age of film, and recollections of Abbie Hoffman, William Burroughs, and Larry Rivers cavort amid the "provocative twitch" of more than a few "pert rumps" and perhaps more than one wants to know about the sexual proclivities of poet Frank O'Hara or one G. Ames Plimpton. Letters to *National Lampoon* make small talk with a *Saturday Review* piece on the Rolling Stones, and a 1968 piece for *Esquire* on the police riots during the Chicago Democratic convention cohabits comfortably with a *Glamour* profile of singer Lotte Lenya. Southern was one of those guys who was everywhere and knew everyone (from Sam Beckett and Henry Green to Allen Ginsberg and the girls of Paris's "famed *Maison de Langue*"), and *Now Dig This* does much to freshen the cocktail that was always his gone (but not forgotten) prose. [Brooke Horvath]

Peter Carey. *30 Days in Sydney*. Bloomsbury, 2001. 248 pp. $16.95.

In the summer of 2000, while the world focused its attention on the pockets of Sydney given over to hosting the Olympic games, novelist Peter Carey returned to the city he had left for New York some ten years before. Carey wrote about his month-long experience for Bloomsbury's The Writer and the City series. While this is Carey's first book-length work of nonfiction, he doesn't seem at all out of his element, as *30 Days* gives him ample opportunity to exercise his interests in rich historical detail and a lively, never dry analysis of the way the past shapes the present, interests always apparent in his novels. Carey subtitles his book "A Wildly Distorted Account," and perhaps it is, since he does talk almost exclusively to his old friends, all of whom he hunts down, has dinner and drinks with, and then tape-records, tapping them for their stories. When Carey comes across a copy of Flann O'Brien's *The Third Policeman* at a friend's house, he thereafter adopts O'Brien's use of an internal interrogator, who questions Carey on his perceptions, testing him on the value of his mission and the trustworthiness of his memory. But whatever Carey trades in objectivity and selflessness, qualities which are, anyway, probably vastly overrated when it comes to travel writing, he more than makes up for with detail and insight. Readers are thus treated to stories about the improbability of Sydney (Captain Cook recommended settling five miles to the south, at Botany Bay), how architecture adapted to the environment, the importance of sandstone, the baroque development of the city's central business district, and the lingering effects of having a master-class and a servant-class coexist in close quarters. Carey's book is, finally, a collection of just the sort of stories one always wishes to hear from travelers. [Paul Maliszewski]

Amy J. Elias. *Sublime Desire: History and Post-1960s Fiction*. Johns Hopkins Univ. Press, 2001. 320 pages. $42.50.

Sublime Desire constitutes a major contribution to the growing body of work on contemporary historical fiction, which Elias dubs "metahistorical romance" because it combines a constant reflection on its own procedures with a longing for the historical sublime. The latter boils down to the "solid ground beneath one's feet" that postmodern consciousness is said to sorely lack. This projection of certainty provides novelists with a motivation to engage with history in a meaningful way, despite their inevitable misgivings about the possibility of historical truth. So although post-1960s historical fiction indulges in metafictionality, achronology, and other literary tactics in an effort to question traditional historiography, it simultaneously tries to find a level of representation on which the ideological aspects of a specific historical situation can be exposed and perhaps even criticized. Elias is at her best when analyzing individual novels (by a series of so-called First World authors including Thomas Pynchon, John Barth, Ishmael Reed, Leslie Marmon Silko, Charles Johnson and Charles Frazier) as illustrations of this paradox. Apart from teasing out provocative readings of single titles, she also manages to organize her discussion of metahistorical romance around a number of significant themes. Parataxis and simultaneity appear as the privileged techniques for indicting and attempting to transcend the familiar methods of historical representation. The popularity of the eighteenth century in recent historical fiction proves the importance of the Enlightenment as a focal point in the debate about modernity and its fundamental concept of progress. Finally, a confrontation with contemporary postcolonial fiction leads to the finding that First World historical novelists consider their own history from the perspective of its Others. While this monograph is not entirely jargon-free and occasionally repetitive, it is definitely a must for those who wonder about the pervasiveness of history in contemporary literature. [Luc Herman]

Philip Tew. *B. S. Johnson: A Critical Reading*. Manchester Univ. Press, 2001. 274 pp. $69.95.

A search in the *MLA International Bibliography* turns up twenty-four references to work about B. S. Johnson, once one of England's most interesting, innovative writers; obscurity would not, however, surprise him. In 1973, the last year of his life, his preface to *Aren't You Rather Young to Be Writing Your Memoirs?* indicates his plight: "I offer [these prose pieces] . . . despite my experience that the incomprehension and weight of prejudice which faces anyone trying to do anything new in writing is enormous, sometimes disquieting, occasionally laughable." Philip Tew tries to set this right with his detailed critical study: "[My] unabashed ambition . . . is to contribute towards the process of rescuing Johnson from what has been a marginal and peripheral position, and to do so th[r]ough applying to his texts exegetical strategies that can sustain the value of his work." Abetted in his crusade by Will Self and Jim Crace as blurb writers and Jonathan Coe, Johnson's biographer, Tew's work is allied with some of the wittiest novelists in England, thoroughly appropriate to Johnson's work. This "critical reading" contains a wealth of information set out in three sections that might be described as, first, background and autobiographical foundations for the texts; second, their intellectual, linguistic, and literary contexts; and, penultimately, "a cartography of self and the city." A coda follows, attempting to draw together the elements of Tew's study and the subject of Johnson criticism. The work would have profited from more careful editing and a clearer sense of the function of the various theoretical sources introduced. [Richard J. Murphy]

A. S. Byatt. *On Histories and Stories: Selected Essays*. Harvard Univ. Press, 2001. 196 pp. $22.95.

A. S. Byatt is at her best in this collection when explaining her own work, not least because she provides very concrete suggestions for interpretation. The two historical novellas that make up her *Angels and Insects* (1992) simply cry out for this kind of authorial direction, and Byatt is careful not to exhaust them, which makes her comments all the more useful. Billed as an analysis of the boom in British historical fiction, *On Histories and Stories* is nevertheless a considerable failure. Indulging in the prime student weakness, Byatt drowns her argument—or what there is of it—in quotation and paraphrase. As a result she often doesn't manage to go beyond the announcement of the essay's topic and a brief treatment of what she considers the most relevant passages from an altogether subjective set of historical narratives that are meant to illustrate her point. Indeed, the ensuing discussion of individual texts resembles a hasty tour through Byatt's personal gallery rather than a full-fledged treatment of the subject at hand. The eclecticism of "Old Tales, New Forms," a piece about the contemporary historical novel on the European continent, is downright embarrassing. To make things worse, the central thoughts of an individual essay frequently remain so underdeveloped that it becomes impossible to dispute them. This is the case, for instance, with the idea in the first essay that historical fiction partly compensates for the inescapable and perhaps frustrating insight that history must remain unknowable. The subsequent presentation of several war narratives could have benefited from this proposition, yet Byatt insists on looking the other way. So while some of her observations are stimulating, the reader interested in present-day historical fiction may do well to turn to more encompassing monographs on the subject, such as *A Poetics of Postmodernism* (1988) by Linda Hutcheon. [Luc Herman]

Ekbert Faas. *Robert Creeley: A Biography*. With Maria Trombacco. Univ. Press of New England, 2001. 513 pp. $35.00.

Ekbert Faas has chosen an audacious style for the first biography of one of the greatest American poets. Faas focuses on the poet's first forty years and relies overwhelmingly on his letters to and from influential figures like Charles Olson, Robert Duncan, Denise Levertov, etc. Most intriguing, though, is that the narrative paraphrases the epistolary style of its sources. Faas mimics Creeley's language and his rhetorical shifts, often to hallucinatory effect. The biography's appendix, which consists of the reminiscences of Ann MacKinnon, Creeley's first wife, heightens this effect, for in important particulars her view does not square with that of his letters. Still, *if* Faas is correct, the facts are disturbing, whatever they are. Because *Robert Creeley* is mediocre in its exploration of Creeley's early poetic and crucial association with Black Mountain College, the indelible impression it makes has more to do with its portrayal of the young poet's dark character than with his innovations. But mark that "*if*." According to people familiar with Creeley, the biography contains distortions, especially in its depiction of Creeley as a sexual predator. What's more, it's definitely sloppy; consider that the book ends with a misquoted poem. According to Faas, the older Creeley is more humane and content—and he is also a sentimental poet. Thus the recent poems "read like those of an aging Rimbaud who, instead of ceasing to write, is pondering in verse the degeneration of his youthful powers or even deploring their once demonic drive." While Faas's book lends credence to this *poète maudit* correlation between anger and artistry, he might have delved its implications more deeply. Though the biography is mesmerizing if breezy, its conclusion is almost facile in its longing for the return of a "Rimbaud-type 'monstrosity'"—as if to say, *great poetry is worth anything*. [David Andrews]

Books Received

Allen, Jack. *When the Whistle Blows.* Dedalus, 2002. $13.99. (F)

Anderson, Donald. *Fire Road.* Univ. of Iowa Press, 2001. Paper: $15.95. (F)

Arlt, Roberto. *Mad Toy.* Trans. and intro. Michele McKay Aynesworth. Duke Univ. Press, 2002. Paper: $15.95. (F)

Askew, Rilla. *Fire in Beulah.* Penguin, 2002. Paper: $13.00. (F)

Auchincloss, Louis. *Manhattan Dialogues.* Houghton Mifflin, 2002. $25.00. (F)

Aylett, Steve. *Only an Alligator.* Gollancz/Orion, 2001. Paper: £9.99. (F)

——. *Shamanspace.* Codex, 2001. Paper: $12.99. (F)

Bail, Murray. *Camouflage.* Farrar, Straus & Giroux, 2002. $20.00. (F)

Baricco, Alessandro. *City.* Trans. Ann Goldstein. Knopf, 2002. $25.00. (F)

Battle, Lois. *The Florabama Ladies' Auxiliary & Sewing Circle.* Penguin, 2002. Paper: $14.00. (F)

Bell, Madison Smartt. *Anything Goes.* Pantheon, 2002. $24.00. (F)

Berberova, Nina. *The Book of Happiness.* Trans. Marian Schwartz. New Directions, 2002. Paper: $12.95. (F)

Bertens, Hans, and Theo D'haen. *Contemporary American Crime Fiction.* Palgrave, 2001. $62.00. (NF)

Black, Michael. *Lawrence's England: The Major Fiction, 1913-20.* Palgrave, 2002. $58.00. (NF)

Black, Stanley. *Juan Goytisolo and the Politics of Contagion: The Evolution of a Radical Aesthetic in the Later Novels.* Liverpool Univ. Press, 2001. Paper: $27.95. (NF)

Bohjalian, Chris. *The Buffalo Soldier.* Shaye Areheart/Crown, 2002. $25.00. (F)

Bök, Christian. *Eunoia.* Coach House, 2001. Paper: $16.95. (F)

Borges, Jorge Luis. *This Craft of Verse.* Ed. Calin-Andrei Mihailescu. Harvard Univ. Press, 2002. Paper: $13.95. (NF)

Boswell, Robert. *Century's Son.* Knopf, 2002. $24.00. (F)

Bourke, N. A. *The Bone Flute.* Univ. of Queensland Press, 2001. Paper: $25.95. (F)

Bowles, Paul. *The Stories of Paul Bowles.* Intro. Robert Stone. Ecco, 2001. $39.95. (F)

Bradway, Becky. *Pink Houses and Family Taverns.* Foreword Michael Martone. Indiana Univ. Press, 2002. Paper: $17.95. (NF)

Brantly, Susan C. *Understanding Isak Dinesen.* Univ. of South Carolina Press, 2002. $29.95. (NF)

Braverman, Kate. *The Incantation of Frida K.* Seven Stories, 2002. $23.95. (F)

Brockmeier, Kevin. *Things that Fall from the Sky.* Pantheon, 2002. $21.95. (F)

Brooks, Geraldine. *Year of Wonders: A Novel of the Plague.* Penguin, 2002. Paper: $14.00. (F)

Bunin, Ivan. *Sunstroke.* Trans. and intro. Graham Hettlinger. Ivan R. Dee, 2002. $25.00. (F)

Burroughs, William S. *The Cat Inside.* Penguin, 2002. Paper: $11.00. (NF)

Byler, Stephen Raleigh. *Searching for Intruders.* Morrow, 2002. $23.95. (F)

Caldwell, Joseph. *Bread for the Baker's Child.* Sarabande, 2002. Paper: $13.95. (F)

Cameron, Peter. *The City of Your Final Destination.* Farrar, Straus & Giroux, 2002. $24.00. (F)

Cannon, C. W. *Soul Resin.* FC2, 2002. Paper: $13.95. (F)

Čapek, Karel. *Cross Roads.* Trans. and intro. Norma Comrada. Illus. Paul Hoffman. Catbird, 2002. Paper: $14.00. (F)

Carson, Anne, trans. *If Not, Winter: Fragments of Sappho.* Knopf, 2002. $27.50. (P)

Carter, Stephen L. *The Emperor of Ocean Park.* Knopf, 2002. $26.95. (F)

Cendaris, Blaise. *To the End of the World.* Trans. Alan Brown. Intro. Margaret Crosland. Peter Owen/Dufour, 2002. Paper: $19.95. (F)

Charyn, Jerome. *Sizzling Chops & Devilish Spins: Ping-Pong and the Art of Staying Alive.* Four Walls Eight Windows, 2001. $24.00. (NF)

Chavkin, Allan, ed. *Leslie Marmon Silko's "Ceremony": A Casebook.* Oxford Univ. Press, 2002. Paper: $16.95. (NF)

Christopher, Nicholas. *Franklin Flyer.* Dial, 2002. $24.95. (F)

Clarke, Brock. *What We Won't Do: Stories.* Sarabande, 2002. Paper: $13.95. (F)

Cleven, Vivienne. *Bitin' Back.* Univ. of Queensland Press, 2001. Paper: $18.95. (F)

Coe, Jonathan. *The Rotter's Club.* Knopf, 2002. $24.95. (F)

Cohen, Rich. *Lake Effect.* Knopf, 2002. $23.00. (NF)

Collins, Hugh. *No Smoke.* Canongate, 2002. Paper: $14.00. (F)

Cornis-Pope, Marcel. *Narrative Innovation and Cultural Rewriting in the Cold War and After.* Palgrave, 2002. $59.95. (NF)

Costello, Mark. *Big If.* Norton, 2002. $24.95. (F)

Cowan, Andrew. *Crustaceans.* Picador USA, 2002. $22.00. (F)

Cowart, David. *Don DeLillo: The Physics of Language.* Univ. of Georgia Press, 2002. $45.00. (NF)

Czuchlewski, David. *The Muse Asylum*. Penguin, 2002. Paper: $13.00. (F)

Davis, Charles. *Allegiances*. Merriman, 2001. $24.95. (F)

De Bolla, Peter. *Art Matters*. Harvard Univ. Press, 2001. $35.00. (NF)

Debord, Guy. *Considerations on the Assassination of Gérard Lebovici*. Trans. and intro. Robert Greene. Tam Tam, 2001. Paper: $15.00. (NF)

De Gramont, Nina. *Of Cats and Men*. Delta, 2002. Paper: $11.95. (F)

Desjardins, Martine. *Fairy Ring*. Trans. Fred A. Reed and David Homel. Talon, 2001. Paper: $18.95. (F)

Dick, Philip K. *Minority Report*. Pantheon, 2002. Paper: $12.95. (F)

Dickstein, Morris. *Leopards in the Temple: The Transformation of American Fiction 1945-1970*. Harvard Univ. Press, 2002. Paper: $15.95. (NF)

Di Prima, Diane. *Recollections of My Life as a Woman: The New York Years*. Penguin, 2002. Paper: $15.00. (NF)

Donoghue, Emma. *The Woman Who Gave Birth to Rabbits*. Harcourt, 2002. $24.00. (F)

Dorrenstein, Renate. *A Heart of Stone*. Penguin, 2002. Paper: $13.00. (F)

Drummond de Andrade, Carlos, and Rafael Alberti. *Looking for Poetry and Songs from the Quechua*. Trans. Mark Strand. Knopf, 2002. $19.00. (P)

Ebershoff, David. *The Rose City*. Penguin, 2002. Paper: $13.00. (F)

Estrin, Marc. *Insect Dreams: The Half Life of Gregor Samsa*. Blue Hen/sPutnam, 2002. $26.95. (F)

Evaristo, Bernadine. *The Emperor's Babe*. Viking, 2002. $23.95. (F, P)

Faccini, Ben. *The Water Breather*. Flamingo, 2002. £12.99. (F)

Fforde, Jasper. *The Eyre Affair*. Viking, 2002. $23.95. (F)

Flanagan, Richard. *Gould's Book of Fish: A Novel in Twelve Fish*. Grove, 2002. $27.50. (F)

Flores-Williams, Jason. *The Last Stand of Mr America*. Canongate, 2002. Paper: $14.00. (F)

Ford, Ford Madox. *Critical Essays*. Ed. Max Saunders and Richard Stang. Carcanet, 2002. Paper: $32.95. (NF)

Ford, Richard. *A Multitude of Sins*. Knopf, 2002. $25.00. (F)

Fowler, Nick. *A Thing (or Two) about Curtis and Camilla*. Pantheon, 2002. $24.95. (F)

Franck, Dan. *Bohemian Paris: Picasso, Modigliani, Matisse, and the Birth of Modern Art*. Trans. Cynthia Hope Liebow. Grove, 2001. $27.50. (NF)

Friedman, Bruce Jay. *Violencia! A Musical Novel*. Grove, 2001. Paper: $13.00. (F)

Fusco, John. *Paradise Salvage.* Overlook, 2002. $26.95. (F)

Gailly, Christian. *The Passion of Martin Fissel-Brandt.* Trans. Melanie Kemp. Intro. Brian Evenson. Univ. of Nebraska Press, 2002. Paper: $14.95. (F)

Galef, David. *Laugh Track.* Univ. Press of Mississippi, 2002. $25.00. (F)

Galloway, Janice. *Where You Find It.* Simon & Schuster, 2002. $24.00. (F)

Garrett, Greg. *Free Bird.* Kensington, 2002. $23.00. (F)

Gatti, Daniel J. *White Knuckle.* Blackmore & Blackmore, 2001. $24.95. (F)

Gerdes, Eckhard, ed. *John Barth, Bearded Bards & Splitting Hairs. Journal of Experimental Fiction* 17. Writers Club, 2001. Paper: $14.95. (F, NF)

— —. *The Laugh that Laughs at the Laugh: Writing from and about the Pen Man, Raymond Federman. Journal of Experimental Fiction* 23. Writers Club, 2002. Paper: $28.95. (F, NF)

Gildiner, Catherine. *Too Close to the Falls.* Penguin, 2002. Paper: $14.00. (NF)

Gilmour, David. *Sparrow Nights.* Counterpoint, 2002. $24.00. (F)

Glass, Julia. *Three Junes.* Pantheon, 2001. $25.00. (F)

Goodman, Allegra. *Paradise Park.* Delta, 2002. Paper: $12.95. (F)

Goodman, Carol. *The Lake of Dead Languages.* Ballantine, 2002. $23.95. (F)

Goodman, Paul. *The Empire City: A Novel of New York City.* Preface Taylor Stoehr. Black Sparrow, 2001. Paper: $17.50. (F)

Gorey, Edward. *The Object Lesson.* Harcourt, 2002. $12.00. (F)

Grossman, David. *Be My Knife.* Farrar, Straus & Giroux, 2002. $25.00. (F)

Hagedorn, Jessica. *Danger and Beauty.* City Lights, 2002. Paper: $16.95. (F, P)

Händler, Ernst-Wilhelm. *City with Houses.* Trans. and afterword Martin Klebes. Hydra/Northwestern Univ. Press, 2002. Paper: $19.95. (F)

Harfenist, Jean. *A Brief History of the Flood.* Knopf, 2002. $23.00. (F)

Hatoum, Milton. *The Brothers.* Trans. John Gledson. Farrar, Straus & Giroux, 2002. $23.00. (F)

Hawke, Ethan. *Ash Wednesday.* Knopf, 2002. $22.95. (F)

Healy, Eloise Klein. *Passing.* Red Hen, 2002. Paper: $11.95. (P)

Hecht, Ben. *Fantazius Mallare: A Mysterious Oath.* Illus. Wallace Smith. Frugoli & Taylor, 2002. Paper: $13.95. (F)

Heppner, Mike. *The Egg Code.* Knopf, 2002. $25.95. (F)

Herbert, Ernest. *The Old American.* Hardscrable/Univ. Press of New England, 2002. Paper: $15.95. (F)

Hill, Kathleen. *Still Waters in Niger*. Triquarterly, 2002. Paper: $15.95. (F)

Hirsch, Edward. *The Demon and the Angel: Searching for the Source of Artistic Inspiration*. Harcourt, 2002. $24.00. (NF)

Hoffman, Alice. *Illumination Night*. Berkley, 2002. Paper: $13.00. (F)

Holmes, Diana. *Rachilde: Decadence, Gender and the Woman Writer*. Berg, 2002. $68.00. (NF)

Honegger, Gitta. *Thomas Bernhard: The Making of an Austrian*. Yale Univ. Press, 2002. $29.95. (NF)

Howard, Maureen. *Big as Life: Three Tales for Spring*. Penguin, 2002. Paper: $13.00. (F)

Hughes, Mary-Beth. *Wavemaker II*. Atlantic, 2002. $23.00. (F)

Inness-Brown, Elizabeth. *Burning Marguerite*. Knopf, 2002. $23.00. (F)

Irwin, Robert. *The Arabian Nightmare*. Overlook, 2002. Paper: $14.95. (F)

Jaffe, Harold. *False Positive*. FC2, 2002. Paper: $12.95. (F, NF)

Jeffers, Jennifer M. *The Irish Novel at the End of the Twentieth Century: Gender, Bodies, and Power*. Palgrave, 2002. $49.95. (NF)

Jefferson, Ann. *Nathalie Sarraute, Fiction and Theory: Question of Difference*. Cambridge Univ. Press, 2002. $60.00. (NF)

Johnson, Adam. *Emporium: Stories*. Viking, 2002. $24.95. (F)

Kakar, Sudhir. *Ecstasy*. Overlook, 2002. $26.95. (F)

Kavaler, Rebecca. *A Little More than Kin*. Hamilton Stone, 2002. Paper: $14.95. (F)

Kavan, Anna. *Asylum Piece*. Peter Owen/Dufour, 2002. Paper: $19.95. (F)

——. *The Parson*. Peter Owen/Dufour, 2002. Paper: $16.95. (F)

Keller, Nora Okja. *Fox Girl*. Viking, 2002. $24.95. (F)

Kennedy, Thomas E. *Realism & Other Illusions: Essays on the Craft of Fiction*. Wordcraft of Oregon, 2002. Paper: $12.00. (NF)

Kesey, Ken. *One Flew over the Cuckoo's Nest*. 40th Anniversary ed. Intro. and illus. by the author. Viking, 2002. $24.95. (F)

Klima, Ivan. *Karel Čapek: Life and Work*. Trans. Norma Comrada. Catbird, 2002. $23.00. (NF)

Koed, Thomas. *Travels in the Unseen Lands*. Illiterature, 2001. Paper: $15.00. (F)

Koprince, Susan. *Understanding Neil Simon*. Univ. of South Carolina Press, 2002. $29.95. (NF)

Korda, Michael. *Making the List: A Cultural History of the American Bestseller 1900-1999*. Barnes & Noble, 2001. $20.00. (NF)

Kraft, Eric. *Inflating a Dog: The Story of Ella's Lunch Launch*. Picador USA, 2002. $25.00. (F)

Kurkov, Andrey. *Death and the Penguin*. Trans. George Bird. Harvill, 2001. Paper: $13.00. (F)

Larsen, Deborah. *The White*. Knopf, 2002. $22.00. (F)

Lasdun, James. *The Horned Man*. Norton, 2002. $24.95. (F)

Lasser, Scott. *All I Could Get*. Knopf, 2002. $24.00. (F)

Lawrence, Mary Wells. *A Big Life in Advertising*. Knopf, 2002. $26.00. (NF)

Lawson, Mary. *Crow Lake*. Dial, 2002. $23.95. (F)

Leithauser, Brad. *Darlington's Fall*. Knopf, 2002. $25.00. (F, P)

Lennon, Brian. *City: An Essay*. Univ. of Georgia Press, 2002. $24.95. (NF)

Lerner, Lisa. *Just Like Beauty*. Farrar, Straus & Giroux, 2002. $24.00. (F)

Lethem, Jonathan, and Carter Scholz. *Kafka Americana*. Norton, 2001. Paper: $11.00. (F)

Leunens, Christine. *Primordial Soup*. Dedalus, 2002. Paper: $12.99. (F)

Lightman, Alan. *The Diagnosis*. Vintage, 2000. Paper: $14.00. (F)

Lovell, Mary S. *The Sisters: The Saga of the Mitford Family*. Norton, 2002. $29.95. (NF)

Lurie, Alison. *Familiar Spirits: A Memoir of James Merrill and David Jackson*. Penguin, 2002. Paper: $13.00. (NF)

Lustig, Arnošt. *Lovely Green Eyes*. Trans. Ewald Osers. Arcade, 2002. $24.95. (F)

Maddox, Bruno. *My Little Blue Dress*. Penguin, 2002. Paper: $13.00. (F)

Major, Devorah. *Brown Glass Windows*. Curbstone, 2002. Paper: $15.95. (F)

Malladi, Amulya. *A Breath of Fresh Air*. Ballantine, 2002. $23.95. (F)

Maraini, Toni. *Sealed in Stone*. Trans. A. K. Bierman. Intro. Alberto Moravia. City Lights, 2002. Paper: $10.95. (F)

Marías, Javier. *A Heart So White*. Trans. Margaret Jull Costa. New Directions, 2002. Paper: $14.95. (F)

Matson, Clive. *Squish Boots*. Broken Shadow, 2002. Paper: $15.00. (P)

Matton, Sylvie. *Rembrandt's Whore*. Trans. Tamsin Black. Canongate, 2002. $24.00. (F)

Mazali, Rela. *Maps of Women's Goings and Stayings*. Stanford Univ. Press, 2001. Paper: $24.95. (F, NF)

McCarthy, Susan Carol. *Lay That Trumpet in Our Hands*. Bantam, 2002. $23.95. (F)

McCourt, James. *Wayfaring at Waverly in Silver Lake*. Knopf, 2002. $25.00. (F)

McGahern, John. *By the Lake*. Knopf, 2002. $24.00. (F)

— —. *The Dark*. Penguin, 2002. Paper: $13.00. (F)

McGirr, Michael. *Things You Get for Free*. Atlantic, 2002. $24.00. (NF)

McGraw, Erin. *The Baby Tree.* Story Line, 2002. Paper: $15.95. (F)

McGuane, Thomas. *The Cadence of Grass.* Knopf, 2002. $24.00. (F)

McKinnon, Karen. *Narcissus Ascending.* Picador USA, 2002. $21.00. (F)

Miller, Andrew. *Oxygen.* Harcourt, 2002. $24.00. (F)

Minot, Susan. *Poems 4 A.M.* Knopf, 2002. $18.00. (P)

— —. *Rapture.* Knopf, 2002. $18.00. (F)

Mones, Nicole. *A Cup of Light.* Delacorte, 2002. $24.95. (F)

Montemarano, Nicholas. *A Fine Place.* Context Books, 2002. $21.95. (F)

Mor, Noam. *ARC: Book I: Cleavage of Ghosts.* Spuyten Duyvil, 2002. Paper: $14.95. (F)

Mueller, Marnie. *My Mother's Island.* Curbstone, 2002. $24.95. (F)

Murakami, Haruki. *After the Quake.* Trans. Jay Rubin. Knopf, 2002. $21.00. (F)

Murguía, Alejandro. *This War Called Love.* City Lights, 2002. Paper: $11.95. (F)

Nesbitt, Marc. *Gigantic.* Grove, 2002. $24.00. (F)

Newell, Stephanie, ed. *Readings in African Popular Fiction.* Indiana Univ. Press, 2002. Paper: $24.95. (NF)

Norman, Howard. *The Haunting of L.* Farrar, Straus & Giroux, 2002. $24.00. (F)

Nova, Craig. *Wetware.* Shaye Areheart/Crown, 2002. $22.00. (F)

Oe, Kenzaburo. *Rouse Up, O Young Men of the New Age.* Trans. John Nathan. Grove, 2002. $24.00. (F)

O'Farrell, Maggie. *After You'd Gone.* Penguin, 2002. Paper: $13.00. (F)

O'Neill, Jamie. *At Swim, Two Boys.* Scribner, 2002. $28.00. (F)

Ouspensky, P. D. *Strange Life of Ivan Osokin.* Lindisfarne, 2002. Paper: $14.95. (F)

Packer, Ann. *The Dive from Clausen's Pier.* Knopf, 2002. $24.00. (F)

Pavese, Cesare. *The Devil in the Hills.* Trans. D. D. Paige. Peter Owen/Dufour, 2002. Paper: $19.95. (F)

Payne, Peggy. *Sister India.* Riverhead, 2002. Paper: $14.00. (F)

Pearson, T. R. *Polar.* Viking, 2002. $24.95. (F)

Pelevin, Victor. *Homo Zapiens.* Trans. Andrew Bromfield. Viking, 2002. $24.95. (F)

Píchová, Hana. *The Art of Memory in Exile: Vladimir Nabokov & Milan Kundera.* Southern Illinois Univ. Press, 2001. $35.00. (NF)

Piersanti, Claudio. *Luisa and the Silence.* Trans. George Hochfield. Northwestern Univ. Press, 2002. Paper: $17.95. (F)

Pilch, Jerzy. *His Current Woman.* Trans. Bill Johnston. Hydra/ Northwestern Univ. Press, 2002. Paper: $15.95. (F)

Pollack, Neal. *The Neal Pollack Anthology of American Literature: The Collected Writings of Neal Pollack.* Perennial, 2002. Paper: $13.95. (F, NF)

Reich, Tova. *Mara.* Syracuse Univ. Press, 2001. Paper: $18.95. (F)

Rice, Stan. *Red to the Rind.* Knopf, 2002. $23.00. (P)

Robbins, David L. *Scorched Earth*. Bantam, 2002. $24.95. (F)

Roberson, Susan L., ed. *Defining Travel: Diverse Visions*. Univ. Press of Mississippi, 2002. $40.00. (NF)

Robson, Lloyd. *Cardiff Cut*. Parthian/Dufour, 2002. Paper: $14.95. (F)

Roth, Joseph. *The Collected Stories of Joseph Roth*. Trans. and intro. Michael Hoffmann. Norton, 2002. $27.95. (F)

Ruffin, Paul. *Pompeii Man*. Louisiana Literature Press, 2002. Paper: $18.95. (F)

Russo, Richard. *The Whore's Child and Other Stories*. Knopf, 2002. $24.00. (F)

Said, Kurban. *The Girl from the Golden Horn*. Trans. Jenia Graman. Overlook, 2001. $25.95. (F)

Sang, Lee. *Crow's Eye View: The Infamy of Lee Sang, Korean Poet*. Selected and trans. Myong-Hee Kim. Illus. Janice Olson. Word Works, 2002. Paper: $20.00. (F, P)

Saroyan, Aram. *Artists in Trouble: New Stories*. Black Sparrow, 2002. Paper: $16.50. (F)

Schneider, Bart. *Secret Love*. Penguin, 2002. Paper: $13.00. (F)

Schnitzler, Arthur. *Night Games and Other Stories and Novellas*. Trans. Margret Schaefer. Foreword John Simon. Ivan R. Dee, 2002. $28.50. (F)

Sellers, Heather. *Georgia under Water*. Sarabande, 2001. Paper: $13.95. (F)

Shumaker, Peggy. *Underground River*. Red Hen, 2002. Paper: $11.95. (P)

Sima, Carol Ann. *The Mermaid that Came Between Them*. Coffee House, 2002. $23.95. (F)

Škvorecký, Josef. *When Eve Was Naked: Stories of a Life's Journey*. Farrar, Straus & Giroux, 2002. $24.00. (NF)

Slaughter, Carolyn. *Before the Knife: Memories of an African Childhood*. Knopf, 2002. $23.00. (NF)

Slouka, Mark. *God's Fool*. Knopf, 2002. $24.00. (F)

Spina, Michele. *Sleep: A Utopian Bestiary*. Trans. Ann Colcord with Hugh Shankland. Colin Smythe/Dufour, 2002. Paper: $19.95. (F)

Srinawk, Khamsing. *The Politician and Other Stories*. Trans. Domnern Garden and Herbert P. Phillips. Intro. Herbert P. Phillips. Silkworm, 2002. Paper: $13.95. (F)

Starr, Jason. *Hard Feelings*. Black Lizard/Vintage, 2002. Paper: $12.00. (F)

Strand, Mark. *The Story of Our Lives, with The Monument and The Late Hour*. Knopf, 2002. $18.00. (P)

Strauss, Darin. *The Real McCoy*. Dutton, 2002. $24.95. (F)

Tanizaki, Jun'ichirō. *The Gourmet Club: A Sextet*. Trans. Anthony H. Chambers and Paul McCarthy. Kodansha, 2001. $24.00. (F)

Tate, James. *Dreams of a Robot Dancing Bee*. Verse, 2002. $23.00. (F)

Tighe, Carl. *Burning Worm*. IMPress, 2001. Paper: £8.00. (F)

Tolstoy, Leo. *Anna Karenina*. Trans. Richard Pevear and Larissa Volokhonsky. Penguin, 2002. Paper: $16.00. (F)

Tremblay, Michel. *The Heart Laid Bare*. Trans. Sheila Fischman. Talon, 2002. Paper: $15.95. (F)

Unger, David. *Life in the Damn Tropics*. Syracuse Univ. Press, 2002. $34.95. (F)

Vallvey, Angela. *Hunting the Last Wild Man*. Trans. Margaret Jull Costa. Seven Stories, 2002. Paper: $14.00. (F)

Vanderborg, Susan. *Paratextual Communities: American Avant-Garde Poetry Since 1950*. Southern Illinois Univ. Press, 2001. $40.00. (NF)

Vera, Yvonne. *Without a Name and Under the Tongue*. Farrar, Straus & Giroux, 2002. Paper: $13.00. (F)

Vesaas, Tarjei. *The Ice Palace*. Trans. Elizabeth Rokkan. Peter Owen/Dufour, 2002. Paper: $19.95. (F)

Vilikovský, Pavel. *Ever Green Is....* Trans. and intro. Charles Sabatos. Northwestern Univ. Press, 2002. Paper: $15.95. (F)

Wagner, Bruce. *I'll Let You Go*. Villard, 2002. $25.95. (F)

Waldrop, Keith, and Rosmarie Waldrop. *Ceci N'est Pas Keith — Ceci N'est Pas Rosmarie*. Burning Deck, 2002. Paper: $10.00. (NF)

Wertzel, Elizabeth. *More, Now, Again: A Memoir of Addiction*. Simon & Schuster, 2002. $25.00. (NF)

Wiesel, Elie. *The Judges*. Trans. Geoffrey Strachan. Knopf, 2002. $24.00. (F)

Williams, Darren. *Angel Rock*. Knopf, 2002. $23.00. (F)

Witchel, Alex. *Me Times Three*. Knopf, 2002. $22.00. (F)

Wodehouse, P. G. *Heavy Weather*. Overlook, 2001. $16.95. (F)

— —. *Jeeves and the Feudal Spirit*. Overlook, 2001. $16.95. (F)

— —. *Laughing Gas*. Overlook, 2001. $16.95. (F)

— —. *The Mating Season*. Overlook, 2001. $16.95. (F)

Womack, Craig S. *Drowning in Fire: A Novel*. Univ. of Arizona Press, 2001. Paper: $17.95. (F)

Zelitch, Simone. *Moses in Sinai*. Black Heron, 2002. $23.95. (F)

Zigman, Laura. *Her*. Knopf, 2002. $22.00. (F)

Contributors

TAKAFUMI AKIMOTO received his M.A. in American Literature from Keio University; the co-author of *A Readers' Guide to Paul Auster* (Sairyusha, 1996), he teaches American Literature at Konan University.

KAZUKO YOSHIO BEHRENS received her M.A. degree from Cornell University in Asian Studies. She is a Ph.D. candidate in School of Education of UC-Berkeley, where she is exploring aspects of parenthood, particularly mother-child relationships through cross-cultural perspectives. She has translated many Japanese postmodern tales and essays into English.

SINDA GREGORY published an interview with and essay about Rikki Ducornet in the Fall 1998 issue of *Review of Contemporary Fiction*; the author of *Private Investigations: The Fiction of Dashiell Hammett* and *Alive and Writing: Interviews with American Authors of the 1980s,* she currently is Professor of English at San Diego State University.

Having received her M.A. in Literature from UC-Berkeley, PAMELA HASMAN is now a poet, fiction writer, housewife, and belly-dancing instructor living in San Diego.

KEITH JOHNSON holds degrees in English and Japanese and is currently a graduate student at Boston University

MARI KOTANI studied pharmacy at the University of Kitazato. A feminist SF and fantasy critic, she published *Technogynesis* (Keiso Publishers, 1994)—which won the Fifteenth Japan SF Award—*Evangelion as the Immaculate Virgin* (Magazine House, 1997), and *On Fantasy: An Introduction* (Chikuma Publishers, 1998). She also co-authored *Blood Read* (University of Pennsylvania Press, 1998).

MICHAEL FUJIMOTO KEEZING studied English at Yale University and received his M.F.A. from Brown University. His avant-porn story, "Anna-chan of Green Gables" was published in 1996 and translated into Japanese in 1997. Formerly teaching English at Keio University and Meiji University, he lives near Amherst with his wife, Mika, and their daughter, Umi.

YOSHIAKI KOSHIKAWA received his M.A. from Tsukuba University and currently teaches American literature at Meiji University. He is the author of a collection of essays, *Beyond the USA* (Jiyu-Kokuminsha Publishers, 1992), and the translator of many books, including Robert Coover's *The Universal Baseball Association* and *Gerald's Party,* and the co-translator of Thomas Pynchon's *Gravity's Rainbow.*

LARRY McCAFFERY's most recent publication was *Federman, A to X-X-X-X—A Recyclopedic Narrative* (San Diego State University Press); currently a Professor of English at San Diego State University, his main activity is hiking near his home in the Anza Borrego Desert.

Currently teaching English at Tokyo's Seikei University, TOSHIFUMI MIYAWAKI received his M.A. from Sophia University and was a visiting fellow at Brown University. The editor of a collection of essays, *The Impact of Puritanism on American Literary History* (Shohakusha Publishers, 1999), he is currently working on a comparative study of F. Scott Fitzgerald and Haruki Murakami.

HIDEAKI OIDE is the editor and publisher of *Paradox,* one of Japan's most prominent SF fanzines, which recently published its forty-first issue. As Hideaki Ibuki, he published such novels as *The Duel of Sherlock Holmes* and *The Space Fighters Angel Links,* which was made into a TV animation.

HISAYO OGUSHI studied English at the University of Oregon 1991-1992. In 2001 she completed her Ph.D. dissertation on Lydia Maria Child at Keio University, Tokyo. She is co-author of *The History of Consciousness in American Narrative* (Nan'undo Publishers, 1998). She teaches American Literature at Keio University.

Currently teaching in the Department of Multi-Cultural Studies at the Siebold University of Nagasaki, KENNETH L. RICHARD's translation of Masahiko Shimada's "Desert Dolphin" appears in *The Oxford Book of Modern Japanese Short Stories* (1997).

AMANDA SEAMAN is a Ph.D. candidate in East Asian Languages and Civilizations at the University of Chicago. She is writing her dissertation on contemporary Japanese women's detective fiction.

TAKAYUKI TATSUMI's recent books include: *New York Decadence* (Tokyo: Chikuma Publishers, 1995), which included queer readings of Melville, Adams, and Duchamp as the cultural engineers of the celibate machine, and *Slipstream Japan* (Tokyo: Shinchosha,1998), which discusses postmodern Japanese writers such as Yasutaka Tsutsui, Ryu Murakami, Haruki Murakami, Masahiko Shimada, Yoriko Shono, and others. He won the Pioneer Award in 1994 for his collaborative essay (with Larry McCaffery), "Towards the Theoretical Frontiers of Fiction: From Metafiction and Cyberpunk through Avant-Pop" (*SF Eye* #12) and the Yukichi Fukuzawa Award in 1996 for his literary historical study, *New Americanist Poetics* (Tokyo: Seidosha, 1995). Currently a professor of English at Keio University, he lives with Mari Kotani in Tokyo.

Born and raised in San Francisco, REIKO TOCHIGI received her M.A. from Sophia University, studying William Faulkner. She is currently Associate Professor of English at Hosei University. A natural born bilingual, she has translated a variety of books including Bernard Jay's *Not Simply Divine* and David Skal's *Monster Show*.

GENE VAN TROYER edited *Portland Review,* including its special Science Fiction Poetry issue in 1981. With Tomoko Oshiro, he co-translated "The Legend of the Paper Spaceship"—later included in *The Best Japanese Science Fiction Stories* (ed. John Apostolou, Barricade, 1997)—by one of the Japanese "godfathers" of SF, Tesu Yano. He lives in Gifu, Japan.

Bard FICTION PRIZE

Bard College invites submissions for its annual Fiction Prize for young writers.

The prize will be awarded to an American citizen, aged 39 years or younger, who has published a first novel or collection of short stories. Writers who have already published two or more volumes are not eligible for the prize.

The winner will receive an appointment as writer-in-residence at Bard College for one spring semester without the expectation that he or she teach any regular courses. The recipient will give one public lecture or reading. He or she will be encouraged to meet informally with students.

The prize consists of $30,000, the residency, and resources at Bard, including office space and housing.

To apply, candidates should write a letter expressing interest in the prize, and submit a C.V. along with three copies of his or her published book. No manuscripts will be accepted. Applications must be received by July 15, 2002. The recipient of the prize will be selected by October 15, 2002, by a panel of distinguished writers associated with Bard College.

For information, call 845-758-7087, send an e-mail to bfp@bard.edu, or visit www.bard.edu/bfp.

Bard College PO Box 5000, Annandale-on-Hudson, NY 12504-5000

Studies in Twentieth Century Literature

Volume 26, No. 1 (Winter, 2002)

A Special Issue on

Perspectives in French Studies at the Turn of the Millennium

Guest Editors:
Martine Antle and Dominique Fisher

Contributors include:

Marie-Claire Bancquart
Yasmine Getz
Mary Jean Green
Leah D. Hewitt
Jacques Jouet
Marc Lony
Boniface Mongo-Mboussa
Warren Motte
Carol J. Murphy
Mireille Rosello
Beryl Schlossman
Dina Sherzer
Stéphane Spoiden
Estelle Taraud

Silvia Sauter, Editor
Kansas State University
Eisenhower 104
Manhattan, KS 66506-1003
Submissions in: Spanish and Russian

Jordan Stump, Editor
University of Nebraska
PO Box 880318
Lincoln, NE 68588-0318
Submissions in: French and German

Please check our Web site for subscription and other information:

http://www.ksu.edu/stcl/index.html

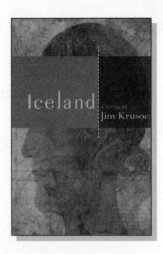

Iceland

a novel by

Jim Krusoe

AMERICAN LITERATURE SERIES
Fiction | $14.95 | 1-56478-314-6

From the author of the critically acclaimed *Blood Lake* (1999), *Iceland* is a novel of melancholic hilarity, which raises questions about the nature of memory, imagination, and desire. Only the narrator's ludicrous perspective holds on course a plot that leaps through time, coincidence, and disjointed logic.

"A work of great originality, humour, cunning, and charm."

–Martin Amis

"Krusoe's offbeat style and the occasional monstrous metaphor . . . make for dizzying satire. A strange and memorable book."–*Booklist* (starred review)

Krusoe's twisted, childlike observations on love, livelihood and the non sequiturs that dominate daily life are consistently entertaining and thought provoking. . . . A writer to watch.–*Publishers Weekly*

DALKEY ARCHIVE PRESS | www.dalkeyarchive.com

Flotsam and Jetsam

by

Aidan Higgins

A Lannan Selection

Short Fiction | $15.95 | 1-56478-316-2

"*Flotsam and Jetsam* offers a vivid illustration of Higgins's range and eclecticism, his out-standing control of atmospheres, his literary development and his importance in the history of twentieth-century Irish literature, in which he can be seen as a missing link between the modernist period and contemporary writing."

—*Times Literary Supplement*

"Higgins captures characters and places with quick lyrical bursts again and again."
—*Booklist* (starred review)

"Higgins is a master of sketching fully formed characters in a few lines or paragraphs, suggesting whole lives and histories with stunningly deft precision."—*New York Press*

DALKEY ARCHIVE PRESS | www.dalkeyarchive.com

L.C.

a novel by

Susan Daitch

A LANNAN SELECTION
Fiction | $14.95 | 1-56478-315-4

"*L.C.* is an important first novel by a promising young novelist, well worth reading for its ingenious interweaving of narrative threads, for its uncompromising treatment of sex and politics, and for the questions it raises about truth and deception in representing self and history."–*Los Angeles Times*

"*L.C.* is simply tremendous: dense, evocative, intellectually and politically taxing; not celebration but critique."–*Listener*

"Susan Daitch's *L.C.* is an important book. . . . Through complex novelistic strategies and acute historical imaginings, she produces a form which encourages us to rethink both fiction and history."–*Times Literary Supplement*

DALKEY ARCHIVE PRESS | www.dalkeyarchive.com

Robert Creeley • Gertrude Stein
ldous Huxley • Robert Coover
hn Barth • David Markson • Flar
'Brien • Louis Ferdinand Céline
www.dalkeyarchive.com
larguerite Young • Ishmael Reed
nn Quin • Camilo José Cela
ilbert Sorrentino • Nicholas Mosl
Douglas Woolf • Raymond Quene
Harry Mathews • Rikki Ducornet
sé Lezama Lima • Aidan Higgins
en Marcus • Coleman Dowell
cques Roubaud • Djuna Barnes
elipe Alfau • Osman Lins • Dav

Your connection to literature.
DALKEY ARCHIVE PRESS

⬚ DALKEY ARCHIVE COLLECTION

Library Alliance Program

- 235 Dalkey Archive titles for $1,000
- Receive our entire list at a 70% discount

—or—

Special Sale

- 100 books : $5 each
- Select any 100 books from the Dalkey Archive list for $5 each

- **Free shipping if you order before August 31st**

For full details, ordering information, and our complete list of books and authors please visit: **www.dalkeyarchive.com**